Don't Let the Lipstick Fool You

LISA LESLIE

with Larry Burnett

Don't Let the Lipstick Fool You

KENSINGTON BOOKS
http://www.kensingtonbooks.com

DAFINA BOOKS are published by

Kensington Publishing Corp.
850 Third Avenue
New York, NY 10022

Library of Congress Control Number: 2008921824
ISBN-13: 978-0-7582-2735-5
ISBN-10: 0-7582-2735-3

First Hardcover Printing: May 2008
10 9 8 7 6 5 4 3 2 1

Printed in the United States of America

Dedicated to my mother, Christine Leslie-Espinoza

Table of Contents

Foreword by Earvin "Magic" Johnson

Lisa Leslie has had a tremendous impact on the L.A. Sparks, women's basketball, and the city of Los Angeles. She has always been the best player, but that has never stopped her from continuing to learn or trying to improve. Lisa cares about the history of the game, and she always asks me what made our Lakers teams so good and what she needs to change in her game to get even better.

When she and my former teammate Michael Cooper teamed up with the Sparks, Lisa became the most dominating player in women's basketball. She was able to take the WNBA to a whole new level because once people saw what she could do, they could not help but appreciate her talents, her work ethic, and her charisma. Little girls started wearing her #9 jersey and wanted to be like Lisa Leslie, and they could not pick a better role model on or off the court. She is a very intelligent woman who has taken care of her money and her image. Lisa was able to pave the way for women in basketball and in sports, but that never affected her willingness to go back into her community, speak at schools, and do whatever she could to help.

I know what it is like to grow up being the tallest in the class and not having clothes that fit right, let alone designer clothes. Lisa knows it, but through her sports and her spirituality, she was able to overcome the many adversities that she faced along the way. Because she was so great at basketball, it allowed her not only to take care of herself, but also her mother, who served double duty as Lisa's mom and her dad. Hats off to Lisa for keeping it all together and leading a successful life—even when her environment might have dictated otherwise.

I remember watching Lisa's stellar career at USC, and I will never forget when she joined my workout sessions with some of my NBA friends and some top-notch college players. It was all men, but Lisa impressed me when she said, "I want to play with you guys, and I don't want anybody to take it easy on me."

This woman would go out there and play. I would always try to team her with me so that I could make the passes and she could make the shots. It was amazing because Lisa would play so hard against those guys, and in turn, they paid her a lot of respect by playing hard against her. They had to because these guys knew if they let up even a bit, she would embarrass them. She never backed down. That was my first chance to see her measure up against men and to see her competitive nature come out.

Lisa took a lot of pride in making herself into a great basketball player, but she was always able to maintain her femininity at the same time. That always came across in the way that she spoke, the way she played on the court, and the way that she dressed off the court. She was a fashion diva, and she still is. Lisa has done many fashion shows for the Magic Johnson Foundation, and she is unbelievable as a model. This woman could have been a runway model full time and could have made a lot of money doing it. I think she shows women, both in sports and out of sports, that you can be a tremendous athlete and still remain a feminine woman. Now Lisa is taking it to another level in her roles as a wife and a mother.

To sum it all up, Lisa Leslie is the best at everything, and

I applaud her for always striving for that. I always try to be the best in anything that I do, and Lisa is the same way . . . times one hundred! She is the best player in the game today, but she is also the best person, woman, daughter, model, and teammate.

Lisa is at the pinnacle of her sport, but her work on the basketball court is not done yet. Now she wants to make the best comeback, and she has set a goal to win one more Olympic gold medal for her country.

I love Lisa because she always represented herself and her mom with the highest level of class and dignity. She constantly has a smile on her face and is always there to support others. Lisa Leslie has reached a rare level of excellence, yet she remains a humble lady who, through all of her achievements, honors, and accolades, has been able to live in the glare of the spotlight without ever once forgetting where she came from.

Prologue

"The United States of America!" blared over the public address system, and the eighty-three thousand fans packed
in Centennial Olympic Stadium went wild. They were all there
to see the opening ceremony of the 1996 Summer Olympic
Games, and since we were in Atlanta, most of the crowd was
from the United States.

The fans got to their feet and applauded, cheered, whistled,
and chanted, "USA! USA!" as our team marched into the stadium. I will never forget this day: July 19. It was one of the
proudest moments of my life. I had worked so many years to get
to this point, and now I was representing my country as a member of the U.S. women's basketball team. I could not stop smiling.

The sights and sounds in Centennial Olympic Stadium were
incredible. There were so many people, so many lights and colors. I had never seen that many American flags, and it took my
breath away. Our U.S. contingent was just a fraction of the more
than ten thousand athletes who were there to participate in the
opening ceremony and compete on the world's greatest stage. I

was living a dream, and walking into the arena gave me goose bumps. The men's and women's basketball teams walked in together, and beside me were NBA superstars Shaquille O'Neal, Reggie Miller, David Robinson, and Karl Malone. But many other athletes I admired were in my line of sight, too: American track stars Carl Lewis, Gail Devers, and Michael Johnson; tennis greats Andre Agassi and Lindsay Davenport; and famed boxer Floyd Mayweather, Jr. Everywhere I turned, there was another familiar face. Clearly, I was in elite company in an incredibly unique atmosphere, and I was soaking it all in. A lot of the athletes were snapping pictures or shooting video to capture the very special moments. I did not have a camera, but I was so busy taking in the sights that I am not sure I would have remembered to take a picture, anyway.

All the U.S. women athletes wore white silk tops, red blazers, and long, blue, poodle-style skirts. We topped it off with red, white, and blue scarves; white hats, which we wore tipped to the side; and these horrible blue shoes with little heels. We looked like we had stepped straight out of the 1940s, but for this occasion, it worked. I waved to the crowd enthusiastically, laughing with my new friends and enjoying my first Olympic experience. Then my right shoe fell off.

I had to grab onto Karl Malone to keep from falling down. I stretched my leg back and managed to find the shoe and get my toes in it, but everyone around me was still moving, and I had to drag my shoe behind me. As I tried to keep pace and avoid getting trampled in the massive traffic jam of people, I could see the headline already: U.S. OLYMPIAN INJURED IN OPENING CERE-MONY STAMPEDE.

But finally, I was able to squeeze my foot into the wayward shoe and continue my stroll around the stadium with the other athletes. I felt awkward and goofy, but relieved and slightly exhilarated. Only I could lose my shoe on live television, with the whole world watching. I laughed out loud at myself for the slipup but also at the irony. My image as a graceful athlete seemed to be still intact. But I was quickly reminded of the less-than-graceful uphill climb that led me to this moment. This made me smile even wider.

Chapter 1

Mothertrucker!

"You were born to play basketball."

People tell me that all the time, but I can tell you for a fact that Lisa Deshaun Leslie was not born with a basketball in her hands or with any desire to play the game. In fact, my road to roundball was more of an obstacle course than an expressway. Whatever basketball genes I did get probably came from my father. I am told that he was a good athlete who played in local leagues in Southern California and some semiprofessional basketball in Alaska. I am told that my legs are built like his, knock-kneed and bowlegged. I am six foot five. They tell me he was six foot four. I do not know. I never knew him.

I do know that my father was always a man on the go. "Papa Was a Rollin' Stone" should have been his theme song, especially the part that goes, "Wherever he laid his hat was his home." His legal name was Walter Lee Leslie, and he was married and had four kids before he moved from Maryland to California. That was when he took an alias, met my mom, and started a whole new family. Mom had no clue. He married her using the name Bernard Leslie and left her when she was four months pregnant with me.

5

Did he leave because of me? I am not sure, and I did not want Mom to think I was unhappy, so I never asked. We rarely talked about my dad, though I did meet him briefly once, when I was twelve years old. Other than that visit, the man was like a ghost to me. When he died in 1984 of cancer, I cannot say that I felt much of a loss. It is true what people say: you can never miss what you never had.

So there was no dad there to greet me when I was born on July 7, 1972, at Gardena Memorial Hospital. Technically, I was born in Gardena, but that is not where I am from. I am also not from Hawthorne or Inglewood or most of the other places you might have heard about. My hometown is Compton, California. In the beginning, it was just my mom, Christine, and my sister Dionne. I was very close to my mom from day one. Dionne was five years older than me. People referred to her as the "dark one" because of her flawless chocolate skin. They described me as "the one with the pretty eyes." Even though Mom tried not to pick favorites, I sometimes heard her tell my aunts, "You know Lisa. She is my shadow, my little helper." I longed to please her.

When I was six years old, we lived in a three-bedroom house on North Castlegate Street, off of Atlantic and Rosecrans boulevards. Mom, Dionne, and I each had our own rooms. Mom's bedroom had a fireplace, which she liked to use on rainy days. Her room also had a sliding back door, which led to a large patio and a decent-sized backyard. Mom had poured cement and put up a tetherball pole out back because she knew that I loved to play.

There was a large tree in our front yard. I do not know what type of tree it was, but it was constantly shedding leaves, and it had a really large root that stuck up out of the ground. Mom and I would always trim that tree or mow the lawn. I remember thinking that those were the types of things a dad would do. Mom always told me that it did not matter if we had a man around or not. We could do anything we wanted. And if we did not know how, we could learn.

The earliest job I remember Mom having was at the post office. She drove a mail truck and did a lot of walking in her job delivering mail in the Wilshire–Beverly Hills district of Los Angeles. Every morning I would hear her get up at 5:00 AM. When I heard her moving about, I would get out of bed to make sure her shoes were by her door so that she would not have to search for them. Her work clothes were neatly ironed and ready to wear. Depending on the California weather, Mom would wear pants or shorts to work. She would get dressed and put on her socks and shoes, and then I would walk her to the door. Every morning I would watch her leave for work, and every morning, when she had gone, I would sit at the door and cry. Dionne would say, "You're just crazy! Something is wrong with you. Crying every day, every time Mom leaves."

Once Mom was out of sight, I would get our family photo album and take it into her room. I'd lie on her bed and look at the pictures until I fell asleep. Dionne would get up and get dressed. Then she would wake me up around seven-thirty and tell me that she was leaving for school. Once my sister was gone, I would turn on the television and let it blare in the background while I got dressed. The *Hogan's Heroes* theme song was my cue to check the back door, lock the sliding door in Mom's room, make sure all the lights were off, close the back door in the kitchen, lock the gate, and, like all the other latchkey kids in the neighborhood, make sure I put my key down my shirt. I was six years old and in kindergarten.

After locking up, I would cross the street, ring the doorbell at Miss Pearl's house (God rest her soul), and tell her I was walking to school, which was just a few blocks down from her house. She would come outside and watch me to make sure I made it safely down the street. I would go to school from 11:00 AM to 2:00 PM.

Dionne got out of school around the same time as me, and we would walk home together. We did that every day for a year. That was our routine.

I looked up to Dionne. She was my big sister, and I wanted her to like me. But Dionne was almost a teenager and did not want her overly sensitive kid sister following her around, asking her questions, or cramping her style. The thing was, it was so important to me to win Dionne's approval, and in trying to impress her or seem cool and fun, I usually just copied whatever she was doing. This only annoyed her more.

In general, if I did anything to irritate Dionne, there was a physical price to pay. She would punch me, kick me, slap me, push me down, and yell at me. This was not playful wrestling. This felt like some sort of combat, and Dionne could be as secretive and creative about it as any CIA operative. But I was never afraid of my sister. I was just confused.

There was the time she reached into the cupboard, with her back to me, and said, "Here! You want some?" then turned to blow salt in my eyes. Another time she smashed a jelly sandwich right in my face.

Dionne could be so mean, and yet I still loved and idolized her. I used to love it when she would put my hair in two pretty French braids, with a part down the middle. Dionne was an excellent braider, and the style looked cute on me. Sometimes the hairstyle would turn out great, and I would be really thankful to her. Then, other times, she would purposely part my hair crooked or way off center so that the hairstyle looked crazy.

When she would rough me up, I would run and hide in the bathroom. She would chase me and then use a butter knife to try to unlock the door. When that did not work, she would go outside, peek in the bathroom window, and scream, "I SEE YOU IN THERE!" She loved to scare me to death.

I would stay locked in the bathroom until Mom came home around five o'clock. When I would hear her car pull up, I would open the bathroom door and see Dionne standing there. But she no longer seemed threatening. Now she was pleading and nego- tiating with me. "Okay, Lisa! If you don't tell Mom, I'll give you some candy." Like a sucker, I would keep quiet, get the candy, and relive the whole ordeal the next day. Mom never had a clue.

The thing is, I was such a timid child. Very timid. I was afraid of lots of things, but by the time I was eight, Dionne's act had gotten old. I was tired of her beating up on me, so one day, when she had pushed me too far, I reached back and socked her in the stomach as hard as I could. She made a "wuh whew" sound and bent over to catch her breath. I ran off to my usual hiding place, locked the door behind me, and tried to keep my heart from pounding out of my chest. I was so scared, but I was so happy, too. I had hit Dionne! I had hurt her. That was the last day that I remember running away from my big sister or getting abused by her. I had finally fought back. I thought our troubles would be over, our battles ended, but that turned out to be the furthest thing from the truth.

Dionne and I were so different. I was very, very neat. She was very messy. I would fold my clothes, organize my socks, sweep my wooden floors, and mop them, too. I was like a soldier's daughter. I would move my bed, rearrange my room, and clean out my closet. Then I would call, "Mom, come and look at my room!" As far back as I can remember, I always wanted things to be clean and organized. I loved having my own room, and I was thrilled that Mom had painted it my favorite color, yellow, to match my curtains and my canopy bed. When the sun would shine in, my room would turn bright, and that would make me happy. It was my private, special place.

When Mom would come to check out my room, Dionne would stand across the hall, with her hands on her hips. She would roll her eyes to show her annoyance. I never realized she worried that

Mom would want to inspect her room next. I just wanted to show off my clean room to my mother and have her appreciate the work I had done. But in the process, it was very obvious that little sister was really getting on big sister's nerves.

It went both ways, though. Dionne had a big problem telling the truth, and if she got in trouble, she pulled me down with her. If Dionne got into Mom's make-up and Mom found out, we would eventually hear, "Lisa! Dionne! Come in here! Who's been in my make-up?"

I had not played a lick of basketball yet, but I already knew how to put up a good defense when I was in a jam. I would begin to protest immediately. "Make-up? I don't even wear make-up. I'm not even old enough to wear make-up."

Dionne would pipe in, lying through her teeth. "Make-up? No, Mom. I have not been in your make-up."

Mom would give us that look that only mothers can give. "There are only three of us in this house. I know I didn't do it. Now, who was in my make-up?"

I would walk up to her, pleading my case. "Mom, look at me. I was not in your make-up. I promise! I swear to God!" I would invoke God's name to try to convince her that I was the innocent daughter.

Dionne always got in the last word, though. "I don't care what anybody says. It was not me!"

This would get Mom really upset. "Go to your rooms. If nobody will tell me the truth, then both of you are getting whuppin's!"

This would send me into a panic. I was a pretty obedient kid and did everything I could to avoid getting hit by my mother. My mind-set was always, *I am not going to do anything to give this lady a reason to whup me.* But on those rare occasions when it did happen, it might as well have been a previously choreographed dance.

Mom would walk into my room and close the door behind her. I was quick and would dive under my bed. Mom would move the bed. I would jump in my closet. She would pull me out. Then she would pick up my sixty-five-pound body, lay me across the bed, and lean on my head so she could spank my bottom. This happened every time I ever got a whuppin'. Running away probably made things worse than they had to be, but I could not fathom sitting still to get a whuppin', especially when I was innocent (not that I always was).

Somewhere in between raising two daughters and working for the post office, Mom found time to date a chef named Max Sanoguet. He was Puerto Rican and had grown up in New York City. Max drove a little yellow Dodge Colt, and he wore his hair in a ponytail. I thought he was really nice. One night I sat on his lap and said, "You're cute. Are you going to stay over?"

He said, "I hope so."

Mom looked at both of us and raised her eyebrows. "I don't THINK so!"

Max was really the first man that I remember being around our house, ever. He eventually moved in with us, and on February 7, 1980, my sister Tiffany was born. I was almost eight years old, and I thought she was the most beautiful thing that I had ever seen. We had a real baby in the house! I remember going to school and then rushing home every day to see my new sister. She slept in Dionne's room, across the hall from me. I would spend most of my free time standing by her crib, staring and rubbing her back. I changed her diapers and volunteered to take a lot of responsibility in caring for her. For some reason, this made Max jealous. "Tell her to get out of there!" he would say to my mother. "She is always around the baby, always around that crib."

I really liked Max, but he and Mom did not always see eye to eye, especially when it came to me; they definitely had their differences. Not long after, in 1981, Tiffany was a year and a half, Max was out of the house, and Mom was ready to stop delivering mail and start a new career.

Mom is an amazingly optimistic person. To this day, she is always filling my head with positive affirmations. When I was growing up, she would always tell me things like:

"Treat people the way you want to be treated."

"You cannot receive anything with a closed fist."

"It is important to be giving."

"Whatever you say in the universe will come back, so speak positively."

And my favorite, the 7 P's: Proper, Prior, Preparation, Prevents, Piss, Poor, Performance.

Her positive outlook always seems to come out strongest when my family goes through difficult times or when one of us needs an emotional or spiritual lift. Mom has always wanted the best for her kids, and that included sending us to college. She realized that her post office salary was not enough to send all three of her girls to universities. So she started considering other job possibilities. She wanted to do something she would enjoy, that would pay well, and that would allow her to build a better life for our family.

So when a friend introduced Mom to a truck-driving acquaintance, her new career path started to take shape. She knew that she liked to talk and loved to travel. And she was willing to try something different. Call her spontaneous, adventurous, or a risk taker, but my mother wound up riding with this truck driver on his trip from Los Angeles to San Francisco, and she helped him unload furniture when they got there. It was hard, hot, and dirty work, but Mom liked it. She saw that driving a truck might be her ticket to see the country and provide the finances necessary to put Dionne, Tiffany, and me through college. The fact that she had never driven a truck, of any kind, did not seem to bother her.

Mom did some research and found out that North American Van Lines was holding a free seminar in Long Beach, not far from where we lived. Their deal was that if you wanted a new career as a truck driver, you could buy a truck from them, and they would teach you how to drive it and teach you how to run your own business. After that, you could venture out on your own. Mom liked the idea, so she signed up for the training classes. Let me tell you what a giant leap of faith this was. My mom did not even know how to drive a stick shift. She had no clue. On top of that, North American Van Lines was headquartered in Fort Wayne, Indiana. That was also where the driving classes were held, and that meant Mom was going to have to leave us for a little while.

In order to save money, she took a bus from Los Angeles to Fort Wayne. North American provided her with a truck for the training sessions. The classes lasted two weeks, and by the end of that time, my mother was driving a big tractor-trailer just like a pro. She was going to be a truck driver, and she was not going to do it halfway. Mom took out a loan on our home and paid fifty-four thousand dollars to buy her own big rig. It was an eighteen-wheeler, an International Harvester 9670 that had twenty-seven miles on its odometer.

Mom was extremely excited, but on the same day that she found out about getting her truck, she also got some news about my big sister. Dionne was eight months pregnant and would have to take a break from high school. On April 18, 1983, my fifteen-year-old sister gave birth to my nephew, Marquis.

It was a crazy time for all of us. There was so much drama and concern. When Dionne brought Marquis home, we had two babies in our house, and I became solely responsible for Tiffany. Mom was in way too deep to even think about giving up her new trucking career. Besides, she was determined to improve our family's quality of life, no matter what. Her plan was still a good one, and she was going to do everything she could to make it successful.

Then came the next bombshell: Mom was going to be head-quartered in Indiana. We would have to stay behind in California. To this day, Mom says that it broke her heart to leave us and head off to her new career. Trust me, it broke my heart, too.

In Mom's new job, she got to drive cross-country routes through all forty-eight states and into Canada and Mexico. Her CB radio moniker was Sugar Chris, and her driving motto was, "I don't go fast, but I do go steady." She hauled all kinds of cargo in that truck, from baby diapers to washing machines to tomato sauce, and when school was out, Mom would haul Tiffany and me in her cab, too. We would spend the summer driving across America, talking, laughing, and, along the way, doing our shopping for the coming school year.

On the road, my mother was always trying to keep costs down, so we would stay at places like Days Inn. Their rooms were inexpensive, and kids under twelve got to eat breakfast for free. One morning the waitress came over to take our orders. Mom told her what she wanted, and then she explained that Tiffany and I would be getting the free breakfast. I was ten at the time but was already very tall for my age. The waitress looked at me, then looked at my mom and asked, with a bit of attitude, "Are you trying to tell me that this big old girl is only ten years old?"

The whole thing made me really uncomfortable. Mom told the waitress that I really was ten, and when the woman got kind of fussy about it, my mother had the manager come to our table. Mom explained the problem to him, and the manager looked across the table at me. Mom said, "Let me explain it this way." She got out of her chair and stood up, all six feet three inches of her. The man seemed to get the picture, and I got my free breakfast.

Mom had all kinds of interesting experiences on the road. One night at a truck stop in Garland, Texas, she saw a poster for a "win a truck" contest that WMAQ Radio was holding. She filled out an entry form, and unbelievably, Mom won the contest and a new 1996 Ford truck. She got to add all kinds of bells and whistles to it, all the chrome and accessories that she liked, and that brand new rig put Mom into the elite fleet of trucking. She started hauling high-priced commodities. Sony rented her entire truck just to send one small computer from New York City to Anaheim, California. T.G.I. Friday's hired her to haul one hand-made telephone booth, worth a half-million dollars, from Hickory, North Carolina, to San Francisco.

Of course, the driving was not easy. Mom had to haul through rain, sleet, snow, gusting winds, and lightning storms. She jack-knifed her truck three times but, fortunately, never got seriously injured. On one trip to Columbus, Mom was driving on a highway in Ohio, and the snow was blowing sideways across the road. Her trailer was empty and very light, so when a fierce wind whipped up, it blew that rig right off the road. The truck was in a ditch, and Mom was stuck in waist-deep snow.

I worried about her constantly when she was away, but the thing that troubled me most was that she could come home only if she got a load that brought her near Los Angeles. After driving from Alabama to Phoenix, for example, Mom would check in with her dispatcher to see if she could get some cargo to haul from Phoenix to L.A.

On those occasions, Mom could usually spend two or three days with us. We could hear her truck pulling into Compton from a block away because it was so loud. She would drive up with her big trailer and then back that rig up, move it forward, and back it up again until she was perfectly parked in front of our house. Tiffany and I would be in our front yard, jumping up and down and cheering her on. We were always so excited. Mom would shut down the truck, step out of her door, and step right back into our lives again, even if it was just for a short time.

Tiffany and I would yell and scream as we ran to greet her, and it did not matter that she was dirty, grimy, and sleep-deprived. For her whole stay, we practically attached ourselves to her hips. She would tell us stories from the road, and we hung on every word.

When it came time for Mom to leave, Tiffany and I would promise ourselves that we would not cry. But when she climbed into her truck, we could not hold back the tears. I would hold Tiffany, and we would watch the truck drive away until it disappeared from sight. Then I would do what I had done so many times before. I would sit by the door and cry, and then I would pull out the photo album and look at the pictures of Mom and me holding hands. She was just so beautiful to me. I would look at her picture and wonder where she was, where she was going, why she had to leave me. I was never angry with her about it, but I was always a little hurt.

One of Mom's friends looked after us the first year she was on the road, but then Mom thought leaving us with family would be a better idea, so my Aunt Pete came in from Texas to help. Her real name was Minerva. She was my grandmother's younger sister, and she brought her teenage daughter, Kriscita, with her. When Kriscita came to California I did not know her, but my favorite cousin Braquel did. Kriscita appeared to be very conservative and proper. She talked with an accent, kept her hair in a ponytail with a bow, and only wore dresses, very long dresses. Kriscita was a breath of fresh air to me because she was so sweet. She was a Christian, always had her Bible, and never cursed, and she would not bow to peer pressure. This girl stood up for what she believed. I was impressed with her. She stayed with me in my room, while Dionne kept Tiffany and Marquis with her. I was excited to have my cousin in our home. I thought Kriscita could do no wrong.

But Braquel had a very different opinion. "Girl, don't believe a word Kriscita says," she warned. "She is such a liar. All this sweet stuff is just an act." I did not believe her.

Maybe it was all an act, or maybe Kriscita's new California lifestyle was a bad influence. I cannot be sure, but before long, Kriscita was completely out of control. She swore, wore suggestive clothes, and even dated one of her high school teachers as a student. She was also really disrespectful to her mother. All that "yes, ma'am" and "no, ma'am" had gone out the window.

Then there was Aunt Pete. She was like a character out of a movie. At times, she was fun-loving. But most times, she fussed and cussed about *everything*. Her negative personality was the complete opposite of my mom's. She barked commands and called me names. "Get your tall, skinny, lanky self and your big feet into this kitchen and come clean up."

I was already Miss Sensitive, so of course, I would start crying. Then, I would go into the kitchen to clean up somebody else's mess. I would plead with her. "Aunt Pete, it's not my week."

"I don't care. Get in there and clean up, anyway."

One night I rebelled and talked back. "No, I'm not cleaning nothing! It is Kriscita's turn, and I'm not doing her work."

I lay down in the hallway in protest, and all I could think about was my mother. I knew that if Mom was home, she would defend me. She would know I was telling the truth, and she would treat me fairly.

Well, I lay in the hallway so long that I fell asleep, and I woke up to Aunt Pete whuppin' me with a belt. I cried and jumped up to protect myself, then walked to the kitchen to start cleaning. I muttered under my breath, "I can't wait to talk to my mom," and I looked over my shoulder to be sure that Aunt Pete had not heard me. Not only did I have to do my chores; now I had to do Kriscita's, too. She was out late, fooling around with her teacher, and I was the one getting the beating. I felt like Cinderella living with her evil sisters.

While I cleaned anything and everything, Aunt Pete taught Tiffany how to curse. Tiffany was still in preschool, but she was smart for her age. Mom did not let us speak baby talk to Tiffany. We had to use real words, so Tiffany was good with language even as a toddler.

Every afternoon Aunt Pete would stand with Tiffany in our front doorway, and if kids stepped on our lawn on their walk home from school, Tiffany would yell out, "Get your a-- off my f------ grass!" Aunt Pete thought this was hilarious.

When I talked to Mom on the phone, I whispered, "Mom! You gotta come home. Aunt Pete makes me clean up all the time. I have to clean up her mess and my mess, everybody's mess. Mom, you are not going to believe this. Tiffany curses like crazy. She says all the bad words, and Kriscita is dating her teacher! She don't come home till late. Mom, they even took the toilet paper out of the bathroom. Now everybody keeps their own roll in their own room. You gotta come home, Mom! You just gotta!"

I spoke quickly because Mom was calling long distance, and I did not want to waste money. I intentionally left out what was really bothering me the most: that I felt abused and taken advantage of. Mom had enough to worry about on the road without worrying about me, too. I always kept quiet.

When Mom finally came home, all hell broke loose. She and Kriscita really got into it. My cousin yelled at her, "Can't nobody tell me what to do!"

Mom said, "You are right. Obviously, you are too grown up to live in this house and abide by the rules."

She threw Kriscita out of the house, and Aunt Pete went packing back to Houston shortly after.

As Mom started to put things back to normal for me and Tiffany, we got more disappointing news. The people she had entrusted with paying the mortgage had done something funky with the money, and we lost our house. Mom had to file for bankruptcy, but thankfully, she was able to keep her truck. We packed up everything we owned and put it into storage. Dionne had left home to be on her own, so Mom got me and Tiffany settled in Carson, with her sister Judy Carol—my Aunt J.C.—and then she went back to trucking. This was just the move I needed.

Chapter 2

How's the Weather Up There?

It took a little work to get settled at Aunt J.C.'s house. She was divorced from my Uncle Craig and lived with her two children, Craig II, whom we all called Craigie, and Braquel. Craigie was my only male cousin. He was eighteen, loved sports, and was creative, smart, and cool. Braquel was fifteen. She was my hero. This girl would not back down from anything or anybody. She was so brave, smart, pretty, and athletic, too. She and Craigie had it made. Aunt J.C. always provided them with the best of everything. They had Barbies, dollhouses, trains, model cars, and very expensive clothes. My cousins had so many things that Tiffany and I did not. I figured they had to be the happiest kids in the world. Oh, they were happy all right, but once we moved in with Craigie and Braquel, I found them to be unaware of just how truly blessed they were.

My cousins did not get along at all. They would really fight. I mean fight with a capital OUCH! I never saw a boy and a girl battle the way they did. He would get on her nerves, and she would kick him. He would choke her. I never knew what to do, except to get Tiffany out of the way while those two went at it. Craigie would punch Braquel. She would punch him right back.

They fought like grown men would fight. It was like I had the family edition of professional wrestling going on right before my eyes, but these conflicts were real.

When Aunt J.C. caught her kids in hand-to-hand combat, she would run in, kick off her heels, and jump on Craigie's back. If that did not break things up, she would run to the kitchen, grab a skillet, and threaten to hit him over the head with it. No kidding! It was serious. Their brawls only happened every few months, but that was more than enough for me. I hated it when my cousins fought. I cried every time. When each free-for-all finally ended, Craigie and Braquel would get a whuppin'. That scared me, too. I knew I had not done anything wrong, but I still worried that I might be next in the whuppin' line. It would not have been the first time I got spanked for something I did not do.

Aunt J.C. had punished me before, so I was overly nervous at her place. I really felt the pressure of trying not to be a bother in a house that was not my own. I made sure that Tiffany and I did not get in the way or ruffle any feathers. We tried to use as little hot water as possible to make sure that everybody had enough, and we always kept the noise to a minimum. Tiffany and I would put out a blanket (we called it a pallet) and sleep on the floor in the living room, where there was soft carpet under us. Aunt J.C. loved Tiffany and me as if we were her own, but I still felt like we were in the way. I knew Tiffany and I were loved, but I also knew it was uncommon for people to take two kids into their home, even if they were related. One thing I can say about my mom and her sisters is that they truly believe that it takes a village to raise a child. They were always there for one another, and since my village was made up mostly of women, I had a ton of role models, Aunt J.C. chief among them.

Aunt J.C. was so glamorous and fun. In a good, interesting way, she was all the things that my mother was not. Mom was more well rounded, but she was not always glamorous. She was bigger and taller than her sister. Mom would pick and choose when she wanted to look really sexy, but she always looked like a lady. Aunt J.C., on the other hand, always seemed to be in Diana Ross mode. She had the big hair, shiny lipstick, and lots of sparkly, unique outfits that made fashion statements. Aunt J.C. always went to work wearing heels and looking sharp. To this day, I have never seen her in sneakers. She wears nylons, really pretty dresses, and blouses that are made of linen, silk, or satin. Her hair is always curled, very stylish, and, do not forget, *big*. Her jewelry is terribly expensive. Her perfume has a scent of class that lingers for hours. When my Aunt J.C. enters a room, people take notice. I wanted to be just like that.

But I was feeling anything but glamorous. I was an awkward, gangly twelve-year-old who stood out at six foot one. I was literally head and shoulders above everybody else. When I was at school or walking home, kids would tease me about my size. They would point and laugh and say, "Wow! You are so tall! You look like Olive Oyl." They called me all kinds of names. Skinny Minnie. Bony. I would come home crushed! Mom would tell me to keep my head up high and understand that when people talked about me, they were only exposing their own insecurities. I tried to see it that way, but it was difficult.

Mom spoke from experience. She had been six foot three since she was nineteen years old, so she knew all about growing up tall. Plus, she wore really thick glasses as a child. Kids made fun of her and called her names, but she never let her height discourage her.

Besides fitting in at school, one of my main concerns was fitting into clothes. I did not understand that when I was growing so tall and so quickly, every pair of pants I wore would look as if they had shrunk. The cuffs would stop well above my ankles. It looked as if I had rolled them up to walk through a flood. Truth was, I constantly outgrew everything that I owned, and nothing ever fit right. Mom started shopping for me in the men's department. I wanted to wear fashionable kids' clothes like everybody else my age, but my days of fitting into children's clothing were over, and it was painfully embarrassing. What twelve-year-old girl wants to dress like a man? Not me.

My feet were size 12, and I walked around wearing these leather shoes that Mom bought for me on a trip to Tijuana. I wore those shoes every day for a full year. Before long, there were holes in the bottoms of them. Rain would seep in, soak my feet, and stain the leather. One day I got on my knees and prayed, "God, when people look at my clothes, make it look like they fit right, even if they don't. Can I please be able to get pants and jackets that are long enough?" Then I would add, "And please let people see me as beautiful."

I prayed a lot growing up. My family was pretty religious, but Dionne in particular used to go to church every Sunday to enjoy the choir and congregate with other people. She always was a people person. When I asked if I could tag along, it was one of the few times that she agreed without getting irritated with me. Dionne and I would walk together to church each Sunday, just the two of us. This gesture is the one thing I will always be grateful to her for; I am not sure if she ever knew it, but Dionne helped bring me to Christ when I was just seven years old.

So I believed in the power of prayer from a very young age, and I have never doubted that God answers prayers. I know that He does not always answer my prayers exactly the way I ask, but He does answer me eventually. To this day, whenever I pray, I say, "May Your will be done," because I understand that God sometimes has something else in mind for me, a different direction, a new focus, or a greater plan that is more important for me than clothes that fit or shoes without holes. But when I entered Whaley Junior High in Compton in 1984, that was exactly what I prayed for. Instead, God gave me basketball.

For years I had to put up with people saying, "You are so tall. Do you play basketball?" I got sick of hearing the question. Before I began junior high school, the game meant nothing to me. It was not even a tiny part of my life. We did not have any basketballs at my house, and I had never watched a game on television, so I had absolutely no understanding of the sport. I had seen some neighborhood kids shooting baskets down the street, but I never considered playing until junior high.

Sharon Hargrove was a very popular girl in school. We called her Shay. She came up to me and asked if I wanted to try out for the basketball team. I was hesitant. After all, I knew I was not tough or strong. My most athletic activities had been tetherball, kickball, and jumping rope. I was very good at double Dutch. Basketball, though, was something completely new and different. But I wanted to fit in, and when one of the most popular girls invited you to join her team, you had to give it some thought. I decided to give basketball a try.

For the first time ever, I was trying out for a team. You could say I was more than a little behind on the learning curve. Our coach split our squad into layup lines. He wanted the right-handed girls in one line and the left-handed girls in another. Of course, I wound up being the only player in the southpaw line. I remember him saying, "Just hit the ball off the top of the square on the backboard." I did, but about all I could do was make a layup. We went through some drills, and I did okay, but I vowed that the next day I would be right-handed so I would not have to be in a line all by myself again.

That tiny insecurity and my desire to feel included forced me to learn how to use my right hand effectively. Over the years, I developed to the point where I could do almost everything I needed in basketball with either hand. That turned out to be a real plus for me throughout my hoop career.

Meanwhile, Mom was still trucking across America. I really wanted to make the Whaley Junior High team. I knew it would do a lot for my popularity, but I was nervous about the results. When the team was finally selected and I realized I had a spot, I

24

could not have been more excited. Mom was fine with the idea and gave me permission to play. I did not really know what I was doing, and I was not all that motivated, but it was something to do. I almost never talked about basketball, so when our team went undefeated (7–0), not one person in my family knew about it. Nobody ever came to see me play. Who was I going to invite? To me, it was no big deal. I kept it low-key so that Mom would not feel badly about not being there to watch me. I played the games, had some fun, and made sure that I got home before dark.

The more I played basketball, the more I figured out the game. I was starting to improve, and when my cousin Craigie realized I played basketball, he started taking me to the gym at Victoria Park in Carson almost every day. I am not exaggerating; we rarely missed a day. Craigie was all about discipline. The first time we went to the gym, he had me do push-ups, sit-ups, and all kinds of exercises before I ever got to touch a basketball. I remember thinking, *Dang!* All I wanted to do was shoot the ball.

He would teach me things and then make me play three-on-three pickup games with the guys. I was unsure of what to do, but Craigie just told me to guard my man. I was already afraid of Craigie; I had seen him fight Braquel. So when he yelled at me, I did exactly what he said. It usually worked out for me just fine. And besides, I remember thinking at the time, Craigie was left-handed like me. That seemed to make it all okay. That made us both a little different than everybody else.

My Uncle Ed helped me, too. He was my mother's youngest brother, and he took me with him when he played basketball on the outdoor courts at a church in Inglewood. I thought it was very cool that my uncle wanted me to play basketball with him. He would make me play point guard and then have me post up.

Uncle Ed was a totally positive human being and encouraged me to get out there when he could have just as easily said, "Go sit down, Lisa. You can't play. You're a girl." Instead, he challenged me to rebound, block shots, and talk trash. I could get away with trash-talking, too. I knew the guys were not going to mess with me, because I had my own personal bodyguard there. My uncle was six foot three and about three hundred pounds. He used to play football at Southwest Community College, and he was huge, so I felt very safe.

Sometimes I would get pushed, tripped, knocked down, or fouled really hard. Uncle Ed would yell to me, "Get up. Come on. Keep going!" Or he would shout, "You can do it! Go hard! Go strong! Don't let 'em take that ball away!" It was like when you got bullied at school and your parents told you, "Go back and fight that bully. If you don't fight *him*, I'm going to whup *you!*" That was Uncle Ed's approach, and it was good for me. I was just learning to play a physical brand of basketball, so his no-nonsense style of encouragement kicked my game up a few notches.

I felt like I belonged in the gym maybe more than I belonged anywhere else. Even though I was a girl, I could play. I was not babied or given any special favors, but there was always a feeling of love and affection for me at the gym, because Uncle Ed and Craigie wanted me to play and gave me a chance. This gave me tremendous confidence. It was a great feeling to find something that I could do well, and it was also very important at that time in my life to have men support me and let me know that it was okay for me to play.

Craigie and Uncle Ed were my only male role models as far as basketball was concerned. I still cannot believe that they spent all that time working with me. I was only twelve years old. They were both closer to twenty. How many guys that age really want to take a young girl to the gym with them? I am sure there were a lot of other things they could have been doing, but their time was just what I needed. I appreciated them so much, and I was thankful for every second that they took out of their lives to be with me. That is why I always tried to be quiet, to not talk back, and to stay out of their way and off of their nerves. I looked them in the eye when they talked, and I listened well. I learned a lot, and I improved. Craigie and Uncle Ed liked my attitude. Craigie set me straight in that department the very first day that he took me to the gym. He sat me down and made it short and simple: "If you are going to have an attitude and want to be in here talking and fooling around, I'll take you home right now and never bring you back." Believe me. I got that message loud and clear. I think that made Craigie and Uncle Ed want to help me even more.

Their attention made me feel good. There was no father at home to watch sports with me and explain what was going on. And there was nobody to teach me the game or help me understand the fundamentals. I was just learning to play basketball on the fly—a pickup game with guys here, a practice with my junior high school team there. It was like on-the-job training. Craigie and Uncle Ed were my teachers, and I was their student. Every time we stepped on the court, I tried to learn as much as I could and make them proud.

At the same time that I was learning basketball, Aunt J.C. was teaching me "girl things." She was the first person to show me how to put Nair under my arms. We would all sit on her kitchen counter while she explained the necessities of underarm hair removal. We walked with books on our heads, and we tried to practice proper etiquette. We worked on the correct way to eat and sit, and we practiced good posture. It was a good reminder of what my mom had already told me. To this day, my friends tease me about sitting up so straight. "You make me sick," they tell me, "always sitting up so straight!" I do try to slouch sometimes, but after a while I go right back to sitting up.

Mom wanted to make sure that her girls knew what girls needed to know. So while she was on the road, Aunt J.C. made sure we learned. I did not know what being feminine was, but I did know what a lady should do and how a lady should act. For example, I knew that when wearing a skirt, a lady should cross her legs so that no one can see what is underneath. This is why I started wearing shorts under my skirts way back in second grade. It was important to me to be feminine, and I liked taking cues from Aunt J.C. and from Mom when she was home. And it is a good thing, too, because I always wanted to look my best.

When we moved in with Aunt J.C. and she saw my hairdo, I think she wanted to dial 911. Dionne had experimented with a Jheri Curl on my head, and it was not going well. My hair was unhealthy and full of chlorine from the local pool and had turned a shade of orange. You also have to keep getting Jheri Curls every few months, but I was not able to manage it well on my own, and Dionne did not really know what she was doing. I had a dry, orange, Jheri Curl. Something desperately needed to be done to repair the damage, so Aunt J.C. brought in Mike the Hairdresser, who came to her house every Saturday to remedy the situation. First, he would do Braquel's hair: wash, condition, blow-dry, press, and curl. Then he would do the same for me.

One Saturday, though, Mike did my hair first. When he was done with me and started working on my cousin, Craigie came home and asked me to shoot some hoops with him. We went around the corner and played for about an hour. It was hot, and I got really sweaty. By the time we got home, my fresh do was not so fresh anymore. My hair was all wet and plastered to my head. I was scared to go into the house because I knew that my hair was ruined. I looked like I had been left outside in a down-pour. I was seriously afraid of how Aunt J.C. was going to react.

When I finally got up the nerve to walk in the house, my aunt spotted me and shouted, "Oh my God! Look what this girl has done to her hair!" She was irate, but for some reason, she was laughing at the same time. "I can't believe it," she said loudly. "You *just* got your hair done!" She stood there in shock. "We were finally getting your hair back nice and clean. It was just starting to look good, and you go out and play basketball? Why did you mess up your hair, Lisa?"

I did not have any answers for her, but Aunt J.C. had an ultimatum for me. "You are going to choose today, young lady. You can either play basketball or get your hair done, but you cannot do both. Which is it going to be?"

Without a hint of hesitation, I told her softly, "I want to play basketball."

My aunt looked at me, looked at my messy hair, and then said, "All right. Fine. Put your hair in a ponytail, and go play basketball."

I knew I had made a big decision that day. I could have said, "Oh, I want my hair done." Mike probably would have done it again for another ten dollars, but who knows what direction my life might have taken if he had. At that time, being cute and stylish was nice, but it was not my top priority. I wanted to play basketball, so I put my hair in a ponytail and went off to play some more. Honestly, I would have played all day and night if I could have. If Craigie wanted to go to the gym early, I was ready. If he wanted to wait until after 5:00 PM, I would do my homework, eat, and get dressed in a hurry just in case he wanted to leave a little earlier.

I had found a passion for the game. It had become a major part of my life. I loved the sport, and somehow, I knew it was going to be a big part of my future. I wanted to be very good, so I would take what Craigie taught me and then try it out in practice sessions and games. I started to put two and two together. When I struggled, I would go back to Craigie, and he would have a ton of criticism and suggestions for me. I would absorb all that he told me, store it in my memory bank, and try to do better next time. I turned into a perfectionist, and that was not necessarily a good thing. Basketball is a game where you strive for perfection but never, ever get there. That can be extremely frustrating. This did not keep me from trying, though. Striving for perfection made me a better player, which came in handy the following spring, when I joined a boys' basketball league and played for a team called the Sonics.

I did not get to play basketball at school during my entire eighth-grade year, because I switched schools in midyear, but I continued to spend a lot of time working on my game with Craigie. A guy at the gym named Vic suggested that I join an organized team to remain competitive and sharpen my skills. There was no girls' team, so I joined the team for boys. I was the only girl in the entire league, and I played in the 14-and-under division. Corey Benjamin, who later played in the NBA, was in my league. Craigie loaned me a pair of his basketball shoes to wear with my brand-new #10 Sonics green uniform. It came with white mid-calf socks that had a green stripe around the top. That was the first "take home" uniform that I ever had. I thought it was very cool, but the uniform was not my size. It was too tight, and I barely fit into it. I wound up wearing very short shorts and a too-snug shirt. I was six foot two, the tallest player in the league, but that was not the only reason I stood out.

At first, the boys on my own team did not want to pass the basketball to me. This really upset me, so on one of our possessions, I intercepted a pass between two of my own teammates and dribbled in to score a basket. I stole the ball from my own team! After that, everybody started shouting, "Give the ball to the girl!" The Sonics soon realized that if they got the ball to the tall girl in the middle, she could put some points on the board and help them win games. They finally listened.

I knew I could play a little, and I soon found out that I could do almost everything that the boys could do. I could jump and block their shots. I could slide my feet and play defense. The boys did have a quickness factor that sometimes left me in their dust, so when I played with them, I really had to focus and play super-hard to stay with them. That extra effort against the boys gave me incredible confidence when it came time to compete against girls. Later, in my professional career, my scrimmages with Magic Johnson and his NBA buddies helped me prepare for the battles I faced in the WNBA. To this day, I like to play with men, because it helps me improve my quickness and my moves. This allows me to be more aggressive and play harder with women.

Someone had obviously been keeping tabs on me while I played on that boys' team or when I practiced at the gym, because in that summer of 1986, I was selected to play in the Olympic Girls' Development League (OGDL). It turns out that the OGDL played its games at the same Victoria Park that Craigie had been taking me to every night to work on my game.

John Anderson was my OGDL coach. He gave me the first pair of basketball shoes that I could call my own. They were Nikes. I loved them, and I knew I would like Nike from then on. Mr. Anderson was a yeller, though. And he was the first coach who cursed at me. Sometimes he made me cry, but I think that hurt his heart, because afterwards he was always really nice to me. He would say, "Lisa, when I yell, I am not really yelling at you. I just want to help you get better."

Even through all of Coach Anderson's shouting, I could sense his caring personality. He was a real sweetheart, and eventually, I learned not to take his shouting personally. Sometimes, I would even go over to his house to hang out with his daughter, Adana. Mrs. Anderson would cook, and we would all have a good time. The Andersons really took care of me. Since Aunt J.C.'s house was nearby, they would even pick me up for practices and games, and then drop me off afterwards.

I knew Coach Anderson saw something special in me, because he was always on my case in the gym, yet so nice at home. He must have liked my game a lot, because before I knew it, he had me playing in the OGDL's fourteen-and-under, sixteen-and-under, and eighteen-and-under girls' divisions, all in the same summer and sometimes all in the same day. I was incredibly busy, but I was excited, too, because Shay had joined the summer league. We would play on the weekends, and when one game ended for me, I would head to the sideline and change into the colored shirt of the next team that I would be playing for. Then, I would get back on the court and start playing again. I could go through a lot of shirts in one weekend. Some days, Shay and I would get to the park at 8:00 AM, and we would play five games before heading home. I loved the competition, and I enjoyed seeing my basketball skills improve with every game.

The OGDL was really great for me. I played against Pauline and Geanine Jordan in the eighteen-and-under division. They were twins who just happened to be two of the best girl basketball players not only in California, but also in the entire country. They were recruited by all of the top college basketball teams. Coaches were constantly coming to watch them play, so the OGDL was a showcase for the Jordan twins. It also shined some of the spotlight on a fourteen-year-old who was playing against them—me! I was not on the twins' level in talent or experience, but I was competitive enough in the eighteen-and-under games. I had to guard Pauline and Geanine (who both got scholarships to UNLV), and that made me better defensively, but I also learned that I could score against the big girls. I could take them away from the basket and hit a short jumper, and eventually, I was driving to the hoop against them and scoring. It was exhilarating. The more I played, the better I got. The better I got, the more fun I had. And the more fun I had, the more I wanted to play.

My metamorphosis on the court was incredible. Within two years, I went from having never played basketball and nervously trying out for my seventh-grade team to holding my own on the court against eighteen-year-olds. I improved so much so quickly, and much of it was due to the basketball mentoring that I got from Craigie. He made sure that I knew the basics, and I made sure that I worked hard and put his teachings to good use. It was all coming together. I was finally really good at something, and I kept growing taller, too. I was up to six foot four that summer, but I was no longer Olive Oyl when I stepped on the court. I was Lisa Leslie, basketball player. I had an identity. I was not awkward. I could move. I performed, and people liked the way I played. My confidence was so high that it did not matter to me what age or gender my opponents might be. In my mind, I had the upper hand on all of them. It was a fantastic feeling.

My schedule was grueling, though. It was all basketball all the time for me, and since it was the summer, I had lots of time. I practiced two nights a week with the OGDL and then played their games on Saturdays and Sundays. I also played two games during the week with the Miraleste High School squad. Mom was trying to transition into more local trucking work, and she wanted to move our family from Carson to Palos Verdes, which was a nicer area. Miraleste High was located in Palos Verdes, so it made the most sense for me to play with the high school girls that I would be joining in the fall. I did not complain; their team was super impressive. We played against athletes like Heather and Heidi Buerge, another set of twins. They were both six foot four, just like me, and they both went on to play in the WNBA, just like me. The Miraleste squad had twin girls who mirrored the Buerges, plus we had a six-foot-seven center, and our point guard was over six feet tall. Our starting lineup featured five teenage girls who were all at least six feet tall. We were expected to have a great season. But as it turned out, I was not going to be a part of it. Mom decided that the move to Palos Verdes would be too much, too fast, and too expensive to handle. So instead, we moved from Aunt J.C.'s house in Carson to my grandmother's house in Inglewood, not far from where the Lakers played NBA basketball at the Fabulous Forum.

That meant that Miraleste was out of the picture, and I would be attending high school in the Inglewood district. The Inglewood district had two high schools at the time: Inglewood and Morningside. I knew absolutely nothing about either of them, but Inglewood was a little closer, so Mom decided to enroll me there. On the day of enrollment, Mr. Dillon, the man in charge of Pupil Personnel Services, made a point of coming over to talk to us. "I know you want to go to Inglewood High because your Uncle Ed went there," he said. "But I really think you should consider Morningside High. They have an excellent basketball team and a great coach. His name is Frank Scott. He takes good care of his girls, and he makes sure that they get home safely. I would really advise you to consider Morningside."

I did not have a preference. I just wanted to get a good education and play basketball. But right then and there, I decided to attend Morningside High. It turned out to be one of the best decisions of my life.

Before I ever stepped one foot on the Morningside campus, I had already received more than a hundred college recruiting letters. I was only fourteen, but my game had improved so much over the summer that college coaches had taken notice and were lining up to let me know that they were interested in me playing basketball at their universities. I was only an incoming freshman and I had not played one second of high school basketball, but I got letters from everywhere, including top Division I basketball programs, like Stanford, USC, Notre Dame, and Tennessee. Harvard wanted me, too. But being highly recruited did not help me fit in.

I was shy to begin with, and I always felt like an outsider, which only made things worse. I hated the fact that I did not grow up in one place, where I could really get to know people. How could I? I went to three different junior high schools. I think that is a big reason why sometimes people misinterpreted my shyness as being closed off or snobby. This still occasionally happens. I have always tried to treat all people nicely, but I am not very good at opening up to people. Growing up without close, long-term friendships made me a loner in a lot of ways. I never had to have a million friends, but it would have been nice to have some of my close friends for more than one school year. I was always the new kid. I was never the outcast, but I was never in any one school long enough to get into the in crowd and at times I felt left out.

My life changed dramatically, though, once I got to Morningside. On the first day of school, I was sitting all by myself on the last bench in the entire lunch area. I did not know one person. I was wearing a long pink skirt with checkers on it, a pink blouse, and black shoes. I had a ponytail and bangs. I was in high school, but I did not have a clue how to dress. A group of girls walked up to me, and one of them asked, "You play basketball?" I found out later that her name was JoJo Witherspoon.

I said, "Yeah. I play basketball."

They ran off, and a few minutes later Coach Scott came over to introduce himself.

"Hi, I'm Frank Scott."

"Hi, I'm Lisa."

He knew who I was. Coach Scott had seen me play for Miraleste during the summer, so I think he was really surprised to see me sitting in front of him right there at Morningside. Just about everybody expected that I would be part of that powerhouse team in Palos Verdes.

"I hear that you play basketball," Coach Scott said. "Would you like to play for our team here at Morningside?"

I told him I would.

"Are you good?" he asked, with a smile.

I answered, "I don't know, but I want to play."

Coach Scott chuckled. "Okay," he said. "Good. Meet me at the gym at two PM." Then he brought me over and introduced me to some of the other girls on the team. I was shy, but I was very excited.

I was in ninth grade—a brand-new freshman—but adjusting to a new high school was not my only concern. Tiffany and I were now staying with my grandmother. She was my mother's mother and was so young looking that we called her Dear instead of the older-sounding Grandma. Dear's house was another new place for us, another sofa bed to sleep on, another set of rules to learn. Every morning Dear would get up around seven o'clock and start yelling, "GET UP! GET UP!" Then she would start playing gospel music and run the vacuum cleaner. There was no sleeping late at Dear's house—not even on weekends.

Tiffany and I would wipe the sleep from our eyes, stumble to our feet, fold up our blankets, fold the sofa, and then just sit there. There was absolutely no reason for us to be awake. We were sleepy, but my grandmother wanted us up, so we were. It was just miserable. I was always panicky at my grandmother's house, constantly making sure that Tiffany did not make any messes or cause any trouble.

Dear would say, "Get your sister dressed, and get yourself dressed, too." That meant I had to shower, bathe Tiffany, get her dressed, and have her all ready to go NOWHERE! My grandmother just wanted Tiffany to be up and dressed. Today, as an adult, I understand that kids do not need to stay in bed until noon or hang around in their pajamas all day, but it sure would have been nice if Dear could have held off on the wake-up calls until at least eight o'clock.

Once again, I found myself talking under my breath. "Oh man! I cannot wait till Mom gets home so we can get out of here." Then a different thought would pass through my mind. *Man, I cannot wait to get out of here so I can go play basketball.* Hoops had become an outlet and my exciting new escape. I had just one small roadblock: my grandmother.

Dear was very hesitant to let me play basketball at my new high school. She was protective of me and did not want me to be take advantage of me. Coach Scott came by the house to introduce himself, and Dear was defensive and downright rude. She asked him point-blank, "Who are you, and what are you doing over here? What do you want with my granddaughter?"

Coach Scott seemed to understand my grandmother's dubi-
ousness and responded in his usual calm, respectful, non-ruffled
way. "I am the coach of the girls' basketball team at Morningside
High School, and I would like Lisa to play on our team. I would
be happy to come by and pick her up for school in the mornings
and bring her back home after practices."

Dear's interrogation continued. "How do I know I can trust
you?" I was so embarrassed. Looking back on it now, I know that
she was just looking out for me, but Dear was really working
Coach Scott over. She had no idea who this man was or what he
might have in mind for me. But Coach answered her questions
politely and gave her a lot of references and phone numbers to
call so she could check up on him. Coach Scott told my grandmother that Mr. Fortune, the superintendent of schools, and our
principal, Mrs. Martin, would verify that he was a good man
who had been at Morningside High for ten years and that he
routinely picked up his players before school and dropped them
off after practice, without any problems at all.

Coach Scott withstood all of my grandmother's blistering in-
quiries, and he turned out to be one of the most invaluable people in my basketball development. He would pick me up for
school every morning. I would go to class, participate in girls'
basketball practice from 2:00 to 4:00 PM, and then practice with
the boys' team until Coach Scott was ready to leave. On some
days, I would stay with Coach Scott to work over and over on my
post moves. He would have me dribble in and take a bank shot. I
would drive to the left, drive to the right, and hit a jump shot.
He taught me how to react when a shot was taken, and how to
box out, grab a rebound, and slide my feet to play more efficient
defense. He was very good with fundamentals and very good for
me. My knowledge of the game and my work ethic improved
rapidly.

After practice, he would drive several players home. I actually
lived the closest to school, but he always dropped me off last. I

begged him to so I would not have to spend too much time at my grandmother's house.

I enjoyed hanging out with him. I still do to this day. Coach Scott would tell corny jokes, and I might have been the only person who laughed, but I thought he was so funny and cool. In a lot of ways, he was the father that I never had. He was a very mellow, soft-spoken man who knew the game and knew how to communicate it to me, but he cared about me as more than just a basketball player. Coach Scott was the only one who knew that my mom was not home and that my sister and I were living with my grandmother under intense conditions. He would check my grades and make sure that I was eating lunch, and he would talk with Mom all the time to assure her that I was doing well. He was interested in me. I was flattered, and I did not want to let him down in any way.

Coach worked with me constantly. He would make me take five hundred shots a day and work on my dribbling. He taught me how to use my height to my best advantage. He would lob the ball up high to me and have me practice my turnaround jump shot. It was catch, turn, and shoot without my ever bringing the ball down below my head, where a smaller defender might grab it. I would do that left-handed, then right-handed. I would do the George Mikan drill over and over: left-side layup with the left hand, rebound, right-hand layup on the right side. Up and down, side to side, and back and forth time after time after time. It was difficult, but that drill helped with my footwork and rebounding, and I was able to get shots off more quickly.

Coach Scott never stopped challenging me to improve. He would bring a broom out on the court, hold it straight up over his head, and try to block my shots with it. That forced me to put more arc on my shots, which really helped when I competed against other tall players. He would line up my teammates and have them dribble and drive at me, one after the other. My job was to block every one of their shots. It was hard work, a real test, but it all paid off. Whatever Coach Scott told me to do, I did. I was not about to cheat myself. I did not cut corners. I worked hard and I got better. Some of the other girls on our team would talk back to Coach Scott or chatter during practice. I did not give him any attitude. I listened and I learned.

I did not talk much with my teammates. I had first lunch period, and most of the other girls had second. I rarely saw them during the day, but then, after school, I had to compete against them in order to win a spot on the team. Everyone was talking about who the starters might be, and more than a few times, I heard someone whisper, "That new girl is not going to come in and take my spot."

It was an awkward situation, but as much as I wanted to be accepted, basketball mattered to me more than going out of my way to be anybody's friend. I had very little competitive basketball experience under my belt, and I had never seen any of my new teammates play. I had no idea what level they were on. My gut told me to just go out and work hard. I definitely knew that I was tall. That was a big plus. I also knew I could shoot and play defense, but I had to learn in a hurry to be competitive. There was no cockiness to my game, because I knew that I had arrived so late to the sport. I knew there were other girls on the team who had played a lot more than me, and I knew that someone out there might be better than me.

As it turned out, I was pretty good. Much better than I thought I would be, at least. I understood the drills and the three-man weave, and I was gaining more confidence day by day. I worked on dribbling, on blocking shots, and I kept improving. I was a freshman, but I was challenging Shaunda Green, a junior, who was the best player on our team. She was coming off an All-California Interscholastic Federation (CIF) season. There was jealousy and some tension in the gym. My teammates were not very discreet when they would say, "She ain't better than Shaunda. She's not going to come in here and start."

My mind-set was, I am here and I can play basketball. I am not going to back down from any player, no matter her talent level. If Shaunda Green was the best on the team, then that is who I wanted to play against every day.

So I was very goal oriented early on. This was just the ninth grade, and I was already writing my goals down, knowing it would help me achieve them. I wanted to get better in math and earn a 3.5 grade point average, and in basketball, I wanted to be "Freshman of the Year" in California. My thinking was simple: *This is what I want to do. This is what I want to accomplish.* And I was so serious about it. On the basketball court, I planned to be the very best that I could be, and it was not just a dream or a wish. It was something for me to work toward, and my efforts paid off. I was the only ninth grader to make the varsity team. Shaunda and I were teammates. We were both very good, and we played well together for Morningside.

My high school basketball career was off to a great start, but six-year-old Tiffany was still my responsibility. I still had to pick her up when she got out of school. Then both of us would go to my practice or game. When the Lady Monarchs traveled, Tiffany would be on the team bus with us, even though that was strictly forbidden. Tiffany would write and keep busy while I did my homework, and I always made sure she got something to eat.

When I had games, Tiffany would sit by herself in the stands. While I was on the court playing, I would glance over from time to time to make sure that she was all right and to make certain that nobody had kidnapped my little sister from the gym. Tiffany was at Morningside High more than some of the students, and she was with me for almost every one of our road games, too.

It was a lot of responsibility for a fourteen-year-old, but somehow Tiffany and I both made it work. She was a healthy, happy, resilient kid, and she thrived in spite of our very unusual circumstances. So did I. I averaged twelve points, nine rebounds, and five blocked shots, and the Monarchs finished with a 27–3 record during my freshman season. And my grades were good, too—mostly As and a few Bs. I was named "Freshman of the Year" in the state of California. The sense of accomplishment I felt tasted so sweet! But it was just the tip of the iceberg.

Chapter 3

Making a Name for Myself

That first year at Morningside was extremely busy for me. Besides playing basketball and taking care of Tiffany, I somehow also found time to play on the Lady Monarchs' volleyball team and compete in track and field, too. I was hoping that those activities would help improve my speed and jumping ability for basketball, but I still cannot believe that I went out for track after the terrible experience I had with that sport back in seventh grade. What was I thinking?

My track coach at Whaley Junior High decided that my long legs were best suited for the 400-meter run, which I believe is the hardest race in the world. In one particular meet, I was running really well. I had the lead with one hundred meters to go, so I kept driving with my legs, pumping my arms, and pushing hard. But I started to tire. My heart was pounding, and my lungs were on fire. I looked straight ahead for the finish line, but I did not see one. I could not find it. The people in the crowd were cheering and yelling, "Come on! Come on! Come on!" As usual, no one from my family was there, but I gave it everything I had just the same. Just for pride. Just for me.

I ran as fast and hard as I could, and then, all of a sudden, I fell down on the track. I just collapsed. I could not believe it. There I was, sprawled in the dirt, all sore and sweaty. I could see my lead disappearing as I lay on the ground. And I could also see a strand of red yarn up ahead of me. It was stretched low across the track. The finish line. It was right in front of me. It was so close, but I could not reach it! I had to get up. I had to finish. I could hear and feel runners breezing by me as I struggled to get to that yarn. My muscles ached, my tracksuit was filthy, and my ego was more than a little bit bruised. But I finished the race. What an ordeal! I knew right then and there that I was finished with running track forever. At least I thought I was.

The track coach at Morningside already knew about me. Coach Ron Tatum had seen me run during basketball season. Coach Tatum kept telling me that running track would improve my physical skills for basketball and also give me more stamina. I knew all that, but I told him, "I do not want to run track."

Coach Tatum was persistent, though, and, just my luck, he wanted me to run the dreaded 400 meters. He thought I would be good at running hurdles as well. The way he put it to me was, "Lisa, with your long legs, you will be able to just glide over those hurdles. You will never hit one."

Of course, the first time I practiced running hurdles, I crashed right into one and went down face-first. The hurdles were made of metal and wood, and they hurt. There I was, sprawled on a track all over again. I told anyone who would listen, "I will never come back out here if you make me run hurdles."

I guess the coach felt really bad, because he agreed that I would have to compete only in the 400 meters, plus three jumping events, and that was fine with me. In the long jump and the triple jump, I would be landing in the sand. That seemed safe enough, but the high jump was a different story. I used the Fosbury Flop method for high jumping, which meant that I would run up, lift off, and go over the bar with my chest facing the sky and my back closest to the bar. Then I would kick and arch my way over. Essentially, I was going over the bar upside down, and I was getting pretty good at it until one painful attempt. I went up just fine and I cleared the bar, but on the way down, I just barely skimmed the edge of the mat on my landing, and I flopped to the ground with a thud. Fortunately, I was not injured badly, and I was able to continue jumping, but after that crash landing, I was never really the same mentally when it came to high jumping. On a good day, I could get up and over a bar set at five foot eight. That was pretty high for me. I knew it was definitely a long way to fall, and everybody who knew me knew that I hated to fall down.

But I did not give up on high jumping, and I am glad that I stuck with it, because I got good enough to compete in the state championships. I cleared the bar at five feet six inches and managed to improve my personal best in the triple jump to thirty-eight feet nine inches. I was so proud to qualify for state, especially since track was just something that I did to help me improve in basketball. I have always wondered just how good I might have been if I had practiced the sport all year long.

I really did feel faster and stronger after track season, and I knew that was going to help me on the basketball court. Any doubts I might have had in that regard were eliminated on a rainy afternoon at Morningside when track practice had to be moved inside, to the gym. I was focusing on my high jump technique, which involved footwork, pushing off, body control, and lift, but we were really limited indoors as to how much practicing we could actually do. My coach said, "Lisa, why don't you work on your approach to that basketball rim over there? It will give you a chance to use a lot of the same skills as the high jump."

I followed his instructions and measured my approach from about sixty feet out. I got my running start, took off, and touched my fingers on the rim. I had never done that before. I was excited, and so were my teammates. Somebody found a tennis ball. I ran in, took my steps, went up, and dunked it. Now everybody in the gym was into it. They found a volleyball, and I dunked it, too. I tried to dunk a basketball that day, but my hands were too small to palm the ball, and I could not get good control. Oh well. But I knew that my time would come. That might have been my most enjoyable track practice ever.

Running track paid dividends for me, but I gave it up after my freshman year because my heart just was not in it. I realized that I spent way too much of my time trying to find excuses not to go to practice. I told the coach, "I dread coming out here because of all the running. It makes me so nervous. When I get to fifth period and I know that track is coming up next, I get sick to my stomach."

It takes a lot to run track. It really does. I think track athletes have more heart than athletes in any other sport. Jackie Joyner-Kersee, a track-and-field legend, is one of my "sheroes" and has all my respect in the world. It takes a lot of heart and a lot of discipline to get on the track every day and to be successful at it. I knew I did not have that kind of heart or desire for track, especially for the running. I told Coach Tatum, "I know what it takes to play basketball. It is hard work, but I never dread going to basketball practice. But this is literally making me sick." That was the end of my track career.

That summer of 1987, I played AAU basketball, and I also played with Morningside's off-season team. When I went back to high school in the fall, I was no longer the "new kid." In fact, my good grades, sense of humor, and success on the basketball court had earned me a lot of respect and had made me pretty popular. I was thrilled when I was elected sophomore class president.

That season our basketball team lost only two of thirty-five games, and despite being one of the smaller schools, we won the CIF Division 5AA title, captured the Division I Regional, and advanced to the California state championship game. Our Morningside squad had a date with Oakland's Fremont High School for the big showdown at the Oakland Coliseum.

That game was hard fought. We should have put Fremont away, but Morningside could not manage to score a single point in the final seven minutes of the contest. Still, we found ourselves trailing just 53–52 with seconds left to play. Coach Scott called a time-out. He huddled us together and said, "This is the play we are going to run." It was an inbounds play from the baseline that we had run ever since I got to Morningside. Our guard, JoJo Witherspoon, would handle the ball and lob it to me at the front of the block. I'd catch it and hit a bank shot. It was nothing complicated and nothing new to us. I make the shot, we win the game, and Morningside wins state. It was as simple as that.

Coach Scott made sure that everybody knew their responsibilities and had the play fresh in their minds. " I want you here," he told each of us as he pointed to the play board and calmly looked around our huddle. "I want you over here. You are going to break this way. Just lob it up there to Lisa, and that will be the game." He never said anything to me. I am sure he figured that I knew exactly what I needed to do on the play and was well aware of the importance of the final shot.

We broke our huddle and stepped onto the court. The play was designed perfectly. JoJo lobbed the ball in. I jumped up to grab it, came down, turned, and put up my shot as time was running out. But it was short. The ball barely hit the rim. What happened? I choked. That was my shot. I made it all the time, but as I turned to make the shot, I could not decide whether to bank it off the glass or try to swish the ball straight in, and I wound up shooting the ball too softly to accomplish either one. My shot was not high enough to kiss the rim, bounce around, and have a chance to drop, and it was too weak to reach the backboard and carom in. If I had just used the glass, I probably would have scored. At least the ball would have had a chance to go in, but the wimpy way I shot it, NO CHANCE. I had choked. I had a triple-double in the game, thirteen points, twelve rebounds, and ten blocked shots, but we lost by one point, and Morningside's season ended on a terribly sour note.

Fremont's players were cheering and jumping for joy in the middle of the court. Their fans were jubilant. Our fans were shocked. Our team was stunned and silent. I know some fans were probably thinking that our senior, Shaunda Green, should have taken the last shot instead of me. Hey. Our play worked. I just could not put the ball in the hole.

That was a major turning point in my life. When I missed that shot, we lost out on a state championship. My miss kept us from getting the title for Shaunda in her last season at Morningside. That was a lot of weight on my shoulders.

Looking back now, I think I needed Coach Scott to say something to me in that final huddle. I needed reassurance that I could do it. Maybe if he had said, "Just shoot it like you normally shoot it, Lisa." Or, "You have made this shot a hundred times. Just use the glass." But I know I should have made the shot.

The whole team cried after the game, and I apologized a lot for letting them down. I cried through the entire flight back to Los Angeles, and I could not stop crying after we got home. I was sick to my stomach and felt terrible, but before I went to bed, I wrote down my goal for next season. I wanted to win the state championship in 1989.

I could not get that loss or that missed shot out of my mind. Maybe that was good in a way, because it motivated me to work even harder on my game. During the off-season, I sprouted to my full height of six foot five, and I was really driven to succeed. In my junior year, I averaged twenty-five points, fourteen rebounds, and six blocked shots per game. Both *USA Today* and *Parade* magazine named me to their first-team high school All-America squad. That was all great, but most importantly, I helped lead the Morningside Lady Monarchs to a 33–1 record and a trip back to the California state championship game.

We played at the Oakland Coliseum again, and fittingly, we got a rematch with Fremont High School, the defending champs. I put up a double-double, and we won the game 60–50 to capture the 1989 California state championship. This time we were the ones jumping and cheering at the final buzzer. That win was extremely important to me. I had to erase the memory of my miss in the previous year's final game loss, but it was also critical for me because I had set a goal, had focused on achieving that goal, and with the help of my teammates, had accomplished that goal. Winning state did wonders for my confidence, my self-esteem, and my ability to believe in myself.

After my junior season, I received a great honor. I was invited to try out for USA Basketball's Junior World Championship squad. They flew me to Colorado Springs, and when I got there, I saw the best women's basketball players in the country. They were all in college. I was sixteen years old, the only high school player in the group.

I blocked Katrina McClain's shot during those tryouts, and everybody told me that was quite an accomplishment. Truthfully, I did not know one player from the other, and I was too young at that time to know who I was supposed to be afraid of.

When we were eating lunch after that practice session, Dawn Staley said, "Oh my God! Do you know you blocked Katrina McClain's shot?" I asked her, "Who is Katrina McClain?" I had no idea at the time, but I came to find out that Katrina was a two-time All-American at the University of Georgia, and she was college basketball's player of the year in 1987 and USA Basketball's Female Athlete of the Year in 1988. I was in very elite company, and looking back, I can tell you that Katrina was one of the greatest players that I ever competed against.

I made the junior national team that year, and we flew off to Bilbao, Spain, for the tournament. I was going to get my first taste of representing my country in international competition. I was really psyched to travel abroad for the first time. My family was really supportive, which made me feel even better about going. Mom was back in L.A. for good now, and Tiffany was with her. They were so excited about my travels.

Debbie Ryan, from the University of Virginia, was our head coach, and future WNBA players Lady Hardmon and Sonja Henning were on our squad. Dawn Staley was my roommate, and she turned out to be my complete opposite. I was six foot five. Dawn was five foot six. I loved bright colors and tie-dye. She loved black and white. I was a California girl, soft-spoken and carefree. She was a Philly girl, tough and edgy. One thing we had in common, though, was passion and heart. We both truly loved to compete and to win. Dawn Staley became my best friend in basketball.

Our team was very young. We averaged nineteen years of age. I was the youngest and the only high school player on our roster, which featured just three players who had any international experience. We lost the first game of the junior world championships, in overtime, to South Korea, then dropped our next game by two points to Australia. We finally got our first victory when I put up twenty-two points and nine rebounds against Bulgaria. Our U.S. squad was in every game, but we finished in seventh place, with a 3–4 record. To this day, that is the only time that Dawn and I competed together and did not win a medal.

Playing for the U.S. junior national team in Spain was an awesome experience. I learned how a group of total strangers could pull together into a team in a very short period of time. I learned about international travel, and I was able to test my talents against some of America's top college athletes and against some of the world's best young players as well. I led the U.S. team in scoring and rebounding at the junior world championships, and I came back to California with improved skills and even greater confidence in my game.

I was definitely ready for my senior season to tip off at Morning-side, and the college recruiters were ready for me. They came out of the woodwork. I got letters and phone calls from them every day. I was getting national media attention as the Lady Monarchs prepared to defend our state championship in what would turn out to be an amazing senior season for a number of reasons.

Early in the 1989–90 season, our game with Centennial High School turned into a brawl. One second we were playing, and the next second, four girls were fighting. I watched the skirmish and then saw three Centennial players coming after me. They cornered me against the wall, so I started swinging, and I kept on swinging. I know I hit some of them in the head. One of their players hit me in the face and scratched some skin off my nose. I just kept fighting back. I had to defend myself until one of the parents saw that I was in trouble. He came over, moved the Cen-tennial girls away, and picked me up out of the corner. I did not even know why we were fighting, but that brawl turned out to have a major impact on me later in the season.

That senior season, I posted the best numbers of my high school career. I averaged twenty-seven points, fifteen rebounds, and seven blocks per game. Those stats could have easily been much higher, but when Morningside had commanding leads in games, Coach Scott would take me out early. He did not want to run up the score and embarrass the other teams. Our Lady Mon-archs had lost only three times all season as we headed into our final home game against South Torrance High.

Now, the tradition at Morningside High School called for the team's top senior to try to break the school scoring record in the last home game of the regular season. In my freshman year, Tia Thomas was our senior, and she scored fifty-two points. The next year, Shaunda totaled sixty-one points, and in my junior season, JoJo Witherspoon set a new Morningside scoring record with sixty-nine points.

That was the number I was trying to beat when we took the court against the Spartans of South Torrance High on Tiffany's tenth birthday, February 7, 1990. We were originally scheduled to finish the home season against Centennial High, but because of our brawl with them earlier in the season, that schedule was changed. The fear was that Centennial might try to hurt me, especially if I was shooting for the record against them. So, we played Centennial High in our next-to-last home game and faced South Torrance in our season finale. Truthfully, Centennial would have been a much tougher opponent for us, and I would have preferred that.

Coach Scott held a team meeting before the final game. He asked everyone on our squad if they were okay with me going after the record. My teammates said, "Let's go for it." That made Coach Scott's pregame instructions pretty easy. He told us, "Get the ball to Lisa."

My job was to shoot the basketball and score as many points as possible. If I missed a shot, my teammates were supposed to grab the rebound and get the ball back to me so I could shoot again. Morningside put on a full-court press from the opening tip to try to force South Torrance into turning the ball over. That strategy worked really well for us. I stayed at half-court, and when one of our players would steal the ball, they would throw it to me. I would dribble into the frontcourt, take it down the middle, and hit a jump shot. Or I would drive the lane and nail a jumper from the side. South Torrance would get the ball back and do their thing. Even if they scored, once Morningside got the basketball back, we would bring it up the court, call a play for me, and I would shoot and score. A lot of times I would go in, score, get fouled, and shoot free throws. I was on fire!

It was almost like I could not miss. I was making shots from everywhere on the court. With the help of my teammates, I scored forty-nine points in the first quarter and another fifty-two points in the second quarter. It was crazy. I made twenty-seven of thirty-five free throw attempts before intermission, and Morningside was winning 102 to 24. When the horn sounded to end the first half, our fans went crazy. They were shouting and cheering as we headed off to the locker room for a team huddle. I took a second to glance up at the scoreboard and was stunned by what I saw. "Dang," I said out loud. "All those points but one are mine!" (Sherrell Young was the player who scored the only other point. She missed her first free throw attempt on purpose, mistakenly thinking that I was supposed to score *every* point for our team. Coach Scott chided her, and Sherrell sank her second free throw try.)

The Monarchs' fans were anxious for the second half to get started. There was a buzz swirling round the gym. Everybody knew that I was closing in on Cheryl Miller's national high school record. Back in the 1981–82 season, she scored 105 points for Riverside Poly High School in a game against Norte Vista. I was only four points away from tying, and five points away from breaking, the U.S. record, and we still had another half of basketball to play. I figured, *No problem*. At the rate I was going, I felt like I could have scored two hundred points that night.

Coach Scott looked at me at halftime and said, "Lisa, we are beating this team pretty badly. I want you to break Cheryl's record, but after you score one hundred six points, I'll take you out."

I said, "Okay, but why, Coach Scott?"

He said, "Enough is enough! Just break the record, and you'll sit out the rest of the game."

I told him, "Okay." I figured that must be the right thing to do.

Our Morningside squad walked back onto the court for the second half, but the South Torrance team was packing up and getting ready to leave. Some of them were already walking out the door. One of the Spartans' players had fouled out in the first half, and the word in the gym was that one other player did not want to play anymore, because the game was so far out of reach. South Torrance High was going to forfeit the game. They were not going to play the second half.

Wait! What about my shot at the record?

I walked across the court to where their coach, Mr. Gilbert Ramirez, was getting ready to leave. I asked him, "Sir, would you please put your team back on the court to finish the game?"

He was obviously frustrated by the situation and more than a little upset, but Coach Ramirez kindly answered, "No, Lisa. You are a great player. I wish you a lot of luck. I am going to cheer for you when you get to college, but we are going to leave."

I was really disappointed, but I told him, "Okay."

When the South Torrance team left the gym, the referee assessed them two technical fouls. One "T" went against Coach Ramirez, and the other "T" went against the Spartans' team for leaving the gym before the game was over. Two technical fouls equaled four free throw attempts for Morningside, and I just happened to need four points to tie Cheryl Miller's record. Coach Scott sent me onto the court to shoot the free throws.

So with the opposing team no longer in the building and the game essentially over, I had four free throws to take to tie the record, and I had to make them all. I was all alone on the basketball court. My teammates were on the sideline. The fans were on their feet, and everyone was watching me.

To say the least, I was very nervous when I stepped up to the free throw stripe. The packed gym went completely silent as I went into my usual routine. I flipped the ball, dribbled it three times, launched my shot, and made sure that I followed through. My first attempt swished in. Cheers rang out through the gym. Then, quickly, everybody went, "Sshhh! Sshhh!" They wanted quiet so I could concentrate.

The second attempt was good, and the crowd roared once again. I needed two more points to reach 105. My third free throw had everybody on edge. The shot was a little bit off line as it flew toward the rim. It did not feel right when the ball left my hand, and when it bounced on the iron, I could sense the crowd leaning with me, rooting for me, and trying to will that basketball into the bucket. Whatever they did, it worked, and when the ball dropped in, a relieved cheer went up from the stands. I was at 104 points and counting.

Just one more to go. Did I feel the pressure on my final attempt? Of course, I did. Did I know the significance of the moment? Absolutely. The cheers faded to a nervous buzz and then to complete silence again as I stepped to the line for the potential record-tying free throw.

Flip . . .

Dribble, dribble, dribble . . .

Shoot . . .

Follow through . . .

Swish!

HISTORY!

I made it. My final attempt went cleanly through the net. I did it, and I was very happy and very relieved. Coach Scott said to reporters that when the last free throw went in, "It was business as usual for Lisa. Just Lisa being Lisa. It was no big deal to her."

He was right. I knew I had accomplished something special, but I did not jump or shout or pump my fist to celebrate. I had expected to make those free throws. That was what all the hard work and practice were about. All the drills, repetitions, and extra hours in the gym were designed to prepare me, physically and mentally, to blot out the bad memories of that missed final shot in the 1988 state championship game, and give me the confidence to succeed in any pressure-packed situation.

The Monarchs' fans thought my accomplishment was a pretty huge deal. The gym went crazy after I scored point number 105. Morningside High was silent no longer, and people stormed onto the court. My sister Dionne led the way with my

Mom and Tiffany following onto the floor to give me a hug. I got mobbed. The fans were ecstatic. They had just seen history made. Move over, Cheryl Miller. Make room at the top for Lisa Leslie.

The 101 points that I scored in the first half gave me a U.S. high school record of my own. I did not have to share that one with anybody except my teammates. Without them, I would never have had a chance to reach those milestones.

I made twenty-seven field goal attempts in that game against South Torrance High School, and I earned thirty-one points from the free throw line. Coach Scott still says that of all the great accomplishments that evening, the most impressive was my canning those four technical free throws, with every eye in the building trained on me and the high school record on the line. I will never forget that feeling. I persevered. I shut out the world for a few seconds and got the job done.

It was a great evening, but when it was over for me, it was over. I did not think a whole lot about it. After the game, I went to the movies with my boyfriend of two years, Eric. Eric was an athlete, too. He was on the basketball and baseball teams as a freshman at California State University at Los Angeles. We were a good couple until I found out he was still seeing his ex-girlfriend. Then I had to cut him loose. Still, for years after I dumped him, he cheered for me at my college games . . . and later dated one of my college teammates.

After Eric dropped me off at home that night, the phone was ringing off the hook. Everybody was calling, including the local television stations. They all wanted to get tape of the game so they could run highlights on the news. I guess I did not know the importance of what I had done or the impact that it would have. It was as if I was in shock. I had no idea what to say, so I told everybody to call Coach Scott.

The next morning, at school, I was summoned to the nurse's office. I saw Coach Scott when I got there, and he told me,

"Lisa, you have a lot of interviews set up. You won't be going to any more classes today."

The TV stations were all coming to interview me. News vans were outside the school. Reporters had crowded into the gym and were stationed at various points around the court. There were lights, cameras, and plenty of action in there. I walked in and worked my way around the room, going from radio people to television to newspapers and magazines. I shared my story and gave my account of the game to reporter after reporter. It seemed endless.

While I was in the middle of the media madness, word came down that CIF was not going to recognize my 105 points that had tied the record. According to league officials, when the South Torrance High team left the gym, they forfeited the game. No technical fouls should have been called, and no free throws should have been taken. The game was officially over at that point, with the final score at 102–24. So, instead of getting 105 points, my performance was marked down to 101 points, and I no longer owned a piece of the national record.

Once that news got out, all the reporters wanted to know if I was disappointed or upset about falling short of Cheryl's mark. I told them that I was happy to set the record for one half and thrilled to be considered in the same company as Cheryl Miller and Wilt Chamberlain, both prominent members of the 100-point club. I thought it was great. I know that I smiled a lot, and tons of photos were taken. Then, when it seemed to be over, I was taken back to the nurse's office to do more radio interviews. In all, I did twenty-three radio interviews with stations all across the country. I was so busy that they had to bring lunch to me in the nurse's office.

In less than twenty-four hours, my entire life had changed. I was excited, but I still did not understand why I was getting so much attention over one game. All of a sudden I was on the news every hour, my story was in the newspapers, and *Sports Illustrated* wanted to visit with my family and me. It was overwhelming.

Some reporters asked me if I thought it was bad sportsmanship to score all those points against South Torrance. I told one of them, "No. I don't feel bad, because I think we played the sport of basketball. It wasn't as if we played with six players or I just camped out under the basket all night. We played the game."

When they asked if I would do it again should the opportunity arise, I answered, "Yeah! I think it is all in good sport. It's not my fault that I am more talented than those players. I do think it is a great opportunity for any senior to try to score as many points as possible and maybe set a record. We played, and we did what we normally would do in a game. It wasn't like South Torrance didn't know that I was going to shoot. It was not a secret."

It has been almost two decades since my 101-point game, and people still ask me about it. I do not know how many points I might have scored if South Torrance had stayed and played the second half. Maybe that question mark—the "what if" factor—is what keeps that night mystical, memorable, and interesting to talk about after all these years. I cannot be sure. But if I had been Coach Ramirez, I would have used a zone defense to try to keep me away from the basket. At the end of the day, though, I acknowledge that his team was full of good sportswomen for the two quarters that they played. They did not try to hurt me, and a less classy team might have tried to. If I had been in their sneakers, I would have taken the challenge to try to stop Lisa Leslie, but I would not deny any player the opportunity to take a shot at making history.

Cheryl Miller's 105-point record remained unbroken until February 2006, when Epiphany Price of New York City scored 113 points in a single game. But nobody has come close to my record of 101 points in a single half.

That season our team went 33–2. We won our third straight CIF title and, for the third consecutive year, made it all the way back to the state championship game, in Oakland. This time our opponent was going to be Berkeley High School, from the Bay Area.

USC assistant coach Barbara Thaxton was there to watch me practice with the Lady Monarchs before the big game. College coaches showing up at our practices and games had become as much a part of Morningside girls' basketball as the hoops and the nets. Southern Cal had been recruiting me hard, and I had gotten to know Coach Thaxton fairly well. I felt strange all throughout practice, so afterwards, I went over to her and said, "I have a bump on my stomach, and it's bothering me."

I pulled up my shirt. She took a look and told me, "Girl, that looks like a chicken pox." Could this really happen to me? I had already had chicken pox when I was seven years old, but surprise, I would be one of the few people to get chicken pox twice in her life, and just in time for the state championship game no less. I was two days away from the last game of my high school career, and I had the prom coming up, too. The timing could not have been worse. And I found out I got it from Tiffany. Great!

When I stepped onto the court at the Oakland Coliseum, I had a fever of 102 degrees. I remember the jump ball that started the game against Berkeley High, but not much after that. I was told that I played every minute of the game and scored thirty-five points, grabbed a dozen rebounds, and blocked seven shots. I was told that we beat Berkeley 67–56 to capture the state championship again. I could not tell you that. I was drained. I collapsed. To this very day, I have no memory of ever playing in that game.

There is a vague recollection in my head of having our team picture taken with the championship trophy, but I never made it to the locker room after that. I fainted. When I woke up, I was on a table, wondering, *What is wrong with me?* I was sweating.

My body was so hot, and I was exhausted. I could not even keep my eyes open. I knew something was terribly wrong.

I was taken to the hospital, where I was treated for fever, exhaustion, dehydration, and the chicken pox. What started out as one little bump had turned into a lot of little bumps all over me. Apparently, the stress of the game and all the sweating that I did triggered a pox population explosion. There were hundreds of them *everywhere!* I could not even enjoy our championship. While my teammates were all out partying, I was lying in the hospital with IVs in my arms and chicken pox all over me. CHICKEN POX!

The next day, my temperature was still up and my fluid levels were still down, but I had to fly back to Los Angeles with the team. Of course, the airlines would not have been real thrilled about having a contagious passenger on board, so I put on a few layers of clothes and a hat so that people would not see that something was seriously wrong with me. Not only did I feel sick, but I also looked horrible, and since I was so tall, there was no way to hide me. I could not even comb my hair. I had chicken pox on my scalp. They were all over me, and they itched. I remember getting on the plane. Thankfully, I was allowed to board first, because I was in a wheelchair. I was so sick and weak that I needed assistance. I did not have an ounce of strength. I took a seat by the window, and I was so tired that I must have fallen asleep before takeoff. The next thing that I knew, I was being helped off the plane in Los Angeles and into another wheelchair. It was terrible.

When we got home, I went straight to bed. I could not go back to school for several days, so while my teammates were basking in the glow of our state championship victory, I was in bed, absentmindedly peeling off all my chicken pox scabs and putting them in a jar. I know. That is so gross! And the thing is, I have no idea why I was doing it. I knew the scabs would leave a mark, but I picked at them, anyway. To this very day, I have a chicken pox scar on my face to remind me of the "Great State Championship Game Chicken Pox Fiasco." And I later poured the jar of scabs on Dionne's car.

By the way, I did make it to my senior prom. Eric took me, and it was my first time getting all dressed up. I had this black, velvety dress with lace at the bottom. It was fun to see the people that I saw every day at school all dressed up for the prom. I had a good time, and then we went to the after-prom party. I wore this hideous white leather skirt and white jacket. Eric wore matching white leather, and we were convinced that we were really styling.

This was a memorable experience for me because it was my first time out. In my four years at Morningside, I had never gone to a school party or joined a club. I had never smoked or drank alcohol. I had never had a one-time "hide in the closet" smoking or drinking experience. I had never had the desire to do those things. I knew that I wanted to be an Olympian, and I also knew that my mom would kill me if she ever found out.

To cap off my senior year at Morningside, I won the Naismith Award as the nation's top high school basketball player, the Dial Award as the top high school student-athlete in the country, and the Gatorade Player of the Year Award, which honors the best high school athletes in the country for their athletic and academic excellence.

That 1989–90 season was filled with highlights, records, and honors, and before the school year was over, I got invited to try out for the USA world championship team, which was scheduled to play in Malaysia that summer. I flew to Florida and competed alongside Cynthia Cooper, Teresa Edwards, Tammy Jackson, and Lynette Woodard, who had played internationally. I held my own against them and made it all the way to the final cut, but I did not make the team.

The good news was that USA Basketball had other plans for me. They sent me to join the junior national team for its summer tournament in Canada, a four-game series in Vancouver. I had never played north of the border before, so it was an adventure for me. Dawn Staley was on my team again.

Canada was not a totally pleasant experience for me. We knew going in that the Canadians played dirty, so everyone on the U.S. team made sure to have their mouthpieces in place before tip-off. I got off to a really good start. I was scoring, rebounding, making my jump shots, and driving to the basket. It was a close, emotional game. We were playing hard, and I was excited. Some of the top people in USA Basketball were there scouting the young talent to see which players might be ready to move up to the next level.

I was playing defense at a crucial time in the second half when I knocked the ball out of bounds off of their center, a big, older-looking lady. I was clapping because we had the ball back, and while all the players were going to the other end of the court, Canada's center walked by and hit me in the side of my head. I was stunned, but I reacted and socked her. I broke the woman's nose.

I quickly backed away and told the referee, "Get her! Get her, and I won't hit her!" I did not want to fight the woman, but I was not going to let her beat me up. I kept shouting, "Get her," but nobody did anything. This big woman kept fussing with her nose and coming after me. I had no choice. I socked her again, in the same spot! Her nose was really broken now! There was blood coming down her face.

Finally, the referee came over and broke things up. I started crying. I knew that this woman was really hurt. My heart was pounding, and I was full of emotion. The referee ejected me from the game, and the Canadian woman went off to get her nose put back together.

I was still crying when I sat down on our bench. I know now that Canada used that skirmish to get me out of the game. But at the time, I was young and naive, and the only thing I could think was this woman hit me; I reacted. I defended myself. But in doing so, I played right into the Canadian team's trap. They knew they could not stop me on the court, so they were willing to try anything. And I'm the one who got thrown out of the game.

It was a tough way to learn a lesson, but I had to understand that fighting was not the answer, especially when it kept me from playing. I had to have the discipline to walk away in situations like that. And I had to remember that I was wearing my country's uniform.

The score on the court was close, and I could not help my team. I knew that I had messed up, and I knew that I could not allow myself to get suckered into fighting again. It was not enough for me to play smart basketball; I had to be a smart basketball player as well.

The game continued as I sat on the bench in tears. That is when Dawn Staley scooted over, put her arm around me, and said, "It's all right, Big Girl. But damnnn, you socked her good!"

Chapter 4

Decisions, Decisions

I was playing on the grand stage. Everything I did during that 1989–90 season took place in the heat of a global spotlight and in front of hundreds of college recruiters. They seemed to be at every practice, at every game, around every corner, and at the other end of every phone call. They were pulling out the stops and coming hard after me, but I was pretty much used to it by then. College recruiters had been a major part of my life since the summer after eighth grade, when I played for the OGDL. That summer I had also competed in the Basketball Congress International (BCI) Tournament in Phoenix, Arizona. BCI hosts local and national tournaments to give boys and girls the opportunity to improve their basketball skills. The players also get to showcase those skills in front of a lot of the nation's college coaches, with the hopes of earning scholarships.

Back in 1986, college coaches could talk more with recruits than they can today. NCAA rules are much more rigid now as far as regulating the number of visits, phone calls, and contacts that a coach can have with a potential recruit. In that summer before I started high school, coaches would come up and introduce themselves to me all the time. I remember meeting Glenn McDonald and Michael Abraham from Long Beach State University. They were the first two college coaches that showed interest in me (years later both men worked with me as L.A. Sparks assistant coaches), and since Long Beach was just down the 405 freeway from Los Angeles, they would come and watch a lot of my local tournaments. Then they'd send me letters with little messages like, "Hey, Lisa! We saw you. You played really well." Both coaches would sign the note. It was very cool and very flattering. They would also call me on the phone two or three times a week, so we got to know each other pretty well.

All this was taking place before I ever got to Morningside. Once I started my freshman year, college coaches from across the country pulled out all the stops to catch my interest. They called my house, and I got tons of recruiting letters. Without exaggeration, I got at least three letters from different college coaches every day. I had so many recruiting letters that I started putting them into photo albums. There were letters from Washington, Alabama, Tennessee, Florida, Florida A&M, Texas, and Texas Tech, and there were some from schools that I had never heard of, like Rice, Xavier, and Bowling Green. You name a school, I got a letter from them. It seemed like I got at least one letter from every Division I, Division II, and Division III college in the country.

I received so much recruiting mail that it got to the point where I would tear open an envelope and look inside. If the letter was not handwritten, I would not read it. I did not like receiving typed letters, so at the age of fourteen, that was how I started sifting through my college suitors. Tiffany became my assistant—screening all calls and organizing my mail.

Coaches would also send postcards, especially when their teams were playing in tournaments in Hawaii. I guess they wanted me to think that I would be going to Hawaii if I chose to attend their university. I cannot tell you how many postcards I got from Hawaii or how many "Happy Holiday" cards I received. Every holiday, my mailbox would be stuffed with cards from colleges. Each card was signed by the entire basketball team and coaching staff.

I have two or three photo albums just full of college letters. Some coaches would write, "We know you are not going to consider us, but we wanted to extend an offer just in case your family is ever out this way and would like to visit our university." It was pretty cool, but it was just mail to me. To this day, I hate mail. Even though my mom once worked for the post office, I HATE MAIL! I cannot stand opening mail, and it is because of all those college letters.

I did develop relationships with many of the coaches who wrote me, though. They would call and ask me about recent games or about how school was going. It was a fun process until it came down to my senior year, when I had to pick the five schools that I would visit. It was an awfully hard decision, but I chose Tennessee, Notre Dame, USC, Long Beach State, and Stanford.

My first visit was to Long Beach State. When I walked into their darkened gym, a spotlight flashed on. It shined directly on a life-sized poster of me, and then a voice boomed through the P.A. system, "ANNNNNNND NOW, STARTING FOR THE LONG BEACH STATE 49ERS, WEARING NUMBER THIRTY-THREE . . . LEEEEEEEESSSSAAAA LESSSSSLIEEEEEEEEE!"

They did this whole production for me, and it was very impressive and flattering. I got to meet, and hang out with, a lot of the players on the women's team, but the fit just did not feel right for me at Long Beach State.

Notre Dame was my next recruiting visit. Coach Scott went with me to South Bend, Indiana, that fall, and it was FREEZING! I knew right away that it was too cold for me in the land of the Fighting Irish, but I loved the gold dome and Touchdown Jesus. Notre Dame was so beautiful, but it was also very intimidating. The campus was really large, there were thousands of students, and South Bend was such a long way from home.

I sure enjoyed my visit, though. It was football season, and at the start of the game, I got to walk through the historic tunnel that the Fighting Irish football players pass through before every home game. I went out into Notre Dame Stadium and stood on the sidelines during the game. I was still really cold, but the experience was great, and I just loved the tradition there.

That evening was also opening night for the men's basketball team, so we went from the football game to Joyce Center Arena and into the men's locker room. I got to meet head coach Digger Phelps. He was extremely nice to me. I listened in as he talked with his team, and then, all of a sudden, this guy walked into the room. He was *so* fine and *so* cute! I found out later that he was LaPhonso Ellis.

LaPhonso was ineligible to play because of his grades, so he was in street clothes while the team was in uniform. He was about six foot nine and really, really handsome. I kept looking at him, but I made sure that he did not know that I was looking. I was thinking, *Oh! I want to come here!* At that moment, LaPhonso Ellis was the only reason that I was considering Notre Dame.

Coquese Washington, whom I later played against in the WNBA, was my host for the Notre Dame weekend. We watched the men's basketball game and then got to hang out with the women's team for a while. Their coach was Muffet McGraw. I liked her, but when my Notre Dame visit ended, I had two thoughts in my head:

1. COLD weather
2. LaPhonso (La Fine so) Ellis

Hmmmmm! What a tough decision!

I did not have to go far for my next recruiting visit. I went to USC in Los Angeles. The Trojan coaches had already been to my home for what turned out to be one of the most memorable and humiliating nights of my life. Head coach Marianne Stanley had come to our door, and I gave her a hug as she entered. Her assistant, Barbara Thaxton, walked in right behind her, and our little shih tzu dog, Semi, jumped on her leg and started humping it.

I could not believe what was happening. It was like something out of a very bad movie. Semi just kept humping away at Coach Thaxton's leg, and I was paralyzed with embarrassment. I could have just *died*. I yelled for help. "Mommmm! Ohmigod, look at Semi!"

I probably could have helped move Semi myself, but I was mortified and humiliated and could not imagine touching Semi while he was . . . in motion. So I did what I usually do: I ran to my room, closed the door behind me, and just sat in there. I had been hoping to make such a good impression because I really liked the USC coaches. Instead, I was hiding out, mortified because of my horny little dog.

Coach Stanley tried to make things easier for me. She called out, "Lisa, come on out, girl. It's okay."

I kept saying, "No! No!" I did not want to come out and face them.

I could hear the coaches laughing and saying, "Nobody is worrying about this dog of yours. Come on out here and visit with us."

I finally slithered meekly out of my room and met with them. Both coaches had big smiles on their faces. They each gave me a hug. They were sweet, but I was so embarrassed. That was, without a doubt, the most humiliating moment of the entire recruiting process for me. I could have killed that dog.

The Women of Troy did not pull out any whistles and bells for my campus visit, but I enjoyed talking with the coaches again, and I had fun hanging out with the team. I really liked how much the coaches talked about winning and turning the program around. I was really interested in the prospect of resurrecting the Trojan legacy that Cheryl Miller, Cynthia Cooper,

Rhonda Windham, and the McGee sisters, Pam and Paula, had built. I knew USC had recently signed some of the nation's top high school seniors, and the team already had some quality veteran players in-house. Tammy Story and Joni Easterly were two of the Trojans' top players. Tammy was a shooting guard who could knock down the 3-ball. Unfortunately, she never really got the chance to excel completely, because she had to play the point guard position. Joni also had a great jump shot, and she worked really hard on both ends of the floor. When I watched them during my visit, I knew that both players would make terrific teammates. I also liked the coaching staff. I knew Coach Stanley had a good personality, and I knew she could be pretty funny, but I was also aware of her reputation for being stern with her teams. Coach Thaxton was very motherly and very nice.

The visit went well. There was not anything earth-shattering about it. There were no fireworks, and I did not need any. I just felt comfortable there. My mom wanted me to go to USC, and I thought the university was excellent. I also figured that a degree from there would be valuable whether or not I continued with basketball after college. I was already thinking about life after basketball, and I knew that at USC, I would get a good education and have some fun, too.

I started to narrow my list of college choices. I told Notre Dame that I was not going to be joining the Fighting Irish. Farewell LaPhonso Darnell Ellis. (He went on to be a first-round draft pick in the NBA.)

I was supposed to visit Stanford next, but their assistant coach, Renee Brown, called and told me, "Lisa. We looked at your classes for your senior year. You have outstanding grades, but we feel that instead of typing, you should take another science class, an AP course, which will automatically give you college credits."

I had already taken my required science courses, and the class

Stanford wanted me to take started at 6:30 in the morning and did not end until 9:00 AM If I added that course to the rest of my class load, plus basketball, I would be looking at some awfully long days. I gave it some thought, but finally told Renee that I did not want to change classes.

She said, "Okay. Then I am sorry to say that we cannot offer you a scholarship."

I told her, "Okay. That's fine."

Renee seemed surprised. "Really?" she asked. "You are not going to change your mind?"

I answered, "No, that's fine. Thank you."

The last words I heard from Renee were, "Okay, Lisa. I wish you the best of luck." That was it. I never talked with anyone from Stanford again, and I had seriously considered going to school in Palo Alto, but now the Cardinal was off my list.

The University of Tennessee was my last school to visit. Head coach Pat Summitt and her assistant, Mickey DeMoss, visited my house during the fall of my senior year, and I really enjoyed them. My mom cooked chicken and waffles and all kinds of breakfast things. They ate, and we all had a good time. Pat was really nice. She had a strong Southern accent and the bluest eyes ever. She was very pretty and very serious. I could tell that she was superintelligent and definitely knew the game of basketball. Her name spoke volumes in women's basketball, and I was awed just to have her in my home.

I had also done my homework regarding Pat. I knew she had worked with USA Basketball. One of my goals was to play for USA Basketball, so I wanted my college coach to have those kinds of connections. Everything was very positive with Pat. The University of Tennessee was already a powerhouse in women's basketball, and I was thinking seriously about going to Knoxville to continue that tradition.

My visit with the Vols was not scheduled until after the first of the year, but Morningside High had a Christmas tournament in Shelbyville, Tennessee, so that turned out to be my first introduction to the Volunteer State and its people.

The Shelbyville Breakfast Rotary Club put on the event and called it the Best of the U.S. Tournament. They picked us up at the airport and gave us silk jackets that said SHELBYVILLE. A fancy coach-style bus took us to a nice hotel, and we got free breakfasts and newspapers while we were in town. It started out as a great experience.

Eight high school teams participated in the tournament. My team had traveled the greatest distance to get there, but teams had come from as far away as New Hampshire and as near as Kentucky, Alabama, and Mississippi. Tennessee had two teams in the tournament, Shelbyville High School and Cannon County High.

We went into the event ranked as the number one high school team in the nation by *USA Today*. Shelbyville was ranked number two. We saw it as a chance to square off against a very good basketball team, to decide which high school really was the best in the country. The competition was designed so that Morningside and Shelbyville would meet in the championship round. All both teams had to do was win their games, and the showdown would be on.

Well, we put an end to those plans in a hurry. Two days after Christmas, Vigor High School, from Prichard, Alabama, knocked off Morningside in our very first game of the tournament. I had twenty-eight points, eleven rebounds, and five blocked shots, but afterwards, Coach Scott called it "the worst basketball game we have played all year."

Our second game was against the Cannon County Lionettes, and it was a real eye-opener in a lot of ways. When we got to the arena, there was already a game in progress. The facility was very nice. It seated about three thousand people, and the place was packed, mostly with Shelbyville fans. As our team milled around, we started to hear comments from the crowd. One man said, "She looks like a monkey."

We all looked at each other like, "Did he say what I thought he said?" The crowd was almost totally white. Our Morningside team was completely black. We acted like we did not hear the remark, but the crudeness did not stop.

When our game tipped off, Morningside scored the first few baskets, and the officials disallowed every one of them because of a foul or a violation. Something was not right. The arena had a "different" feel to it, and I felt completely out of place. Cannon County jumped out to a 19–6 lead. The referees were cheating. They were taking away points, taking away baskets. They would not let me play my game. Cannon County's players were all over me.

When Coach Scott got up off the bench to question a referee, the fans started yelling racist remarks again, and the official moved away. He would not acknowledge our coach, so Coach Scott walked all the way across the court to get to the ref and let him know exactly how he felt. That cost him a technical foul.

Cannon County High pulled out to a 40–15 lead. The game was obviously rigged. We were set up to go in there and lose our number one ranking. It was a terrible experience, and I was devastated. The game was completely out of our control. That was probably the hardest part. It did not matter what we did; we were going to lose. These people took away my joy of playing the game, and I felt like we had taken a bad trip back into the 1960s. I was angry and powerless.

As the game progressed, the racist remarks became louder and even more crystal clear. "Get that monkey off the court." We could not believe what we were hearing. The fans would mix in, "Get those niggers off the court!" I remember them calling us niggers a lot.

Nobody was controlling what the people were saying, because it obviously was not offensive to the other folks in the

stands. None of them seemed to care, but it was just too overwhelming for me. I had never experienced anything like that. I
had read about prejudice and I had heard of the Watts riots and
I knew about Martin Luther King, Jr. and his march. A lot of
people, like me, think that we are educated about racism, but I
had no understanding of the hate and the hurt that went with it
until I actually experienced racist people firsthand.

Color had never been an issue with me. I had been around
people of different backgrounds all my life. I did not look for differences between whites, Mexicans, Italians, blacks, and people
of other heritages. Our skin colors were different, but so what? I
believed we were all God's children. That was the way my whole
family thought. Two of my aunts had husbands who were white.
Our family had a mix of biracial couples and children, so for me,
race was never really a big deal. I had never felt racism personally before, but it hit home now.

The comments from the crowd and the behavior of the referees were already a shock, but then the game started to get physical. Coach Scott visited with the refs in hopes of getting them to
keep the opposing team from roughing me up. While they stood
there talking, one of the hometown fans in the stands yelled to
the official, "Come on. Let 'em play." My mother, who was
standing right there, heard the ref turn to the man and say, "Do
you really think a black man is going to get a call in this arena
tonight?"

That is what we were up against in Shelbyville that night. We
lost the game 72–43, and I was heartbroken. It was one thing to
go in with the #1 ranking and lose the first game to Vigor High.
They beat us and that hurt, but in Morningside's loss to Cannon
County, we got cheated! It was blatant! What made things so
much worse, though, was the racist fans. I still cannot believe the
things that they yelled at us. I will never understand the venom
that came out of their mouths. Maybe the people of Shelbyville
were good, caring people who just took their sports too seri-

ously, but based on the way they treated us, they were horrible excuses for human beings.

I remember crying and asking Coach Scott, "Why did you bring us here?" I could not comprehend what had taken place. It made me confused about life. Why were we there? Why did that happen to us? I remember it like it was yesterday. How could something like that happen in 1989?

Coach Scott sat us down, and he apologized to us. I think he was in shock, too. We were all baffled, and at that point, all we wanted to know was when our flight was going home. We wanted to get out of there as soon as possible, and I could not wait to leave Tennessee.

The morning that we left Shelbyville, there was no free breakfast, no free newspapers, and no fancy coach-style bus waiting for us. Instead, we rode a raggedy old school bus to the airport. When I got on the plane, I swore that I would never go back to the state of Tennessee. I should have known that Shelbyville was just one small town and that not everybody in Tennessee was racist, but that entire experience made me so sick that when I got home, I just climbed into my bed and stayed there.

It was not long before Pat Summitt called me. I told her right away, "I am not coming to Tennessee," and I explained to her exactly why.

Pat's response was very sympathetic and sweet. She assured me that Knoxville was not like Shelbyville. "Lisa," she said, "it's a whole lot different here."

All I could say was, "Pat, I am really sorry. I like you guys. I respect your program, but I could never play for people who are racists. I just could not. I would not even want to be a part of a program that had to deal with hate like that. I don't know what to tell you, Pat. I will never come back to Tennessee."

Time has passed, of course, and I have been back to Tennessee, but I will never forget what happened to me there. It is the only time I have thought about my race when I played a sport. I just want to play, and I want to be good. And I want to play with other people who are good. To me, race is irrelevant. The ball does not have a face on it. You play with your team-mates, and you play against your opponent, but Shelbyville was the first time I saw people make the distinction.

The University of Tennessee was immediately crossed off of my list of prospective colleges. That left Long Beach State and USC as my final two choices. At the time Long Beach had the better team, but to me, USC had the better lifestyle. Basketball vs. lifestyle? It was a tough decision. I had to look at the big picture. I wanted to get into broadcasting, and USC was strong in that department, but just when the scale tipped in favor of the Trojans, Long Beach State offered Coach Scott a coaching position. That meant if I joined the 49ers, I would get to keep my high school coach with me. This made things really complicated for me. I loved Coach Scott. The man was truly like a father to me, and Long Beach State was going to give him the opportunity to move up to the college ranks after coaching high school basketball for so many years.

My heart told me to go to Long Beach State and stick with Coach Scott. When Coach Stanley called from USC, I told her that I was planning to join the 49ers because they had offered Coach Scott a job. Honestly, I was feeling pressured, because I knew that Coach Scott's job offer from Long Beach State was contingent upon my signing to play there. All of a sudden, my coach's livelihood was in my hands. The man had done so much to help me over the past four years, and I wanted to help him. Wasn't I obligated?

Coach Stanley said, "Don't do a thing. I'll get back to you."

Amazingly, a coaching position for Coach Scott was also open at USC. I was ecstatic. Long Beach had a lot of strong points, but when it came right down to it, I did not want to go there. I really wanted to go to USC and I really wanted to play for Coach Stanley and I really wanted Coach Scott to go there with me. When that coaching position opened up for him, I said, "That's it. We are going to USC!" Everything worked out perfectly. I signed my letter of intent in the career center at Morningside, and Coach Scott had a new job. Finally, it was all decided. And it was ideal in every way.

I was going to be a Trojan, but because my SAT scores were just average, I had to go to summer school before I could actually attend classes at USC in the fall. The SATs were a real sore point with me. While I was still in high school, I gave an interview in which I said that I did not think our students at Morningside were properly prepared to take the SATs. That interview turned into a newspaper article that upset a lot of people at Morningside High and in the Inglewood school system, but I was just expressing my opinion.

When I entered high school, I set a goal to earn a 3.5 grade point average. I achieved that, but I was not really sure what I had learned in my four years there. During my senior year, I started going to an SAT prep class in Brentwood, an affluent area. Each week, our instructor would give us one hundred vocabulary words to learn. We had to define them and know how to use them in a sentence. We would get tested only on ten words, but because we did not know which ten, we had to know all of them. I was baffled when I first looked at the vocabulary words. I asked others in the prep class, "How do they expect us to know these words? Where do you learn them?"

They told me, "In the books that we read in high school."

I had never been around so many kids before who had access to a better education than me. I could not believe how much they knew or how much they had read. They rattled off a long list of books that I had never heard of. I had read *1984*, *Gone with the Wind*, and *Lord of the Flies*. I had probably read seven of the books that were on their lists, and I had read most of those on my own. They had not been assigned reading at Morningside, so I felt as if I was at an educational disadvantage.

I was not trying to make the Inglewood school system look bad. It was just the reality of my educational experience. I thought somebody needed to say something to make sure that every student had access to the right information, the right books, and the right opportunities. Some parents, teachers, and administrators took offense, but I told them that I was not saying that they were not doing their jobs. I was simply asking if the students at Morningside High School were being properly prepared not only to get good grades, but also to do well on standardized tests, which is crucial to college acceptance these days. I was not about to take back what I said.

Looking back now, I realize it was not just an issue at Morningside. It was, and still remains, a shortcoming of California's public schools and probably of schools across the country. I think there is a serious problem with our educational system, especially in the inner cities. If our government ever gets serious about fixing the matter, a good place to start would be by increasing salaries for teachers.

Anyway, summer school at USC was pretty cool. It was the first time I stayed in a dorm and had a roommate. I was taking classes, learning time management, practicing basketball, and meeting interesting athletes.

When fall classes finally began, it was time to get serious about my basketball and my studies. I liked going to school, and once all the students got there, I learned something very quickly about USC. Everybody partied on Friday and Saturday. Sundays were for studying and doing homework.

Chapter 5

Trojan Wars

I entered USC as the top recruit in the nation, and when the USC sports information department found out that I could dunk, they had posters made up with pictures of me dunking a basketball. The big caption read, WHEN WILL SHE DUNK? So, there was just a little bit of attention focused on me as an incoming freshman. Coach Stanley was not too happy with the poster. She was all about winning and not much for hype. In fact, she actually limited some of the media access to me in my first season just to keep some of the heat off and allow me to focus more on basketball.

When I got to USC, Coach Stanley was in her second season as head coach of the Women of Troy. Her first team went 8–19, but she had a terrific track record of success and was one of the primary reasons I chose to enroll at USC. The woman had been an All-American point guard, had won two national championships in the 1970s at Immaculata College, and when she was twenty-three, she had accepted the coaching job at Old Dominion University (ODU) and had become the youngest head coach in the country. Coach Stanley had helped develop great players at ODU, like Anne Donovan and Nancy Lieberman, and she had turned the Monarchs into a college basketball powerhouse that won the NCAA title in 1985.

Coach Stanley spent two seasons at the University of Pennsylvania before moving to USC in 1989. She took over a Trojan women's team that had gone from the glory years of conference championships and NCAA tournament appearances in the mid-1980s to a sub-.500 team that finished sixth in the Pac-10.

Coach Stanley had a reputation for being very strict and disciplined, and she could definitely be strong. But she was loving, too. If she trusted you and you were in her circle, then you would always be in her circle. The structure was good for me. I needed a strong coach who was going to help me become a better basketball player. I had experienced different coaches in the USA Basketball system, and I found that I truly loved working with passionate coaches who stressed discipline and had some intensity to them.

Coach Stanley possessed those qualities, and she would work with me after practices to improve my game. Some days, she would come in early to teach me a drill or a skill, which we would demonstrate later, when the entire team arrived for practice. She was an excellent teacher and had a deep understanding of the game, and she could communicate that knowledge to her players. She could also get in your face, and when that happened, Coach Thaxton would step in and put her motherly graces to work. She balanced out the strong and forceful personality of Coach Stanley. Coach Thaxton would take a player aside and say, "I know she gets on you, but everything is okay. Just get back in there, and do your best." Her soothing voice and calm demeanor could be very comforting when Coach Stanley was steamed. Coach Thaxton was also our fashion police. She made sure that we dressed nicely and acted like ladies. I appreciated that. Even though I did not have the nicest, most expensive clothes, I still thought it was very important to dress well and act appropriately, especially when we traveled as a team.

Not all of my teammates agreed with the dress code. Some wanted to dress casually, and some were downright bummy. It was clear that they did not correlate our team's image with that of the school. But it seemed like a clear, straight line to me. Besides, I liked the transformation from my persona as a Wonder Woman athlete to my normal, regular self, which usually felt more like Lucille Ball. I liked the difference.

But we somehow managed to get along well. The team was a melting pot of personalities, races, and backgrounds. But we were more alike than we were different, and everyone was pretty friendly.

In my first game at USC, I scored thirty points and pulled down twenty rebounds. We beat Texas, and my career with the Trojans was under way. There was a lot of hype surrounding me, and plenty of expectations, too. In our first season, the Women of Troy posted an 18–12 record. That was ten more wins than the year before. We finished third in the Pac-10 and got all the way to the NCAA West Regional in Las Vegas before Long Beach State—the school that I had passed on—beat us 83–58.

In my first college season, I led the nation with nineteen points and ten rebounds per game, and I was honored to become the first Pac-10 freshman to be named first-team All-Conference and NCAA Freshman of the Year. Those were great individual awards, but the Trojans still had lots of work to do as a team.

The summer after my freshmen year, in 1991, I played for USA Basketball in the World University Games in Sheffield, England. It was a sixteen-team tournament that featured Spain, Canada, and the Soviet Union. Stanford's Tara VanDerveer was my head coach again, and I got to play with Ruthie Bolton, Suzie Mc-Connell, and, of course, Dawn Staley. We had a lot of top-notch talent, and we beat Spain in the gold medal game, finishing with an 8–0 record and outscoring our opponents by an average of forty-two points per game. That was a pretty good way to spend my summer vacation.

I loved the responsibility I felt to contribute to a first-rate team. Having grown up with so many adult responsibilities—especially taking care of Tiffany—it took a lot to make me feel burdened or pressured. I thrived under the weight of expectations that I could play well.

Back in Los Angeles, Coach Stanley was trying to build the USC program back to national prominence. If my family's cheering alone at the games could have done it, it certainly would have. Everybody came to my USC games. Mom, Dionne, Tiffany, Aunt J.C., Craigie, Uncle Ed, the whole gang. And they were the loudest, most animated group there. Dionne even used to come hang out with me on campus sometimes. We were trying to have a normal sisterly relationship with one another, and it was nice going to parties with her or just coming back to my apartment to cook and talk. I was enjoying my freedom away from home and away from having to take care of Tiffany. Mom was being a full-time parent, and everyone was happy. Oddly enough, when Tiffany came to spend time with me, *she* was now the younger sister trying to assert her independence and act older, and I was now the irritated big sister who had to put her back in her place and remind her who she was talking to.

The whole family loved the sport, and they respected Coach Stanley's attempts to make the USC team better by bringing in excellent talent and emphasizing hard work, teamwork, and Trojan pride. She was very protective of us and wanted our women's team to have its place in the USC athletic world. That was no easy task due to the pecking order that existed at the university. Men's football was the highest priority, followed by men's basketball, and if you looked really hard, you would find women's sports somewhere well down the list.

It was an uphill climb in the "good old boy" society on campus, so our coach was very territorial about the team's practice sessions in the gym. She got agitated when people barged into our workouts, and she got really upset when campus tours marched through. Tours were forbidden in the gym when the men's team practiced, but they were allowed to come in and disrupt our training sessions.

A lot of times, men in the athletic department acted as if the women's teams did not matter. There were many situations when we were disrespected as a team. To me, that was one of the most disheartening things about playing college basketball, and Coach Stanley was not the type of person to just stand still and take it. She was not a subtle person, and at times, she did not seem to care much about political correctness, but the coach did everything that she could to defend our program. It was like using a nail file to carve out a niche for women's basketball. But she was determined to do it, even if it had to be one scratch at a time.

As a team, we were taking baby steps, but we were moving in the right direction. In my sophomore season, I averaged over twenty points and eight rebounds per game and shot 55 percent from the field. The Women of Troy won twenty-three games that year and moved up to second place in the conference. We got back to the NCAA tournament, and this time, we made it to the West Regional finals in Seattle before losing to Stanford, the eventual national champs. The Associated Press ranked USC number twenty-three in its final poll. I was picked first-team All-Pac-10 again and was named All-America by the U.S. Basketball Writers Association and *Basketball Times*. In my mind, individual honors were great, but they were not what college basketball was all about.

Off the court, things were looking up, too. I was really comfortable with my body. The awkwardness that I had felt as a girl was gone. Now I was a strong, fit, shapely woman. And though my athleticism usually made me more of a homegirl among the guys than a love interest, I found myself head over heels in love for the very first time.

Marcus* and I were practically inseparable as freshmen. We started out as the very best of friends, and progressively, we got more serious about one another. He was an athlete, too, and he seemed to understand me—the on-the-court me and the off-the-court me. Being in a loving, stable relationship brought a lot to my life, and I was happy to have it.

In May of 1992, I got invited to the U.S. Olympic Trials in Colorado Springs. There were fifty-six ladies there, each of us hoping to make the team that would play in the Barcelona Olympics that summer. I was nineteen years old, the youngest player ever invited to try out for the U.S. Olympic squad, and I was competing against the likes of thirty-two-year-old Lynette Woodard and thirty-three-year-old Nancy Lieberman. I also had to battle three excellent former USC players: Cynthia Cooper, Pam McGee, and Cheryl Miller.

Theresa Grentz of Rutgers was the head coach of the U.S. national team. Lin Dunn and Linda Hargrove were on her staff, and Coach Stanley was one of the court coaches for the trials. Team USA had already qualified for the Olympics back in 1990, when it won the world championships in Malaysia. Now it was just a matter of finding the right combination of players and getting them ready for Barcelona.

There were only a dozen roster spots available on the U.S. women's team, so you can imagine just how competitive things were at the trials in Colorado. I held my own against the older players. Most of them were collegians, but many had also played professionally overseas. I hung in there through one cut-down day after another, but on June 12, when the U.S. women's Olympic basketball team was announced, my name was not on the roster.

It was heartbreaking. I had worked so hard, and I desperately wanted to be on the U.S. squad in Barcelona, but I noticed that a lot of excellent players had been left off the team, including the

*Not his real name.

legendary Cheryl Miller. The only former Trojan to earn a spot on the team was Cynthia Cooper. Man, I wanted that Olympic experience, but when I looked at the big picture, I realized how much I had learned and accomplished from competing against some of our country's greatest female athletes. I was only nineteen, and I knew there would be Olympic Games in my future.

Most of the basketball fuss in the 1992 Olympics surrounded the U.S. men's Dream Team. That was the first year that the International Olympic Committee allowed NBA players to compete, and Michael Jordan, Magic Johnson, Larry Bird, and company blitzed through Barcelona to the gold medal.

Our women's team was not as fortunate. After winning gold in Los Angeles in 1984 and Seoul in 1988, Team USA could do no better than the bronze medal in Spain. Medina Dixon of ODU was the team's top scorer, and Katrina McClain was their leading rebounder, but the American women finished behind the Soviet Unified Team and China. That was unheard of and simply not acceptable. USA Basketball officials knew, right then, that our women would have to prepare much differently if Team USA was going to have any chance of striking gold when the Olympics moved to Atlanta in 1996.

I saw every one of my experiences with USA Basketball as an opportunity for me to grow as a person and as a player. My understanding of the game was constantly evolving, and I was always excited to get back to USC to show my teammates some of the things that I had learned. I wanted to help them so that we could get better as a team. I was winning at the USA Basketball level, but our Trojan team kept getting roadblocked at the Final Eight. It was so disappointing. Every year I would return from USA Basketball and think, *This is the year*, but it always wound up being, *Wait until next year*.

Our USC program was getting better and moving forward. The weak did not survive under Coach Stanley, no matter who they were, and there were times when she would just chew into people—me included—to get them in step with her agenda. I remember she called me into a room once at Washington State, and I walked out crying. Coach Stanley would always find ways to push me to make the most of my abilities. My coach looked me right in the eyes, shook her finger, and said emphatically, "If you want to be the best, Lisa, you gotta act like you wanna be the best."

Coach Stanley set the standard for the kind of program that she envisioned us having at USC. It was the standard that a top five college coach would set—not just any old college, but a perennial contender for the national championship. Coach Stanley had no use for slackers. She set the bar very high. Unfortunately, only about half of our team was on the same page with Coach Stanley in terms of what she was trying to achieve. This frustrated me beyond belief.

I could never understand why players would go to college if they really did not want to be there. Why play a sport if you are not going to give it your all? I understand that everybody has an off day, but not *every* day. It drove me nuts when certain players on my team would not put in the effort but still expected to win games, capture Pac-10 championships, and compete for the national title.

Our team would hit the track for conditioning around 5:30 in the morning, and then we had to lift weights. Some of my teammates would stroll into the weight room at 6:30 and be gone by 7:00. They would come late and leave early, and that really upset me. They were cheating on the track and they were cheating on their weights, which meant that they were cheating themselves and cheating our team.

There were times when USC would lose games because we did not play well together as a team. Maybe we did not pass the ball around or play good defense. That always disturbed me, because those losses related right back to when players cheated themselves in practice, in the line drill, or in the conditioning workouts. When you cheat yourself early, it always catches up with you in the end.

Things like that really drove me crazy, but I made it a point to cry only one time per season. I know that must sound strange, but I never wanted to be the one crying at the end of a season, so I would find a game earlier in the year in which to let the tears flow. It might be a game that had very little meaning. We might have even won the game, but I would be hurting because we did not play the game well, did not follow the game plan, or maybe we just did not come close to playing the game the way it is supposed to be played. For some people, I know sports is all about winning and losing, but to me, it is also incredibly important how you go about winning and losing.

As for the wins, USC posted twenty-two victories in my junior year. We went 14–4 in the Pac-10 but still finished second to Stanford. This time our season ended in the NCAA West Regional semifinals. We lost by twenty points to Sheryl Swoopes and Texas Tech. That marked the second straight year that the Trojans had been ousted by the eventual NCAA champ.

I continued to play well, averaging nineteen points, nine rebounds, and three blocked shots per game that season and shooting at a 56 percent clip. I was named first-team All-Pac-10 for the third straight season, and I was a finalist for the Naismith Award as women's college basketball player of the year. Sheryl Swoopes beat me in that contest, too. The Associated Press ranked USC number fifteen at season's end, so we were climbing up the national rankings every year, but the Women of Troy still could not get over the hump that kept us from going to the Final Four.

That off-season, I played with USA Basketball in the 1993 world championship qualifying tournament in São Paulo, Brazil. There were eight teams in the event. Canada, Chile, and Mexico were in Group A with us, while Brazil, Cuba, Puerto Rico, and Argentina were in Group B. The top four finishers in the tournament were guaranteed automatic berths in the 1994 world championships in Melbourne, Australia.

Tara VanDerveer was our head coach, and Nancy Darsch and Coach Stanley were her assistants. Our U.S. team breezed through the first three games in the championships, and then something happened in our matchup with Cuba that has only happened once in my entire basketball career. Not too many people know this, but I pushed a referee. (Dawn Staley *loves* to tell this story.)

I took a jump shot in the game against Cuba, and one of the opposing players shoved me out of bounds. I landed on top of the referee, and the man was nice enough to help me up, but he was not smart enough to call a foul on the play. I was blatantly pushed off the court, but when no foul was called, I kind of shoved the ref. I did not mug or maim him, but I did put my hands on the official. I knew right away that it was wrong, but my teammates thought it was hilarious! They were all laughing while I was trying to sweet-talk the ref to keep him from giving me a technical foul. "I'm sorry, sir! Excuse me! I am so sorry," I pleaded. "Really, I did not mean it." I must have said the right words, because the referee did not "T" me up.

I do not recommend getting physical with officials, far from it. But there were times, especially as a young player, when I would just react badly to situations. I would be playing and everything would be fine, but then a player, or a referee would do something that just set me off. Boom! I would react in an instant without even thinking. I never thought about fighting premeditatedly, but I was not above speaking my mind. Thankfully, I have learned to control my emotions on the court. I have learned to compartmentalize the Lucille Ball and Wonder Woman personas and make sure that they seldom play on the same playground. My approach is much more pragmatic these days. But for the record, yes, I did push a referee, but just that one time, and it was not very hard.

Our U.S. team put away Cuba and Canada to set up a showdown in the semifinals with the host team, Brazil. Now remember, we were playing in São Paulo. They had more than ten thousand fans jammed into the Gimnasio de Ibirapuera, and it seemed as if everybody in the arena was wearing Brazil's green and yellow colors. There were people standing in every open spot in the building. A fire code in Brazil? Not likely. People were cheering and making noise with tambourines. They were stomping their feet, shaking and banging just about anything they could find, and the shouting never stopped. It was like a raucous crowd at an international soccer game, and it gave every indication that Brazil's matchup with Team USA was much more than a regular basketball game.

The two teams went into the semis as the only undefeated squads in the tournament. That meant that no matter which team won the semifinal game on July 2, the same two teams would have to meet again to decide the championship on the Fourth of July.

Janeth Arcain was on Brazil's team, but she was only their third best player. Hortencia was Brazil's top athlete and, arguably, the best player in the world. Their point guard, Maria Paula da Silva (aka Magic Paula), was the world's best at her position. She could come across center court and just fire away. These ladies had international and Olympic experience together, and they could really play.

Team USA was still a young group. I had not turned twenty-one yet, but I was the leading scorer. Ruthie Bolton, Jennifer Azzi, and Katy Steding averaged double-digit points as well. Carla McGhee topped our squad in rebounding, and Dawn Staley ran the show for us at point guard. Our U.S. squad played even with Brazil in the semifinal game, but they wound up beating us in overtime 99–92.

That set up the championship duel, fittingly, on America's Independence Day. I dropped in twenty points in the first half, and Team USA led by fourteen at intermission. Arcain and Magic Paula combined for fifty-eight points for Brazil, but we had five players with double-figure points, and Dawn was incredible. She got me the ball all game long and finished with six assists. We beat Brazil 106–92 on their home court to win the world championship qualifying tournament.

I remember thinking, *Oh man! We beat Brazil, in Brazil.* We were screaming and cheering as we ran off the court. The people in the arena were shocked and upset, but we were incredibly happy. Our joy carried over to the locker room. The smiles and the cheering never stopped as we all got cleaned up, dressed, and ready to leave.

We had to go directly to the airport to catch our flight home, but when we got on the team bus, everybody kept telling us to get down. People were moving up the aisle and closing the curtains over the windows. The Brazilian fans started rocking our bus. We were on the floor, in the dark, and they were trying to kill us! We did not know what they were going to do, or how far things were going to go, but we knew we needed help from the police. How can anyone take sports so seriously? It was just a basketball game. Granted, it was an important basketball game, but not something to get violent about.

The herds of people kept pushing our bus back and forth. I do not know how it kept from tipping over, because we were doing some major rocking. The local police finally surrounded the bus and moved the angry crowd back enough so that the police cars could pull in and escort us out of the pandemonium. Everyone on our U.S. team was still down on the floor when the bus finally started rolling toward the airport. There was a collective sigh of relief when we got away from the arena and the chaos. It felt great to be safe, but we were all thinking, *Brazil is nuts. These people are crazy!*

I was thrilled to be alive and excited to get back to the States, even more so when I found out that I was being honored as USA Basketball's 1993 Female Athlete of the Year. Everything was going so well for me at the national level, but there was still work to be done at USC. I had one more year to get it right, but as it turned out, Coach Stanley was not going to be around for my senior season. I was shocked to find out that my coach would not be back for my final year.

How could that be? She had brought the USC program back to life. We had gone to the NCAA tournament three straight years, and we were coming off a season in which we went to the Elite Eight. Coach Stanley was the reigning Pac-10 Conference Coach of the Year, and she had a great recruiting class coming in that included Tina Thompson, the top high school recruit in the nation, and Karleen Thompson (formerly Karleen Shields), the number one junior college player in the country. Karleen scored just under forty-two points per game the previous year at Contra Costa College, and she led the nation in scoring. USC was picked to go to the Final Four in my senior season and could possibly win the national championship, so what had gone wrong? What had happened to my coach?

News started filtering in that Coach Stanley had asked for a new, multiyear contract equal to the one that USC had given to George Raveling, the Trojans' men's basketball coach. Raveling was believed to be earning between $130,000 and $150,000 per year. Coach Stanley wanted equal pay for equal work.

I remember her telling me that she had met with Athletic Director Mike Garrett to discuss the issue. Coach Stanley said that he had agreed with her position on the equal pay issue, but then the salary he later offered her did not line up with that at all.

(Garrett never publicly acknowledged this.) I am sure that Coach Stanley felt that if she stayed, she would be abandoning her principles and doing herself and her gender an injustice. The two sides could not agree, and just like that, Coach Stanley was no longer USC's women's basketball coach.

I was heartbroken.

I remembered that before all this went down, Mike Garrett would occasionally come to our practices. He and Coach Stanley would go to lunch, and I would ask her, "Coach, do you like him?"

She would tell me, "Yeah. Why?"

I was never quite sure how to respond. Because Mike Garrett seldom spoke to me and we had not had a conversation beyond an occasional "Hi, how are you," I did not know where I stood with him. I respected Garrett because he had been a Heisman Trophy–winning running back at USC, and he had gone on to play in the NFL. But he seemed unapproachable and I did not think women's sports interested him.

I think Coach Stanley tried to fight for what she thought was right. There are times when women have to take a stand. If you look at the facts, it was not fair for my coach to be paid less than George Raveling. Just compare our record to the men's record. In the four-year period (1989–90 through 1992–93) that Coach Stanley was at USC, our women's team earned a 71–46 record. We went 45–27 in Pac-10 play and finished seventh, third, second, and second again in the conference. In that same time frame, the USC men's basketball program posted a 73–44 record, went 40–32 in the Pac-10, and finished seventh, third, second, and fifth place in the conference race. Our women's team went to the NCAA tournament in three of the four years that Coach Stanley was on the job. During that same time span, George Raveling's teams made two visits to the NCAAs and one trip to the National Invitation Tournament. Coach Stanley was putting up winning numbers if not better numbers, and it seemed reasonable that she should be rewarded for it.

But there were, of course, other issues involved. At USC I noticed there were differences between the men's and women's basketball programs when it came to marketing, support, and respect within the university. I believe Coach Stanley wanted to see improvements in those areas as well. Initially, money was the key issue, but more and more, the stalemate became a matter of principle. She thought that Garrett and the university had discriminated against her because she was a woman. She contended that even though she and Coach Raveling performed the same duties in their respective jobs, she was compensated less and received fewer benefits than he did.

It was all too much for me to handle. I did not even want to come out of the house. I did not want to play. Our team was hoping that somehow Coach Stanley's position would go unfilled. We figured that any coach with a hint of conscience, especially female coaches, would turn down the job out of respect for the principles that Coach Stanley had been fighting for. As a team, we were united in our support, so we held a news conference at a hotel across the street from the USC campus to let everybody know that we were 100 percent behind our embattled coach. We were asked in front of cameras, microphones, and reporters, "How many players are planning to transfer to other colleges if Coach Stanley is not reinstated?" We all raised our hands. It was unanimous. We did not know if our show of solidarity would change anything, but we were holding on to hope that Coach Stanley would somehow get her job back.

It was not long, however, before we heard that Cheryl Miller would be the new head coach for women's basketball at USC. This is the same Cheryl Miller who scored 105 points in a California high school game, then went on to a brilliant career at USC, where she rewrote the record books and won two national championships, three Naismith Awards, and, just for good measure, a gold medal in the 1984 Olympics. *That* Cheryl Miller.

Once she took the job, our team had to face the harsh reality that Coach Stanley was definitely not coming back. When Cheryl came in, she kept Coach Scott and Fred Williams as her assistants, but I had mixed feelings about her taking the job. I remember the official meeting when Cheryl was introduced as our head coach. Several of us were sad and crying. I was stunned.

On the one hand, I thought, *Cheryl Miller is a legend. This woman played, and she was great.* I had never seen Cheryl play in person, but I knew that she could play ball. And it was kind of exciting. On the other hand, I thought, *This woman has never been a coach before. She probably doesn't know anything about coaching. It is one thing to be a player, and it is a whole different thing to be a coach.*

My teammates had similar concerns, and we dealt with it as a team. We knew that nobody was going to come to USC and be better than Coach Stanley. Not Cheryl Miller. Not anybody. We would have resented whoever tried to step into Coach Stanley's shoes. Cheryl just happened to be the one. Our team decided right then that we were not going to like Cheryl and we were not going to talk to her. We really thought that shutting out the new coach would bring us closer together as a team. In all honesty, we did not know what to do. Our team was just confused and grasping for straws.

I will give her this: Cheryl came in completely confident, and she exhibited her strong motivational speaking skills right from the get-go. She said to us, "I know it is going to take time for you guys to get to know me. I am not here trying to replace Coach Stanley. I am just trying to help. This is our university. We can win!" In retrospect, I can see why she thought this approach would work with us. But emotions were running high, and I just could not let go of my allegiance to Coach Stanley. (Incidentally, it is moments like this that taught me what professionalism is.)

After that speech, we had even more mixed emotions to deal with. Some of the things that Cheryl said to us sounded pretty good, but we did not want to betray Coach Stanley. It was like your father divorcing your mother and then finding a new girl-friend. The girlfriend might be nice, but if you like her, are you betraying your own mother? If you fight against the girlfriend, doesn't that hurt your dad? The child cannot win in that situa-tion, and that is how our team felt when Cheryl Miller arrived.

I was the team captain, and I was going into my senior year. What was I supposed to do? Did I want to stay and play for a new coach, or did I want to transfer and sit out a year before I could play again? Could we all transfer as a group or decide as a team that we would not play for the new coach? Would we be turning our backs on Coach Stanley if we supported Cheryl and bought into her system?

We had a lot of questions and very few answers. I was the leader of a team in disarray. Some players were practicing, and some were not. I was one of five seniors on the squad. We had quality veterans in place and some excellent young players join-ing the team. We had potential, but we had no direction. Coach Stanley was out as head coach, but she gave us a lot of positive encouragement and tried to make things easier for everyone on the team by telling us, "Don't leave USC. Stay there and finish your college career. You guys are going to win it."

I do not know if Coach Stanley really had her heart in what she said, but in some strange way, she had given us her blessing to move ahead. I felt as though we might as well play, even though it seemed as if we did not exist at the university. We kept getting slapped in the face by disappointing realities.

When Mike Garrett finally came to talk to our team, our pro-gram was in turmoil and filled with uncertainty. He could not have been more blunt or heartless when he addressed the team and basically told us that if we did not want to play at USC, we should leave. He also said that the university and the women's basketball program were going to go on with or without us. If we wanted to play, we could stay. If not, we should let him know.

We were in tears. Garrett's words sounded like threats to us. We felt as if our own university was abandoning us. New players did not know what to think. Things were such a mess.

I was never sorry that I chose to attend USC and to this day, I feel a connection with the university. But my experience in my senior year prepared me for the harsh realities of the real world.

Chapter 6

Women of Troy

USC put pictures of Cheryl Miller and me on the 1993–94 women's basketball poster. I was not thrilled with the idea. Our team was not happy to have a new coach, but we decided that we would play and work hard for Cheryl. There were times in practice when Cheryl would explain a drill or a strategy to us, and we would all just look at each other, thinking, *That is nowhere close to how Coach Stanley would have explained it.*

It was inevitable that we would make comparisons, but like it or not, we had to deal with our situation. I tried to keep an open mind about it, and that was not easy, but Cheryl was the coach and I was the player, so it really did not matter how I felt about her. My job was to play the game. I never let Cheryl know that I did not like the fact that she was my coach, though she probably sensed it. I just moved on and played the game. That made some of my teammates mad. They even called Coach Stanley and told her, "Lisa likes Cheryl. She's acting like everything is okay and nothing happened."

I had to tell them, "It is not that I like or dislike Cheryl. It is just that I believe that we have to move forward. We have to move on. Let's go. We have got to win. Cheryl is on the bench, but she is just one aspect of the game." I wanted my teammates to know that I was not digging Cheryl any more than anybody else was, but we still needed to respect the game plan and try to make it work for us.

As the captain, I told them, "We are the ones playing. We are in control of our own destiny. I know that we all love Coach Stanley and we all miss her, but she wants what is best for us, and right now what is best for us is to win the national championship. When we accomplish that goal, it will show everybody just how strong Coach Stanley's program at USC really was."

Despite having a new coach and tense circumstances, our team eventually started to act like a team again. Not one player transferred out. We went through our conditioning workouts on the track, and things went pretty well. When we got to the weight room, players were getting after it. They were not cheating anymore.

In practice, Cheryl would explain how she wanted us to get over a pick, how to get through a cross pick, or how to play against a certain type of man-to-man defense. Oftentimes, when workouts were over, the core of the team would stay after practice. We would shoot around until the coaches left the gym, and then the other seniors and I would show the new players how to get on the midline, how to be on "help side" defense, how to rotate, and how to "help the helper" when contesting shots. Sooner or later, every player on the team became a part of those extra sessions, and our efforts started to pay off.

I think defense is the most important facet of basketball, but Cheryl's defense was completely different than anything we had learned before. We had been playing under one system for three years, and it had worked. It was the same system that USA Basketball used. But Cheryl had her own ideas and her own way of saying and doing things, and it was all foreign to us.

I must give her credit, though. As a player, she was one of the greats because of her solid work ethic. Cheryl simply outworked her opponents, and she coached with that same intensity. We could see and feel her passion for the game, but there were often times when we did not understand her terminology. With our team, if we did not understand you, we could not be on the same page with you. And if we were not on the same page with our coach, USC basketball had little chance for success.

We definitely had talent. Tina Thompson turned out to be really good. She was the reigning California AAA Player of the Year, and the freshman stepped right in to start for us at forward. That meant that she and I had to work together and have a total connection on the court. I would tell her, "Tina, if you get back first on defense, be sure to take my man. I will take yours." It was just basic basketball, but they were critical connections that Coach Stanley would have broken down for every player on our team. With her, we all used the same terminology. We would write it on the blackboard and jot it down in our notebooks. Sometimes, Coach Stanley would quiz us on the information. She showed us the basics, and every one of us had to know them.

Tina and I got to be very close. We had both attended Morningside High, and now we were playing together at USC. She always wanted to learn, so Tina would pick my brain for everything that I knew. A lot of times when Cheryl would teach us something, Tina would stand by me. For instance, our coach would say, "You can go over the top of the pick or underneath." I would tell Tina that she had to understand her opponent in order to make that decision. Coach Stanley always taught us to make that determination based on how well the opposing guard could shoot, pass, or penetrate. If she was a shooter, we would go over the top of the pick in order to stay in the player's face.

Cheryl admits now that when she started her coaching career at USC, there was a lot that she did not know. At that time, I felt I had very good knowledge of the game, and believe me, I did feel a responsibility to make our team a winner that would claim the national championship. I worked a lot with Tina and Karleen after practices. Karleen became my very best friend. Still is. She was also a single mom, and right away, I took a liking to her young daughters, Ayesha and Keisha. I think it was Karleen's work ethic and perseverance through adversity that impressed me most. Before she went to Contra Costa Community College, Karleen had been working at Burger King while her daughters slept on blankets in the back room. She had been through a lot, and she was still standing. Being a mom is a full-time job by itself, and Karleen was handling all of those parenting responsibilities at the same time that she was a full-time student-athlete at USC.

Karleen was an excellent shooter with three-point range, but she had a habit of taking a lot of her shots from inside the arc. I kept telling her, "Kar, you have to back up. I need you to get farther away from me so we have more space to work with. Throw me the ball, and then *move*. I promise I will throw it back to you, and you are gonna get an open jump shot."

We worked endlessly on defense after regular practices, too, first just the seniors, then eventually the whole team. Karleen told me, "I cannot believe that I have played the game this long, and I never heard of the midline or the help side. I have just been out there getting by on my athleticism." Every day after practice, we would work on something different. Karleen had amazing talent, but she will tell you to this day that she hated not getting to work with Coach Stanley. She knows she would have been so much better. Karleen Thompson is currently the head coach and general manager of the WNBA's Houston Comets.

Before the coaches could legally work with the squad, my teammates and I played some pickup games in the gym. In one game freshman guard Erica Jackson was doing a lot of faking and dribbling between her legs, but she was not having any luck getting the ball up court against Nicky McCrimmon. I told her several times to take the ball straight down the middle and get it into the frontcourt as quickly as possible. Erica would tell me,

"Okay," but then she would continue to dribble between her legs and take forever to get us into our offense. Tina was saying, "Oh my god! When is she going to get across midcourt?"

When Erica finally found her way past the center stripe, I popped out to get a pass from her, but she did not throw the basketball. I went back inside, popped out again, and yelled, "Erica! Throw the ball!"

Erica had been a star in high school the year before, but in her first days at the collegiate level, the newcomer had a bit more than she could handle. She was frustrated, flustered, and more than a little embarrassed. Erica got angry and threw the ball at me. I caught it, whipped the ball right back at her, and yelled, "What is your problem?" Before I knew it, we were in each other's face. I grabbed her by the hair, and started pulling. I was so wrong, but I wanted to drag this girl over to the brick wall and smash her head. She had a bad attitude, and I was about to jack her up. I snapped. My teammates were yelling, "Lisa! No! No! Let her go!"

I finally let Erica loose and stormed out of the gym. I was so upset with myself. I had reacted without thinking again. I had exploded with instant anger. Cheryl found out about the incident, and when I calmed down, I went to her office. She closed the door, and I just knew she was going to give me a lecture. Instead, the coach gave me high fives. "That's what I'm talking about," Cheryl told me. "You don't let nobody disrespect you! You stand up for what you believe." She was praising me, but I told her that I was not proud of what had happened, and I wanted to apologize to Erica and the team. After all, I was the team captain, and I was supposed to set the example. Cheryl called Erica in, and we apologized to each other. I found out later, though, that when Cheryl talked privately with Erica, she told her the same thing. The word in the locker room was that Erica was given the same speech the coach had given me. What the . . . ?

I immediately wondered what Coach Stanley would have

done in this situation. I know she would have been very disappointed in me. She probably would have had me apologize to everybody and then made me run, and run some more. Coach Stanley would have known that would be serious punishment for me. She might have removed me as team captain, and I would not have blamed her. What I did to Erica was totally unacceptable. I was disturbed by my own behavior, but I was more concerned about the effect it might have on our team and our camaraderie.

Our basketball team turned out to be very resilient. We won the first six games of my senior season at USC, and we lost only one time in our first eighteen games. Karleen had clearly shown that she was our top guard. She earned the starting role, but as the season progressed, Cheryl moved Tracy Atwater, a senior, into the starting lineup.

Wait a minute. Shouldn't a coach start the most talented players on her team? Shouldn't she put the players on the floor that will give her squad the best chance to win? What was going on? The team never understood the logic behind her decision.

No matter what Cheryl's reason was for making the change, it would have been more palatable to the players if she had told them that she was making the change for the good of the team or because she wanted more firepower off the bench.

The way Cheryl did it, our team wound up with one senior happy about starting, one new player unhappy about not starting, and two USC players upset with each other because of ridiculous team politics. Cheryl said so many different things to so many players that her credibility really came into question. She was always trying to make every player happy. If the coach is not strong, consistent, and in control, the team will eventually fall apart. I realize that Cheryl was probably doing what she thought was best to keep the team going strong. She knew that our squad had been through a lot with Coach Stanley's departure, and she did her best to create a friendship with all of us. I must admit that there were times when I shared laughs with Cheryl and wished that we had met under different circumstances, but without my favorite coach at the helm, I just could not let her in. It was an awkward relationship at best.

I was the California player who for *years* had been compared to Cheryl Miller. Now I was playing for her at USC, where she had earned her legendary status. Cheryl was the coach, but she had to share the spotlight with me and constantly answer media questions about her star player. Maybe I was a threat. I cannot be sure. All I know is that the relationship was not that strong. Cheryl would put her arm around me and smile when the cameras were on, but I was not sure if it was sincere because we were both equally as open with each other as we were closed.

I was just thinking Cheryl being my coach after Coach Stanley was bad timing. In a lot of ways, I could relate to her as a player more than as a coach. One incident was a practice that I remember. We were working on zone defenses in practice. Tina, Nicky, Karleen, and I were moving the ball around and scoring easily against the zone. One of our walk-on players was part of the defense, and Cheryl yelled out to her, "Give me that jersey!" Our coach took the girl's shirt, pulled it on, and stepped in to play the middle of the zone.

I asked Cheryl, "Are you just demonstrating, or are you playing?"

"No, I'm playing," she said.

"Are you sure?" I asked.

"I'm sure. I'm playing. Let's go!"

In all my years of playing basketball, I had never seen a head coach actually play in a scrimmage. It was one of those things that was so weird, it was funny. Cheryl had forced her way into the action, so there was no way that we were going to take it easy on her. We figured she could hold her own. In fact, some of us looked forward to mixing it up with the new coach. Cheryl was only thirty years old, and she was a solid six foot three. Everybody knew what a great player she had been during the 1980s. I had no idea how good she still might be, but I did not want to take my chances and get beat by her. I knew she would have some game left and might try to muscle me and block my shot, so I was going to play hard, just as I would in any practice.

But Cheryl's competitive instincts took over. Our coach was trying to make a statement, so she dug in defensively, stole the ball, drove to the other basket, and scored. In that instant, I thought, *I wish she was my teammate!* Cheryl was feeling pretty good about herself, too, and then we switched, and her team went on offense. Cheryl was showing the reserves how to attack the zone. I was in the middle defensively, with Tina and Jualeah Woods on the wings. Nicky and Karleen were at the top of the zone for us, and as only Karleen can do, she started to challenge Cheryl verbally in a lighthearted way. "Come on. Bring it in here, Coach. Let's see what you've got."

Cheryl took the challenge. She drove hard, squeezed past our guards, came right at me, put up a finger roll, and scored. The coach was pumped, and started joking and talking trash. Our starting five was beginning to feel tested. That was when things began to get more physical on the court.

The next time Cheryl dribbled through the top of our zone, Karleen bumped her a bit with an elbow and put our coach on a direct path to me in the middle. I went up in the air, with the intent of blocking her shot, and I did get a piece of the ball, but on my way down, my elbow accidentally caught a piece of Cheryl's face. I busted her lip, and she was *pissed*. My teammates looked at Cheryl, and then they looked at me. All I could say to them was, "Hey. When she put on the jersey, Cheryl stopped being the coach and became one of us. That play was just good, hard basketball." Everybody laughed, even Cheryl. I think we truly gained respect for each other's competitiveness that day.

In Cheryl's first year on the job, our team finished 14–4 in Pac-10 play and won the conference championship. That earned us an automatic bid to the NCAA tournament, and we went in as the number two seed in the Mideast Regional, right behind Tennessee. We caught a break as well. The first two rounds were on our home floor, at the L.A. Memorial Sports Arena, right next to the USC campus. The Women of Troy took advantage of that home cooking and knocked off the University of Portland and then George Washington University to advance to the regional semifinals in Fayetteville, Arkansas.

Our first foe in Razorback country was the University of Virginia. We made quick work of the Cavaliers. That victory put the Trojans back in the Elite Eight, but the question remained, Could we take that giant step to the Final Four? I told my teammates, "We have got to get past this point. We are not here to be crying again. We have got to play!"

USC met up with Louisiana Tech in the Mideast Regional finals. They were a powerhouse team coached by the legendary Leon Barmore. The Lady Techsters had squeaked by Tennessee in the semis, and they were a tough matchup for us, but we got off to a good start in our biggest game of the year. We led by three at halftime and were playing great, but I had been on the floor just about every second. I started to get tired down the stretch, but Cheryl would not take me out of the game. I was drained. I ran out of gas. I played as hard as I could for as long as I could, but I needed a break. I needed just a minute or so to catch my breath, so I asked for a sub, but Cheryl would not remove me from the game. All she said was, "You got to suck it up, big girl."

That game was neck and neck for a long time, and then Louisiana Tech started to pull away. We could not hold on, and we could not catch up. USC went flat, and the Lady Techsters beat us 75–66 to move on to the Final Four in Richmond, Virginia. I had played thirty-eight minutes, and I was exhausted. Exhausted and disappointed, once again.

My biggest disappointment was that Coach Stanley did not

coach me for my senior year. I truly believe that played a huge role in our team's not winning the national championship. As it was, we never got to play for the national title. We never even made it to the Final Four. Individually, that senior season was my best statistically. I averaged twenty-two points, twelve rebounds, and three blocked shots per game while shooting 56 percent. I left USC as the Pac-10's all-time leading scorer and rebounder; and I became the only player to be named to the first-team All-Pac-10 list four times. The postseason accolades just kept coming my way. I finally won the Naismith Award as the top player in women's college basketball, and that was a tremendous honor for me, but in the four years that I played for USC, my teams never accomplished college basketball's ultimate team goal. That was another disappointment to me.

I did feel a tiny bit better when I was named to the 1994 Kodak All-America team. The Kodak team might not have been the biggest honor to some players, but it was the ultimate award to me. Cheryl Miller had been a four-time Kodak All-America pick. She was the best, and I wanted to be the best. I would always look at what people before me had accomplished and try to do even better. That was my top goal. That is what I had to go for. So one of the goals I had written down was to make the Kodak squad.

I was a three-time All-America pick, but I still coveted the Kodak squad. Every year that I got slighted, I would look at the players who had been chosen, and I would say to myself, "I am at least as good as this player." But I knew with hard work, I would one day achieve my goal.

I cried in my freshman, sophomore, and junior years when the Kodak team was announced and my name was not on the roster. I faced the same problem every season: USC would fall short of the Final Four, and I would be ignored by the Kodak selection committee. But it finally happened for me, and it confirmed once again that my habit of writing down my goals and staying focused was a good way to achieve them.

In an ironic twist of fate, USC decided to retire my number thirty-three Trojan jersey on November 10, 2006. That was the night that the university opened its brand-new Galen Center to basketball. USC decided to retire Cheryl Miller's number thirty-one jersey on that *same* night, in the *same* halftime ceremony. The Women of Troy hosted Long Beach State that evening, and I sat near midcourt, watching the game and signing autographs. When Cheryl came in, she took her seat right next to me. For the first time, we hugged and congratulated each other with true sincerity. I think we both realized that our struggles had been the same struggles. We may have chosen different paths, but our goals were identical. We both wanted to be the best players that we could be, and we always wanted to win. I think being honored by USC at the Galen Center that night helped us realize that there was enough room at the top for both of us.

When intermission rolled around, the ceremony began. Several of Cheryl's former USC teammates—Paula McGee, Rhonda Windham, Melissa Ward, and LeAnne Sera—stood on the north end of the court. Some of my former Trojan teammates came, too—Tammy Story, Michelle Campbell, Jodi Anton, Nicky McCrimmon, and yes, Erica "You Pulled My Hair" Jackson— and they were lined up at the south end. The lights went down, and a video montage of my USC highlights was shown on the overhead scoreboard. When I was introduced, the fans erupted. It was an incredible feeling to be honored and appreciated after so many years. I was able to address the crowd and thank everybody for their support and kindness. I also challenged the kids in attendance to "follow their dreams," just the way that I had and just the way that I continue to set goals and chase my dreams.

Then it was time for a video montage of Cheryl's legendary career at USC. She spoke to the crowd, too, and then, there we were. Lisa Leslie and Cheryl Miller, two of the Trojans' most illustrious women's basketball players, standing together at center court. And get this: USC Athletic Director Mike Garrett and his associate, Carol Dougherty, brought flowers out to us. Then, as the Trojan marching band played the USC fight song, the number thirty-three and number thirty-one jerseys were unveiled and slowly raised to the rafters. I had always hoped to have my number retired at USC, and it was quite an honor to have it retired with as great a player as Cheryl Miller. Cheryl and I locked arms and smiled a lot as we both enjoyed our very special evening. As I look back, I am thankful for the life lessons that I learned while at USC, and I am proud, once again, to be a Trojan.

Chapter 7

Grande Liza!

When my playing days ended at USC, my basketball career did not come to a screeching halt. In fact, it kicked into high gear. That June I played for USA Basketball in the 1994 world championships in Sydney, Australia. It was the first time that our future Olympic team played together, and Dawn Staley, Ruthie Bolton, Teresa Edwards, Katrina McClain, and Sheryl Swoopes were all key members of that squad. Tara VanDerveer was our head coach once again as our U.S. national team went after its third consecutive world championship.

We wound up facing our old rivals from Brazil in a semifinal game, but this time they got the better of us. Katrina had a monster performance, but Brazil hit all ten of its free throw attempts in the final minute and eliminated us. We had to settle for the bronze medal, and we were not happy about that at all. I did get further proof, however, that Katrina was one of the greatest players that I had ever competed with or against. She averaged fifteen points and eleven rebounds in the world championships and shot a very impressive 63 percent from the field. Katrina's athletic skills were phenomenal, and just between me and you, she might be the only athlete that I ever played against who

107

made me nervous when I knew that I would have to guard her. I was very happy to have Katrina McClain on my side.

The interesting twist to our encounter with Brazil was that all the teams that played against one another had to ride on the same bus. So our team had to share a bus with the very energetic women's team from Brazil. They put one team on each side of the aisle. We did not know it, but the Brazilian players had made a deal with their coach that if they beat us, the players could shave his head. So on the ride to the hotel after the game, our U.S. team watched from across the aisle while Team Brazil shaved their coach's head. That was something you did not see every day, even at the world championships. All the U.S. team could do was watch in silence.

I continued to play for the national team anywhere and every-where. The Goodwill Games in St. Petersburg, Russia, were a great experience. After our third-place finish in Australia, we were considered underdogs to China and their six-foot-eight center, Haixia Zheng. She was a very big girl who had a lot of talent and took up a ton of space. We went head to head with China in the semifinals, and we beat them. Then we beat France in the finals.

I loved playing with this national team because we were a very sisterly team. We hung out together, played cards, talked trash, and gave each other advice. We had played together for so long that we were like a little family. The veterans played hard, and they were not afraid to teach the younger players like me what they knew. There was no ego; everyone just wanted to win. And the high intensity of their game made me elevate mine.

The next thing I knew, it was late August 1999, and I was heading to Alcamo, Sicily. Representatives for the Sicilgesso team, in the Italian League, had heard of my collegiate exploits and had seen me play with USA Basketball. They offered me a contract worth $110,000. Those were 110,000 good reasons why I was jetting my way to the northwest corner of Sicily, to a spot right near the Gulf of Castellammare. Alcamo was just west of Turkey, a short hop north of Africa, and a long way from home.

My flight went from Los Angeles to Rome, to Palermo, the nearest large city to Alcamo. I packed my huge USA bags with clothes; toiletries and cosmetics; a few boxes of Cheetos, Crunch Berries, Frosted Flakes, and oatmeal; and a few movies to keep me entertained.

My new coach, Vito Pollari, picked me up at the airport, and I stepped into a whole new world. He drove me to a beautiful two-bedroom apartment that the team provided for me. It had one bathroom, a kitchen, a living room, hardwood floors, and a balcony. The weather was warm and beautiful in Alcamo, a lot like Los Angeles.

I could open my windows, let the sun in, and always get a nice warm breeze through my apartment.

I found a former Trojan hoop star in Sicily, too. Cynthia Cooper was my teammate. She had been the best player in Italy for seven seasons with Parma and was starting her first season playing for Sicilgesso. I had met Cynthia when I tried out for the USA Basketball team in 1990. She was very nice to me then, and now she was living upstairs from me in Alcamo.

Shortly after I arrived in Sicily, Cynthia and I went to a luncheon to meet everybody associated with the team. I did not speak a word of Italian, so I just smiled a lot. They must have thought that I was an incredibly happy person, but honestly, I did not have a clue what to do or say.

At this luncheon, they brought out a big bowl of pasta with marinara sauce. It looked and smelled delicious, and I ate my share. It was quite filling. Then they brought out *pette di pollo*, a chicken dish. When I travel internationally, I try to be open and respectful to the people and their culture, so I ate a tiny bit of *pette di pollo* to be polite. But that made me feel really stuffed. Next came the salad. Then a plate of vegetables. This was an Italian-style, seven-course meal, and I had not realized it. I had never heard of such a thing, and my goodness, there was enough food to feed a small country. They just kept bringing out food. I laughed and tried to say, "No more," but they just kept telling me to keep eating.

Cynthia was sitting at the end of the table, trying to translate for me. "Do they always serve this much food?" I asked her.

"They always serve a big lunch and a small dinner. You'll get used to it."

(And I did.)

Driving was also a new experience for me in Alcamo. The team had promised me an automobile, but I did not know how to drive a stick shift, and there were no automatics to be found. Apparently, you had to have some serious money over there to get an automatic transmission in your vehicle.

The owners of Sicilgesso eventually bought me a Fiat to drive, but it was so small, they had to cut out the driver's seat, slide it all the way to the back of the car and then weld it in place just so I could squeeze inside the thing. There was absolutely no room for anything behind my seat. One of my team managers eventually took me into the hills and taught me how to drive a stick shift. After a few hours of trying, I eventually got the hang of it and drove myself home. But for my first month or two in Italy, whenever I needed to go out, somebody from the team would pick me up, or Cynthia would give me a ride.

Cynthia and I had a really good relationship. Players over there would always ask me, "What is it like playing with Cooper? Is she mean to you? Does she pass you the ball?"

I have never been much of a gossiper, and I was not going to fall into that trap. I heard so much of it while I was playing with USA Basketball. Athletes talked about one another all the time, like they had nothing better to do. I did not want to keep that going. But there was nothing to say, really. We only ever had one minor dustup. It was, of course, on the court in Sicily.

In practice, I would rebound the ball and toss it out to half-court, to Cynthia. She would catch it, put a crossover move on a defender, then do her one-two step and go in for a layup at the other end of the court.

We followed that routine in almost all of our games. It was so effective that there was no reason not to. In one game, though, I threw several of those outlet passes to Cynthia and everything was good, but the one time that I did not pass the ball to her, she got angry. I had looked for Cynthia after clearing the boards, but I saw a defender coming up behind her. I knew that I could not get the ball to her cleanly, so I threw it to our other guard. Cynthia went nuts and yelled at me, "Pass me the f---ing ball!"

At the next time-out, I immediately went over to sit next to Cynthia on the bench. I told her, "Look! I pass you the ball nine times out of ten, and you get on my case the one time that you do not get the basketball? You were covered. Don't ever yell at me about getting you the ball. You should be able to trust the decisions that I make. If I don't throw it to you, there must be a reason."

Cynthia came back later and apologized. That was it, end of story. We never had another confrontation or problem. I think we just had a high level of respect between us. I totally respected her as a veteran of the international game. I was a good, young player in my first season overseas, but I was never mouthy, brash, or arrogant. I was always polite, I always listened, and I always wanted to learn and get better. I deserved respect, too.

I never spoke to anyone about the incident with Cynthia because we really had a good relationship, especially on the court. We each went out of our way to be helpful to one another, but we did not try to force a friendship that was not there. We did not hang out like we were buddy buddies, but we were there for each other, and that was important. If I needed a ride, Cynthia would drive me. Sometimes we cooked and ate together, and it was not uncommon for me to bring her a plate of food pregame, and vice versa. The mutual respect was very cool.

Cynthia did most of the translating for me when I got to Italy, but I wanted to learn the language. I bought some books, and when I was not practicing or playing games with my team, I was learning Italian. I got a lot of help from Guisi, a very nice, young Italian woman who lived across the street from my apartment. We got to be such close friends that her family called me their new Italian daughter. I loved hanging out with Guisi and her brother, Alfredo. They were older than me, but we all got along great. Guisi wanted to speak better English, so we worked together and helped each other. I would go over to her place for lunch, and some nights we would head out to the discotheques.

I loved to dance and Guisi did, too, so we would dance all night. The men loved to blow kisses at me since we did not speak the same language. And the ones who did speak a little English liked to recite common American phrases, which never seemed to fit into the conversation at hand. It was always a great time, and getting home at three in the morning was the usual.

My coach, Vito, was not a big fan of his players having fun, however, especially one of the team's high-priced stars. Vito told me, "Liza [they spelled my name with a z over there and pronounced it Lee-za], we do not want you going out to the discotheques."

I asked him, "Why not? How many points do I average for you?"

"Twenty-two points."

"How many rebounds?"

"Eleven."

"Is that what you hired me to do?"

"Yes."

"Then I am doing my job. As long as I do my job, you cannot tell me what to do in my personal life. I can do whatever I want to do."

Wherever I might be staying or traveling, if I decided to go out, I would go out regardless of how big or small the town was or who knew about it. If I wanted to go out dancing, I was going to go dancing. I knew I was not doing anything wrong. I did not do drugs, and I was not drinking. As long as I came to work and performed to the best of my abilities, how I spent my personal time was my business.

After listening to my side of things, Vito agreed.

That was a big victory for me, because at that time in Italy, the owners and coaches really wanted to control their players. In fact, they *did* control the Italian players. Those ladies had a laundry list of rules to live by, which hampered their social lives completely.

The Italian fans called me Grande Liza, and they were very loyal supporters. Watching our Sicilgesso team play basketball was *the* big thing to do in Alcamo. It was a huge social event, a chance to get together with friends, maybe drink some wine, blow off some steam, and root for the home team.

Fans really liked to bring sparklers to the games. And I mean sparklers like the ones that we light and shake around on the Fourth of July in the United States. The fans in Alcamo would light their sparklers while our games were in progress indoors! We did not play in a huge arena or an open-air facility. Our court was the size of a high school gymnasium in the States. The fans were also allowed to smoke in the building, so while Sicilgesso played, we had to inhale cigarette and cigar smoke as well as those stinking sparklers. My eyes would be burning and watering, and all the players would be choking. Every time there was a jump ball, the game would have to be held up because someone would be coughing or struggling to breathe. And this was on our home court, in front of our home crowd! So much for home court advantage.

Sicilgesso fans really did get into the games, though. They would chant, "Grande Liza! Liza!" for me and, "Chin-see-ya!

Chin-see-ya!" for Cynthia. They cheered hard and loud, almost like European soccer fans, but without the violence. The fans in Alcamo were very cool.

The basketball in the Italian League was highly competitive, but the gyms were average, and the weight rooms and facilities were a joke. Since my team was not in the top division, we only played one game per week, but we still practiced twice a day, so we went through an awful lot of practice sessions just to play one game.

The European players were very good scorers. Offense was a top priority overseas. Defense was not. They wanted us to score, score, score, score as many points as possible, but when the opposing team scored more points than us, the defeat was usually blamed on the American players on the squad. And there were a lot of us.

In Italy I played against Ruthie Bolton, Carla McGhee, Andrea Stinson, Kym Hampton, Michelle Edwards, Edna Campbell, Bridget Gordon, and many others from the United States. We all loved the game, and this was the only place to play it as a professional at the time.

The coaches in Alcamo wanted me to play their Italian style of basketball, which really emphasized footwork. Players were allowed to take that extra step in the international game, and it really made a difference. My coach taught me some useful things about facing up, using my feet to my advantage, and making one move, then following it with a second move. I learned to play that international brand of hoops, but ironically, I wound up using it mostly against Americans. Just about every Italian team had an American post player or a scorer from the United States.

I remember the first time I went head-to-head with Jennifer Gillom in Italy. We each put up thirty-six points and just kept scoring back and forth until we both fell on the floor. Jen looked at me and said, "Girl! You are making me earn my money tonight!" I was just a rookie then. Jennifer was a seasoned veteran and an amazing scorer. She could use her body so effectively and was excellent competition for me. But our skills canceled each other out in that game.

That happened a lot in Italy; the Americans on each team would negate each other's points, so the teams had to hope that their Italian players were better than the opponent's Italian players. Sicilgesso's Italian players were not very good, except for a young guard named Francesca Zara, who eventually made it to the WNBA.

At the start of the season, my team was the sorriest squad in the Italian League. It was like a high school team playing against professionals. Sicilgesso had never been competitive, but our owners thought that Cynthia and I would take them directly to a championship. We tried to. Cynthia averaged about twenty-five points, and I posted twenty-three points and twelve rebounds per game that season. Our team started to improve, but to get over the hump, we needed one more experienced player or a point guard who could really pass the ball. I would run the floor all game long, but my teammates could not get the basketball to me. It was frustrating. I was in a foreign country. I was alone. I was only playing one game per week, and I was losing. But I was still happy to be playing and learning more about the game.

Playing overseas is not for everybody. It takes a lot of strength and discipline to handle being that far away from your loved ones. You do not understand the language, and most of the time, you sit in an apartment when your team is not playing, practicing, or traveling. You do not know anybody, and if you are not open to embracing the culture, life overseas can be really depressing.

If I had never opened up my balcony, I would never have met Guisi and her wonderful Italian family. If I had stayed locked up in my apartment, I would never have enjoyed the wonders of true Italian food. It was so fresh! I have never been to an Italian restaurant in the States that serves food the way they do in Italy.

I had to buy milk every two days at the market in Alcamo because it was not pasteurized. I would walk to the butcher shop, and there would be an entire cow hanging in the store and chickens, too. It was quite a sight. The ground beef and turkey meat were always fresh, and the vegetables, pastas, and bread were, too. I get hungry just thinking about it.

My favorite thing to eat in Italy was a brioche. It was plain, circular-shaped bread, kind of like a croissant. There was nothing on it and nothing in it, but a brioche was warm and fresh and delicious. I had it every morning. At the store, I liked to buy three brioches at a time, but the merchants would look at me and say, "Three? That is too many." They were not used to serving such a large meal to one person that early in the day. But I loved it.

Once you have had authentic Italian food, you do not want the American version. In Italy they do not use cheddar cheese . . . on anything. They do not use a lot of meat sauces the way we do, either, but the Italians do a lot with mushrooms, fish, and eggplant. The food is fantastic! You can get baked lasagna in Italy, but it is nothing like the lasagna we get stateside. If you want pasta with cheese on top, or your spaghetti all cut up, you are out of luck. Oh, and one more thing. Do not ask for Alfredo sauce in Sicily. It does not exist. I remember when Guisi came to California with me. We went to an Italian restaurant, and she said in her strong accent, "Liza, who is this Alfredo guy?" Her brother, Alfredo, thought it was pretty funny, too.

I had so many great learning experiences in Italy. But living there was hard for me. Sometimes I was so sad and homesick that I was ready to pack up and go home. But then my family would come to visit me for several weeks and I would feel better. I usually found ways to make the most of my time there. It felt like an adventure, and I tried to keep a good attitude about it all.

I was playing the sport I loved in a beautiful city, and I was being paid well to do it.

That holiday season, in 1994, I was really excited to go home for a break. I love that time of year, but this particular Christmas was not so very merry for me. When I got back to Los Angeles, I found out that Marcus, the man I had been dating for three years and was engaged to, was seeing another woman, while I was away in Italy. I thought I was going to be sick.

Marcus was my first true sweetheart, and I thought I was going to spend my whole life with him. He was my best friend, and we had made plans for a life together. Now that was falling apart. My love for him ran so deeply that I tried to find a way to forgive him and keep the relationship going. We even moved in together. But our fourth year as a couple was rocky at best. I kept trying to believe I could somehow get past the pain and trust issues and start over again with Marcus, but when his post-collegiate plans did not pan out, he went from never drinking alcohol to drinking heavily. This new Marcus was not as patient or as kind or as attentive as the man I had grown to love.

One time, in particular, Marcus and I had plans to go out for the evening. He had a few male friends over, and I cooked and let the boys be boys. A few hours later, I asked Marcus when we were leaving to go out, and this set him off. He had been drinking and did not want me to question him. He got very angry with me—angrier than I had seen him before—and for the first time ever with Marcus, I was scared. This was not the man that I knew. This was not the man that I loved. His rage had turned him in to another person.

The altercation I had with Marcus that day was brief, but I was not about to stick around to see what else might happen. I grabbed my keys, my purse, and ran the hell out of there, and I did not see Marcus again for almost five years. It was a tragic ending to a relationship that meant a lot to me.

Life threw me another curveball when I got back to Italy in the New Year. My team had improved enough to climb into third place in the league, and we were playing a big road game up north against first-place Como. I was doing well, and then my knee locked. I was so scared! I kept trying to play, but the coaches told me, "No, Liza. You sit out. You wait. Put on a knee brace." I tried to run, but my knee just kept catching and locking. They thought I had torn my meniscus.

I said, "That is it. I am going home," and I did not mean home to my apartment. I meant home to California. I was already heartbroken and spending way too much time listening to sad Celine Dion songs and romantic Barry White songs. Now I was hurt. In all my years of playing basketball, I had never really been hurt. Now, here I was injured, and I was in Italy. We Americans always think that our country has the best of everything and is the best at everything, and that nobody else can compare. Well, that was exactly what I was thinking when I told the team officials, "You are not doing surgery on me in this country." In actuality, I received excellent medical care during my entire time in Italy, despite all the stereotypical "operations gone bad" thoughts that went through my head. But I was still hesitant to have surgery away from home. I was in pain. I was alone, and I was frightened.

I told Vito that if I could play, I would stay, but I was hurting too badly. My knee would seem fine for a while, but then I would start doing some light running and OWWW! The knee would lock straight as a rod, and I would be hobbling again. I was not going to keep playing and gambling that the knee would not act up. It was catching way too often. I think my body was telling me that it was tired. I had never taken a break since I started playing basketball back when I was twelve. Every school year, there had been lots of basketball, and every summer there had always been lots more. Enough was enough. I threw my hands up and made up my mind to go home immediately.

I went back to my apartment and started packing, but Vito came over and pleaded with me. "Liza! No! No! Stay at least until we can get another player over here." But there was no way I was going to stay. There were no bad feelings. They loved me in Alcamo. When I left on February 7, 1995, the people were sad and crying. I was sad, too. I had built many strong relationships in a very short time, but I had to go. I could not risk it. The Olympics were coming soon. I had to go home and get my knee checked out.

When I got back to Los Angeles, I sought out Dr. Stephen Lombardo, the L.A. Lakers' orthopedist. I had dye shot into my knee and MRIs taken, but Dr. Lombardo did not find anything wrong. He told me that when my knees got extremely tired, they would just stop and lock up. If I put ice on my knees and got some rest, it usually would not take long for me to recover, but there was no way that I could have continued competing for the Sicilgesso team in Italy. No way.

According to Dr. Lombardo, structurally, my knees were a lot like those of Kareem Abdul-Jabbar. They were strong and solid, and would probably allow me to play into my forties. But when my body began to wear down, it would send me a signal that said, "That is enough. Shut it down, Lisa, or we will shut it down for you!"

I knew I had to listen. With the 1996 Olympics around the corner, there was too much at stake. I needed to get healthy and start training again as soon as possible.

The Olympic prep process for the U.S. national team was much different for the Atlanta Games than it was for Barcelona in 1992. The 1992 team was selected in May and then played in the Olympics that July. The U.S. team for Atlanta was picked in

May of *1995*, then trained, played, and toured for more than a full year to get ready for the 1996 Games.

With a lot of rest, my knee got a lot better, and I made that team. I cannot tell you how excited I was to be preparing for my very first Olympic Games. There were so many amazing people and personalities that made that U.S. women's basketball squad so very special. Looking back on it, our preparation for those Summer Games was more difficult than playing the actual Olympic competition.

After the team was selected, we worked out in Colorado Springs, at the U.S. Olympic Training Center. One of our conditioning requirements was running a timed two miles. Our entire team went out to the track. It was so cold out there that your nose would freeze, and if you sneezed, your snot would ice up as soon as it came out. I was the only California girl on the team and had never been a fan of cold weather. I wore tights, gloves, and layers of sweats to try to stay warm.

I was a pretty good runner in high school, so I figured I would have no trouble finishing within the sixteen minutes that head coach Tara VanDerveer had allotted. The clock started, and we all took off. Jennifer Azzi and Ruthie Bolton were the best distance runners. They ran hard and were really strong on the track. They finished first, with Nikki McCray not far behind. Dawn Staley was a very good runner, too, but she would do precisely what needed to be done in the time she was given, nothing more and nothing less. Sheryl Swoopes turned out to be better than we had expected. She finished in the middle of our group, but Teresa Edwards, Carla McGhee, Rebecca Lobo, and I were at the back of the pack.

Here is the thing. I can run, but I cannot run in *cold weather*. Mentally, I was done before I ever stepped on that track. Even with all the layers of clothing I had on me, it was just TOO COLD! I could hear the wind blowing at me, stinging my face and making my eyes water. I am usually a pretty positive individual, but on this day, I felt totally down and defeated. I hated running. I was not used to the weather. I had never run more than a mile. Yet here I was, trying to run two miles in freezing temperatures. Ruthie, Jennifer, and Nikki all loved to run. Lisa? Not so much.

I was done. Finished. When I could not run anymore, I walked the rest of the way, and when I finally finished the two miles, I stopped and put on my warm clothes.

Rebecca and Carla did not finish in time, either. In fact, it was so cold that day, I think half of our team failed to complete the running assignment.

That was not good, because every time a player did not finish in time, she had to go back later and run the two miles again. The slowpokes in the group, like me, wound up running those miles over and over. We had to keep trying until we got it right. Some of our teammates who had beaten the clock would come out to cheer the rest of us to the finish line. That was the kind of camaraderie we had on that team, but the cheerleading was not enough to help me get the job done. I never made it. I could not get over that mental block of running in the cold. I did not know how to pace myself, and the sound of my own breathing drove me crazy. And believe me, my lungs were working overtime in the thin Colorado Springs air.

I was the only player on the U.S. national team that could not complete the two-mile run on time. It took Rebecca four tries, but even she made it.

Our exhibition tour began in late November. We beat the Athletes in Action team in Ohio and then went to the University of Georgia to play the Lady Bulldogs. The tour was under way and the games had begun, but that did not mean that I was off the hook for my running assignment. Tara VanDerveer was not going to let that slide.

I like to compare Tara to Rain Man, in the good sense. She was all about consistency, and her favorite saying was, "Repetition of errors shows a lack of intelligence! You cannot keep making the same mistakes over and over." So I knew that sooner or later, I was going to have to run those two miles. But I did not expect it to happen when it did.

Tara gathered us for practice in Athens, Georgia, and told the squad, "Lisa is going to have to run her two miles, and if she does not make it in time, the whole team will have to do the run again."

Oh Lord! I thought to myself. I had some big pressure on me when I went out to the track, but thankfully, I was not alone. Nikki McCray said, "Lisa, I will run with you."

I was shocked. "You would really do that?"

"I will run with you every other lap. That will help you keep your pace."

Maybe this was going to work out after all. "Okay, Nikki. Thanks."

The clock started ticking. I ran my first lap, and then Nikki came up in the lane beside me. She had great form and really looked like a runner. I did my best to keep up with her on the second lap, and then I was on my own again for lap three. When I came around for lap four, Nikki was waiting, all prepped and ready. I was rolling. I had nice form, and my teammate was helping me keep the pace up. When I got to the final laps, I asked, "Nikki, run these last two with me so I can get a really good time, okay?" She agreed and we ran hard together and when I finally finished, my time was the best of any post player on our team and better than some of the guards' times. I was completely out of breath, but I had beaten Tara's sixteen-minute monster. I hugged Nikki and barely had enough breath to shout out, "Thank you!"

My teammates were ecstatic because they had been spared the agony of doing that two-mile run again. When Tara found out what my time was, she told everybody, "That time was so good, none of you will ever have to do that run again!"

Everybody was jumping around and slapping high fives, and we all had Nikki McCray to thank. I have to give Nikki her due. Without her, I would have never made it. I might still be running to beat that clock. Even now she will come up to me and say, "Lisa, do you remember when I helped you with that run?"

"Yeah, Nikki. What would you like for dinner?" We both know I still owe her big time.

Playing with this national team was one of the best experiences in my career. The players were extremely talented and hungry, and Tara was the kind of coach who would push you as far as she thought she could. She knew I would have needed counseling if I had let my teammates down. She also knew that I was physically capable of the running challenge but had to overcome the mental aspect of finishing that run. She pushed the right button when she challenged me in front of my peers, and Nikki's willingness to help me did a great deal to strengthen our team bond. Tara understood team dynamics, and she understood the game completely. She is the best coach I have ever played for.

I loved to learn from her, but Tara rarely said anything to me in front of the team. Whenever she had anything negative to say about me, she would pull me aside or she would enlist Dawn Staley, our point guard, to get me going. "We have got to get the big girl going," she would say to Dawn. "The big girl has got to crash the offensive boards."

During my private evaluations with Tara, she would say, "Lisa, you are very consistent. I like this about your game. What do you think you have to do next? What do you think you can improve on?" She was constantly challenging me.

I would tell her, "I need to crash the offensive boards more. When I shoot, I don't go in and rebound."

"That's true," she would agree. "You need to watch film."

Our team watched more film than Leonard Maltin and Roger Ebert combined, but that was crucial for Tara's teams. We used to dissect film forever, but it was not Tara's way to criticize anyone directly. "Good job," was about the most I would get, but there were a lot of high fives. That was her way of saying, "You really did good."

The youngest player on our 1996 Olympic squad was Rebecca Lobo. I do not think Rebecca had a really good tryout, but she made the team, anyway. Some say it was primarily so that USA Basketball could use her name for marketing purposes. After all, Rebecca Lobo was the 1995 Naismith Award winner, and she was fresh off of UConn's undefeated NCAA championship season. Skill-wise, she was considered the best player in college basketball that year, but when compared with the talent on our Olympic team, she was not that impressive.

Most of the players looked at it this way: if you had Lobo on your squad during a scrimmage, you were playing shorthanded. Players would attack wherever she was because she was the weakest link. I think Rebecca sensed that some of the players doubted her selection to the U.S. national team, and I bet she felt a lot of pressure about it. I know I would have.

Rebecca was our backup center, so she looked at me as the one to challenge to prove that she truly belonged. The coaches always encouraged her to play tough against me. They wanted her to rough me up, push me, and get me ready for the physical international competition that was ahead. It was difficult for her, but Rebecca worked really hard, showed a lot of heart, and found a way to fit in. She was nice and sweet, and she gave her best effort every day. That was all you could ask of anybody. Rebecca stepped up, and the team respected her for that.

The team as a whole was enormously talented. Teresa "T" Edwards was the greatest of the greats. I remember the first time I saw her play. She was incredible! T's intensity level was amazing, and thankfully, it was contagious. She lifted every player up a notch and truly made all of her teammates better basketball players. T was so good that I would feel sick when I missed one of her passes. If I dropped one, I did not even want to look at her face. She would just give me a look, and I worried to myself that she might never pass the ball to me again. Of course, T was not like that. She would not like that you missed her pass, but if you were open the next time down the floor, she would get the ball to you. Teresa Edwards made us all want to play a better brand of basketball.

Dawn Staley was the same way. I hated to miss her passes or mess up a play, because when I did, Dawn would make a face that had frustration written all over it! It made my heart sink. She would walk back down the court, and I would feel terrible about botching things up.

Watching Dawn and T battle each other every day in practice was incredible. Dawn is the most competitive person that I have ever met, and T just plain ole hates to lose. When you put "most competitive" against "hates to lose," you have got a war on your hands. Both of them possessed so much drive and heart. It was amazing to watch, and I know for a fact that Dawn and T really helped me become the player that I am today.

Sheryl Swoopes was our small forward. I would not want to leave the country without her. With Sheryl on my team in the Olympics or a world championship competition, I always felt confident that we would be victorious.

Katrina McClain was our best post player. She was only six foot two, but Katrina was something to see. She could jump, and in the air, she was graceful and beautiful. Not many women can do the things that she could do. Katrina could do one-hand tip-ins, and she was athletic enough to do reverse layups while she was working in the post with defenders all around her. Katrina could grab tough rebounds and make it look so easy. She barely broke a sweat, but the girl could do it all. She could score, hit the free throw line jump shot, and drive left and right. She could rebound, and she could score down low. Strong! I wanted to be like her. Playing against Katrina forced me to take my game to another level.

Katrina is one of the major reasons that I had so much success in the 1996 Olympics. All the other countries knew about Katrina McClain, but they did not know much about me. The other teams had seen her play on ten U.S. national teams and had watched her win Olympic gold in Seoul in 1988 and a bronze medal in Barcelona in 1992. Opponents respected Katrina's talents and tenacity, so most teams put their main focus on stopping her. That gave me lots of opportunities. I could shoot threes, or I could drive to the hoop. I got so many chances to score because the opposition was dead set on dealing with Katrina. The fact that Katrina was very strong in the post and unselfish with the ball only made her an even better teammate. I loved her game.

Just thinking about that team gives me goose bumps. We were athletic and smart and had excellent skills, but our team chemistry might have been our best asset. I had never seen anything like it before. We absolutely knew in our hearts that every one of us had the common goal of winning the Olympic gold medal, and we were determined to accomplish that without egos or petty selfishness getting in the way. We always wanted everybody to do well, and we cheered for each other, no matter who made a basket. I still do not know how a group of eleven competitive women played together for one whole year and never had a conflict. Before I played for the 1996 Olympic team, I never thought it was possible. But the friendship and the love we had for each other would be necessary to get through the roller coaster of emotions we felt once the Olympic Games started in Atlanta.

Chapter 8

Bombs Bursting in Air

After my whole lost-shoe incident during the opening ceremony, I could tell that the 1996 Summer Olympics in Atlanta would be something very special to remember.

The opening ceremony went on for hours. Thankfully, each country entered the stadium alphabetically, so athletes from the United States and Zambia did not have to stand nearly as long as those from Afghanistan and Aruba. The evening was like a dream sequence of music, pageantry, history, and choreography. It was a big theatrical production, and there was an amazing celebration of both Southern culture and the one hundredth anniversary of the modern Olympic movement.

President Bill Clinton inaugurated the XXVI Olympiad, and there were lots of speeches in several languages, but the highlight of the night came when "The Greatest," Muhammad Ali, was introduced to light the Olympic flame. There had been a lot of speculation leading up to the Games as to who that person might be, but somehow Olympic officials managed to keep Ali a secret. When he stepped out of the shadows and onto the platform, the fans immediately realized who the mystery man was.

The entire stadium went crazy. After all, Muhammad Ali is one of the most recognized and admired people in the world.

This, however, was not the bold, young, and brash Ali from his boxing days. This Ali was heavier and greyer and was moving more slowly. He was not "floating like a butterfly." He was shuffling and unsteady. Muhammad Ali was living proof that our time as elite athletes is short and extremely precious. I remember thinking at that moment, *Wow, even the greatest grow older. I better make the most of the opportunities that I get.*

On this night, Ali was standing in Centennial Olympic Stadium, and his body was shaking from Parkinson's disease. When he grasped the Olympic torch, I worried that he might not be able to hang on to it, but when Ali turned slowly and pointed that torch toward the giant cauldron, the shaking seemed to stop for just that moment. Muhammad Ali ignited the flame and got the 1996 Summer Olympics off to a rock-solid start.

Having played together for a year already, our U.S. women's basketball team was very prepared. Our U.S. national team went 52–0 on the tour, which covered ten months and over one hundred thousand miles, and led us right up to the 1996 Olympics. We won in Russia, Ukraine, China, Australia, and Canada. We also defeated twenty-one U.S. college teams, beating them by an average of forty-five points per game. So, by the time July 2006 rolled around, we were ready to strut our stuff on our home turf. And we were in the hunt for the gold medal.

Two days after the opening ceremony, we played our first Olympic game. We beat Cuba in our opener. Later in the week, we knocked off Ukraine and pummeled Zaire by sixty points. The Games were running smoothly, television ratings were soaring, Team USA was rolling, and everything was looking good in our quest for the gold medal. Then, something terrible happened that made the Olympics, Team USA, and the world stand still.

It was nighttime in Atlanta on July 26. Shaquille O'Neal and I were talking in my room at the Omni Hotel. He was at the Olympics, playing for the U.S. men's basketball team, the latest edition of the Dream Team. Shaq also had business on his mind. He told me that he was about to leave the Orlando Magic and sign a free-agent contract with the Lakers. I was one of the very first to know, and since I was from the Los Angeles area, I was really excited. The Lakers had fallen on hard times in recent years. Magic Johnson and James Worthy were retired, and the team had not had a dominant big man since the glory days of Wilt Chamberlain in the 1970s and the "Showtime" days of Kareem Abdul-Jabbar in the 1980s. With Shaq coming on board, the Lakers would have that unstoppable force in the middle again and a great shot at becoming NBA championship contenders once again.

As we talked, Shaq and I stepped on to the balcony that faced Centennial Olympic Park. It was just across the street from our hotel. In fact, we could easily throw a rock from my balcony and hit the park. It was so close, I could see the corporate venues that were set up for the fans, tourists, and Olympics visitors. Nike, AT&T, and a bunch of other companies had displays, exhibits, and shops in the park. There were rides, food stands, and amusements, too. I could easily see where the basketball courts had been set up for games, clinics, and demonstrations. People were trading pins in the park, and there was a band performing on the stage. The park was a very busy place.

Shaq stopped looking at the people below and turned my way. He had that gleam in his eye and that crooked smile that meant the wheels were turning in the big man's head. Shaq is a huge guy, but he is also a big kid. He loves comic books, Superman, and all kinds of gadgets. There is a fun-loving, mischievous ten-year-old hiding inside that seven-foot frame.

Shaq looked at me and said, "Wait a minute." Then he went

into the bathroom, soaked some tissues with water, and then brought them out to the balcony. Shaq had that wide grin on his face. "Let's have some fun," he said.

Well, I am not a party pooper. We started throwing tissues off the balcony, then watched them drop, floor by floor, to the ground below. Most of them splattered harmlessly on the sidewalk, but some were right on target for unsuspecting people walking outside the hotel. When that happened, Shaq and I would quickly duck down on the balcony to make sure we were not seen. We would look at each other and crack up laughing. We were having a great time running back and forth to the bathroom, giggling, and tossing soggy tissues. Then Shaq's bodyguard came to my door. My supersized partner in crime had to leave, and our Olympic tissue-tossing event was officially over.

It was starting to get late, but shortly after Shaq left, Mom and her new husband, Tom, stopped by my room to tell me that they were going over to the park. Mom had known Tom through her job for several years. He started out sending her cookies and flowers around the holidays, and eventually, they struck up a friendship and began to date. They had been married just a year, and I liked Tom. He made Mom happy, and I was happy that she had found someone to love. Going out with them to the park sounded like fun, and I wanted to go. But the realities of my situation made it difficult. At my height, there was no way for me to blend in with the crowd, and being recognized had been an overwhelming experience.

When we first got to Atlanta, I tried to go to the McDonald's that was in my hotel, but there were tons of people there. So many fans wanted to get close, say hello, and get an autograph or an Olympic pin. They were reaching out and calling my name. I was surrounded. I had to have a police escort take me back to my room to make sure I got there safely. That was the first taste for me of what Michael Jordan must have been dealing with every day of his career. If it was that crazy in my hotel, there was no way I was going into the masses of Olympic visitors and tourists outside the hotel.

So I was pretty much on self-imposed hotel room arrest, and I was not happy about it at all.

I told Mom, "Stop by the Nike booth, and see how it looks."

I endorse Nike. They were supposed to have some big pictures of me, Team USA, and a lot of other Nike athletes in their display. "Take some pictures of the Nike area so I can see what they have set up, okay?"

"Okay. Are you sure you don't want to go?" Mom asked.

"I'm sure. I don't want to go anywhere that involves crowds. Have fun. I love you guys."

I gave kisses to Mom and Tom. They headed for the park, and I got ready for bed. Sometime after 1:00 AM, I was blasted awake by a loud BOOM! BOOM! BOOM! and violent shaking. The whole hotel shook. My window was rattling. The room was dark. I was not sure where I was. I thought I was in L.A., in the middle of an earthquake, so I got out of bed and ran to brace myself in the hallway door frame. I knew from growing up in California that that was the safest place to go during an earthquake. My eyes stayed locked on that big window the entire time. The glass was closed, but the sheer curtain was open. I kept thinking that window was going to shatter and send glass flying my way. My ears were ringing. Everything was shaking. I was shaking. What was happening?

When the noise and the banging finally died down, I looked out my window and into the park. People were running, screaming. There was smoke everywhere. I was HYSTERICAL! Before I knew it, I was in the hotel elevator. I could not think. I could not remember how much time had passed, but I knew that my mom was supposed to be in that park.

Shaq was in the elevator. "Where are you going?" I asked.

He said, "I gotta get out of here!"

Charles Barkley and Reggie Miller were there, too. All kinds of different people were jammed together: men, women, athletes, and celebrities. All of us were shocked, shaken, and scared. We rode the elevator down to the ground floor and got off. People were yelling and asking me where I was going. I was not sure exactly, but I had to find my mom and stepfather.

I kept trying to get out of the building, but the security guards would not let me. "No! You can't go out there," they told me. "We don't know what has happened or what is going on. It is not safe."

I said, "Look! I gotta go! My mom is in that park."

Reggie and Charles chimed in. "Our wives are out there."

So many people were rushing down in the elevators, most of them with loved ones unaccounted for and no idea what might have happened to them. We stood together in the Omni lobby, half hysterical, pacing, and in shock. Then I realized that I was standing there with a scarf on my head. My hair was in pigtails, and I was wearing pajamas. I did not have socks or shoes on, but I did not have time to be embarrassed. I was too worried for that. I was anxious, frightened, and concerned about Mom and Tom.

Frantic people were hugging, holding hands, and trying to comfort each other. We waited, hoped, and prayed.

Before long, people started to trickle in from the park. Some of those who were close to the explosion were having hearing problems. They were devastated by the noise.

Reggie's wife and Charles's wife pulled up in a limo. They were okay. I still wondered, *Where is my mom?* I had no idea what was going on, and security still would not let me out of the hotel. So many thoughts were zipping through my mind, and most of them were not good.

Finally, after about forty-five minutes had passed, my mom came running in with Tom. I got to them, and we all hugged. "Mom, where were you? Were you in the park when the explosion happened?" I asked.

Mom was still breathing hard, but she told me, "You are not

going to believe this, Lisa. We were going to the park, and Tom said, 'First, let's go to the souvenir shop that we saw earlier.' So instead of being inside the park, we were walking down the street outside the park gate when we heard the noise and felt the ground shake. People told us a bomb had exploded."

Mom was visibly shaken. Tom was, too. Sirens were blaring! People were still scurrying outside the hotel. I told Mom, "Don't go anywhere else! Stay here!"

I was a nervous wreck. So much had happened so fast. What were the odds of me having that hotel room facing that park? Most of my teammates were on the other side of the hotel. Just think, a few hours before, Shaquille and I were laughing and throwing tissues off my balcony. If that bomb had gone off while we were out there, we would have been knocked out. The way the hotel was rocking and that window was shaking, who knows what might have happened.

That early Saturday morning in Atlanta was an absolute nightmare. The reports said that a bomb had gone off right by the stage where the concerts were held. Ironically, Jack Mack and the Heart Attack were performing when it happened. Thousands of people were in Centennial Olympic Park at the time. One person was killed. More than one hundred were injured. It was unbelievable.

Our Olympic world in Atlanta had been soundly rocked. Now there was a cloud hanging over the Games, and, unbelievably, our women's team had a basketball game to play that same day. Tara VanDerveer, our head coach, kept telling us to stay focused. "Do not let anything or anybody take away our joy. You cannot let people put fear into you. We have been through so much this year," she told us. "These are the Olympics. We came here to do a job. Let's do what we came here to do."

That is exactly what we did. We managed to put the bombing behind us for a few hours and knocked off Australia to remain unbeaten. Two days later, we defeated South Korea. Then, in the quarterfinals, I set the U.S. single-game Olympic scoring record with thirty-five points in our victory over Japan. Team USA was kicking butt. I was feeling very confident on the court. The Olympics, however, were taking a backseat to the tragedy of the bombing and the hunt for the person who did it.

Safety was now everybody's ultimate priority. USA Basketball officials set down rules in an attempt to protect America's athletes, especially the Dream Team. The restrictions were for our own good, but they really put a damper on everyone's Olympic experience away from the basketball arena. It was my first Olympics and the first for every player on our team, except Teresa and Katrina. These games were on our home soil, but now none of us could go anywhere in Atlanta. We had no idea how to handle the situation. No one had been arrested, and nobody knew if a bomber was still out there planning to blow up the hotel, the venues, or something else in Atlanta.

We were all jittery. It was hard to believe that somebody would come to the Olympics and do something like that. There had not been an attack at the Olympics since Munich in 1972, when the Israeli athletes were kidnapped and killed. We had never experienced anything like this. When we had gotten to Atlanta, we had felt really safe. We had not had one thought in our heads that there might be a bombing or someone out there plotting to kill us. Things like that just were not supposed to happen at the Olympic Games.

Security got so much tighter after the bombing. We had to have our bags, our shoes, and all of our belongings screened by security personnel. Everybody had to have the proper ID. We could not have guests at the team hotel unless they were cleared by security. Things had really changed! Getting around was more difficult than ever, and those people who had lots of family and friends in Atlanta really had it tough.

Now, when our team went to practice or to games, we had to take the hotel elevator all the way to the basement. There was no more parading through the lobby and going outside. Security guards with bomb-sniffing dogs would inspect our bus. While we waited, they checked inside, outside, under the seats, in the luggage compartments, and everywhere. Mirrors were used to make sure there were no explosives underneath the bus or on the chassis. When security decided that the bus was clean, we were finally allowed to get on board. It was scary, and every one of us was on high alert.

So much had changed in Atlanta since the opening ceremony just eight days before. Back then the Olympics were all about international competition, the world's top athletes battling to see who was the best. Now, all anybody could talk about was the bombing.

The Olympic Games continued, but amid an air of uncertainty. In our semifinals rematch against Australia, we fell behind early and had to claw our way back into the game to win. That victory put our team on a collision course with Brazil—our biggest rival—in a showdown game that would decide the gold medal.

Both Team USA and Brazil were undefeated when we tipped off in the Georgia Dome for the gold medal match. Thirty-three thousand fans packed that place. The stands were filled with acres of red, white, and blue. I was psyched, focused, and prepared for battle. Our team was ready to complete our mission. There was no way we were going to let Brazil take home the gold from our Olympics. We jumped on our opponents early and ran away to a 111–87 victory. I scored twenty-nine points. Sheryl, Katrina, and Ruthie all scored in double digits, and Team USA staked a claim to the gold medal in women's basketball. It was finally over! We did it! We went undefeated, and our squad set another U.S. single-game Olympic record by shooting better than 66 percent in our impressive win over the Brazilians.

Our long road had come to a successful end. All the hard work had paid off. We had come to Atlanta and had done what we had set out to do. Team USA had conquered the competition. What a great feeling! The bombing was behind us, at least for those few moments, and we were more than ready to get some new gold jewelry around our necks. I had won gold medals before and had been through ceremonies, but never at the Olympics. And I was certain of one thing: I was *not* going to cry, like so many athletes do on the medal stand.

When our team was not playing, I watched a lot of other Olympic events and ceremonies on television. Everybody was crying! It was ridiculous! I saw this big, burly wrestler. He was so strong and tough in winning his match, but when the guy got the gold medal, he just started bawling. I thought to myself, *Whatever! That looks so phony and rehearsed.*

A swimmer won gold, and he started blubbering. Our U.S. women's gymnastics team went to the podium with their hero, Kerri Strug. They all got gold medals, and every one of them started crying. I was like, "Oh come on! Give me a break. These people are just really overdoing it."

When it was time for our basketball team to get gold medals, the entire squad went up on the podium. We had barely gotten settled when it happened to me. I started boohooing. I was *crying* and looking in the stands for Mom. When I saw her face, she was crying. That made me weep even more. So many feelings were going through me all at the same time. There was exhilaration, but there was also fatigue. After a full year of working toward our goal, all of a sudden we were there. We had done it, and the quest was over. But the ending was so abrupt. My teammates and I shared such a strong bond, and knowing that we would now go our separate ways was hard to digest. We all knew that we had restored the Team USA name, which had been marred after the team struggled in international competition. But it was hard to think about moving on without my trusty teammates. I just tried to enjoy the moment.

The emotion of winning an Olympic gold medal was beyond

words. It was the ultimate reward for a year of hard work, travel, dedication, and sacrifice. Having the gold medal placed around my neck was exhilarating, and smiles and hugs flowed as easily as the tears. Then the American flag started to rise.

I was filled with incredible patriotism. My team and I had done something special on our home soil, and everyone took notice. We had proved that talent plus hard work and a solid strategy could bring success. Is that not the American way?

All the Americans in the Georgia Dome stood up to sing our national anthem. I beamed with pride and elation, and as I stood shoulder to shoulder with my teammates, worn out physically and mentally and with the gold medal around our necks, I suddenly realized, *Okay, I get it now. This is why people cry.*

Chapter 9

Model Citizen

Ireceived a huge surprise when I got back to Los Angeles after the 1996 Olympics. I was fixing up my condo and I needed household items, so Mom, Tiffany, and I drove to a department store. I picked out some towels, and the bill came to about four hundred dollars. When the cashier ran my credit card, I could tell right away that something was not right. She got on the phone, and I got a very uncomfortable feeling. After several minutes, the woman told me that my credit card had been rejected. That made no sense to me, because I always paid my bill. I figured I would straighten things out with American Express when I got home, but to move things along at the store, I decided to write a check to pay for the merchandise.

The cashier ran my check, and it was no good, either. Now I was getting embarrassed and upset. I knew I had plenty of money in my checking account, but she told me that my file showed several outstanding debts. My check was about as worthless as my credit card. I had no idea what was going on, but I was going to find out. Mom paid for the towels, and we headed home.

I called American Express, and I was told that my account had been frozen because I had not made payments on the seven-hundred-dollar bill that was on my corporate AmEx card. What? I had never owned a corporate card!

The people at Bank of America told me that there were a bunch of delinquent checks on my personal account, but the account number that they were looking into did not sound familiar. Wait. I only had one account at the bank, and that number was not mine. Had someone opened another checking account in my name? The bank official told me that anyone opening an account had to have a valid ID or driver's license. He suggested that I might get some answers at the Division of Motor Vehicles, so that is where we went next.

There is a small office at the DMV that is tucked away behind the cubicles, the photo spot, and the written test area. That was where I met with one of the DMV's detectives. I explained my situation to him, and he pulled out my entire file. He showed me the first driver's license that I had ever had, and I got to see my second license as well. I had had to get that one to replace the one that I had lost during my sophomore year in college. Next, the detective showed me my third driver's license. It had my name and information on it, but the picture was not mine. The face belonged to my sister Dionne.

I was shocked. Mom was stunned. Tiffany just held my hand. We had just seen Dionne's fake ID, in my name, and she was smiling in the photo as if she had done nothing wrong. Mom and I could feel our hearts breaking. This was too much. It was too devious, even for Dionne.

When the detective saw our reaction, he figured that we knew the culprit. He asked, "Do you want to press charges?" I thought about it for a while. What was I supposed to tell him? What could I do? Should I send my own sister to jail? What was Mom supposed to do? Send her own daughter to prison? All I could think about was my sister's four children. What would they do without their mom? Her kids needed her, especially my little niece who was only two years old at the time. I had a very tough decision to make. It was not the kind of choice that I could make in a hurry, especially not at that moment. There were too many emotions in play, and too much was at stake. I took the detective's phone number and said, "I will get back to you."

When we got home from the DMV, I called Dionne and said, "Just tell me why. I would have given you a hundred thousand dollars if you had just been patient. I would have put you guys in a house."

Her answer was, "You get everything. I don't get anything. Everybody loves you. Everybody loves Lisa, but I am the black sheep of the family."

I could not believe my ears. My sister was pretty and smart. She was smarter than me. At least that was what I thought until this identity incident. She had her kids and a family, and she was doing fine. It was not like Dionne was struggling and I had abandoned her. Everything I had, she had. If I got a new car, she got my old car. I bought her clothes, and we shared my clothes. It was not like my sister was some forgotten outcast. Wherever I moved, she moved. When I moved up, she moved up, too. When I was at USC, Dionne would visit me in the dorm. We hung out. I never disconnected from her in any way. I never tried to make her feel like I was better than her, but then I never expected her to turn on me and steal my money and my identity, either.

My credit was trashed, and my sister was at the root of the problem. She had taken my Social Security number and had used it to get the driver's license in my name. Then she had stolen my identity and had started writing checks all over the Los Angeles area. She had bought a BMW using my name, and then she had missed payments. She had even put her utilities in my name and then had not paid her bills. She had run up outstanding bills at grocery stores and with merchants all over Los Angeles. She had even tried to start her own business using a corporate American Express Card that she had secured in the name of Lisa Leslie. That was where the troublesome corporate card had come from.

I was crushed. My credit was an absolute mess, and it had all happened because I had given my sister a chance. This was the same sister who had tortured and terrorized me as a kid. And this was the same sister who had used a knife to break into my piggy bank when I was in grade school. Of the $150 that I had earned by watering neighbors' lawns, Dionne had left me with just three dollars and a couple of "I-owe-you" notes. Still, I could not believe that my sister would steal from me like this.

It was after the piggy-bank incident, in fact, that I started to close myself off to people and became very difficult to get to know. Suddenly, trusting people was extremely hard for me, especially trusting girls. That incident affected my life then, and it still does today. I love people, and I enjoy hanging out. When I am on the court, I am 100 percent there for my teammates, but off the court, I always resist getting too close. That reluctance was born when my own sister broke into my piggy bank. It remains one of the most heartbreaking experiences of my childhood.

Years later I forgave Dionne for all of those childhood dramas and traumas, and I began to trust her once again. Dionne and I were adults now and had gotten close; I loved her unconditionally. I would call her to see how she was doing and would invite her over to my apartment at the college so we could cook dinner together. Things were so good between us that when I finished college and went to play basketball in Italy, I left my checkbook with Dionne. While I was away, she was supposed to pay any of my bills that came up and make sure that my mom had money if she needed it. I told her, "I will just sign some checks so you can take care of things."

She said, "Yeah, okay. No problem, Lisa. You know you can trust me. I would never do anything to hurt you."

Well, in the time that it took me to play in Italy in 1994, travel with Team USA in 1995, and play in the Olympics in 1996, Dionne had invaded my life and destroyed my credit. I had left her with some very small responsibilities to see how she would handle matters. I thought if Dionne could do this simple job, then maybe as I made bigger money, we could do more together. My heart was in the right place, and her tasks took very little effort, but she managed to turn the opportunity into a crime.

I do not think like a criminal, so I never once questioned Dionne about her personal business or her money. I thought it was great when I found out that she had purchased a used BMW. She needed a good, safe car. I had no problem with that, but I had a real problem when I found out that she had used my name and my money to buy the car. What hurt the most, though, was that my own sister had betrayed me. I could almost accept somebody else stealing my identity, but knowing my own sister had stabbed me in the back hurt.

I was angry with myself, too. In the words of my mother, trusting Dionne with my checkbook was like locking up Jesse James in the bank and telling him not to touch the money. Maybe I should have known better. But I thought that after all those years of distrusting Dionne, we had put all the bad stuff behind us, and I thought it was okay finally to let my guard down.

Dionne was obviously envious of what I had accomplished and felt overshadowed. I was gaining more and more notoriety in my sport and was getting more and more attention. I did a lot of interviews, so I was in the newspapers, on the radio, and on television, and my name was starting to grow in Southern California. But family always came first with me, and I never pulled rank on my sister or tried to demean her. I never felt as if she owed me anything or was somehow beneath me. I never rubbed my success in Dionne's face. Yes, I was Lisa Leslie the basketball player, but playing hoops was what I did; it was not who I was. Dionne knew that I loved her completely, so getting burned again by her was one of the worst things that ever happened to me. I still find it hard to believe that my sister would steal my identity.

When Tiffany lived in the condo with Mom and me after I started playing in the WNBA, she would cook a few days a week, so I paid her for that. I would have given more to Dionne, but she had already stolen my identity. Tiffany never asked me for anything, but I gave her everything, anyway. Dionne? I would have taken care of her first because she was the oldest. I would have made sure that she and my nieces and nephews were okay, but for some reason, Dionne felt like I owed her something. She felt as if she deserved something and was not being treated fairly. She reminded me of my USC teammates who would not put in the effort on the track or in the weight room, yet still expected to win championships. Dionne's reasoning was twisted. She actually said to me, "Everything comes easy to you. I have to work hard!"

I almost lost it. "What are you talking about? You have watched me practice, train, and play. You know how much time I put into going to school and working at my craft. You have seen me do it all, and that seems like nothing to you? You don't think that I work hard?"

Dionne was totally irrational. I had to deal with the reality that my sister was a con artist, and I had to decide if I should push her completely out of my life or forgive her and pray for her. When it came down to it, I had to forgive her. I honestly believe she has a sickness, some chemical imbalance that has plagued her since she was little or maybe all of her life. That may not be medically accurate, but sometimes I have to tell myself things like that so I can try to understand her.

And it is such a shame. My sister can be a beautiful, loving person who will do anything for you and, nine times out of ten, will kill you with kindness. But on that tenth time, watch out for your wallet.

I cannot afford that kind of friend, let alone that kind of family member. So I decided to love Dionne from a distance. When she was close, my weakness was too obvious, and my vulnerability to her deviousness was much too high. Whatever Dionne got from her scam against me was nothing compared to the distance she created in our family. I was the victim, but I felt sorry for my sister and the sorry mess her life had become.

People kept asking me, "Do you have any idea who stole your identity?"

The DMV detective wanted to know. "Do you plan to press charges?" he asked.

Dionne's future was in my hands. I hated what she had done to me, but she was still my sister, and she did have four children. I was concerned about them. I struggled with my decision, and I prayed about it. At the end of the day, her kids—Marquis, Brionne, Jacquise, and Artavius—were the only reasons that I did not put my sister behind bars.

With that decided, my focus shifted to the task of getting my identity back. There was so much red tape in dealing with the bank, the stores, and the credit card company. I had to fill out numerous affidavits and sign every one of them. Then Dionne had to sign them all and acknowledge that she was responsible for creating my debts. Then I had to send out all the paperwork and wait. My driver's license, bank account, and credit cards were all in limbo. If I wanted to buy something, I had to spend an hour on the phone ahead of time, explaining my situation to bank officials or some store manager. Even after all the paperwork and the hassles, my credit was still rocky.

Two years later, when I was looking into buying a house, Dionne's misdeeds continued to follow me. I had to show all my affidavits and prove that I was not the one who had been running up debts, writing bad checks, and decimating my finances. My credit report was loaded with negatives, and that was so unlike me. I am way too organized to have that happen, and I am too conscious of things like that to have bad credit. I always pay.

I learned some tough lessons from that ordeal with Dionne. I had not been conscious of it before, but I knew now that she could not be around me. I had too many valuable possessions to let her get close again. There were times when my cousins would come over, and I would let them go through some of my things. They could take whatever they wanted, and if they needed money and I had it, eight times out of ten I would give some to them. I would explain to everybody, though, "Look, I've got bills to pay, too. I have to pay the IRS. I cannot give, give, give." But they knew that if it was really important, I would almost always come through for them, at least until I got married and started a family of my own.

God has blessed me with a comfortable life, and I like to give. Besides, everything that I give I get back tenfold. That is the way that I function, and because people know that, sometimes they try to take advantage. But that does not work with me anymore. They know that if they go too far, the relationship is over. And when it is over, they are cut off completely. I learned from my very own sister not to let anyone use me.

I never told anyone about what Dionne did to me, but she started to feel bad vibes from the family soon after it happened. Maybe my extended family knew about the identity theft. I do not know, but life in Southern California got to be too much for my sister, so she moved to Fresno. Her story did not end there, however, and neither did the drama that seemed to follow Dionne.

One day she called Mom from a hospital. Dionne said she had been rammed by a hit-and-run driver while standing at a bus stop, and Mom immediately went to Fresno to see about her. I told Mom to bring Dionne to my house so that we could take care of her.

When she arrived at my house, Dionne looked sickly and skinny, and she could not walk very well. We put her in bed. Based on my past experiences with Dionne, I did not believe one word of her hit-and-run story. Maybe she had been in an accident and maybe not. She was awfully sore, but it seemed to me as if she was on drugs. I was jaded to the point where I had to think of worst-case scenarios when it came to my older sister. That was how things usually worked out with Dionne and me, but my weakness started to surface again. I loved her, regardless of all that had happened. When my family needs me, my family needs me. I knew I was taking a chance again, so I prayed about it a lot. I know that the Lord forgives me for my sins, and I know He wants us to be forgiving. So if I said that I forgave my sister, my actions had to show it. I wanted to show Dionne love and forgiveness, but I was not blind to her ways. Before she arrived at my place, I made sure to have a lock put on my bedroom door.

Mom and I fed Dionne and got her to the point where she could get out of bed and walk around. It took about two months for my sister to recover and improve. I could see that she was starting to feel better, and I was getting more comfortable having her around. But I was no fool. I looked at the calendar, and I told Dionne, "You need to find some other place to stay."

She nodded and said, "I really need to get a car."

"I do not know what you plan to do," I replied, "but I am going to give you five thousand dollars. You can do whatever you want with it, but you have got to leave my house."

Dionne was very smart. She got on the computer and started looking into apartments. She also found something else. "I can get low-income housing," she told me. "I can do things with kids, like a foster home or something."

I thought, *Foster home? You cannot even take care of your own kids.* Dionne had four children, but only one, Artavius, was living with her at the time. She gave away her daughter, Jacquise, to a friend to keep for a few years, and the lady never gave the child back. Jacquise thinks that Dionne is her aunt. How could my sister dare to think about trying to make money as a foster parent to anybody? How could she possibly think about caring for other kids when she did not even care for her own?

All I knew was that she had to get out of my home, so I gave her the money, and Dionne moved in with our cousin Craigie, who was living in Long Beach. Before long, she had gone through the money and did not have a place to stay, or a car to show for it. So, that was that. I washed my hands of the situation. I talk to my sister every now and then. She will call and sometimes drop by or catch one of my games.

The whole situation with her is amusing in a very sad sort of way. I do love Dionne, but if she were not my sister, there would be no way that she would be in my life. My relationship with her now is that of an associate or an acquaintance. We are cordial, and I will give her a hug when I see her because Dionne is family, but I will never put anything of value into her again. There will never be any closeness or substance to our relationship.

I guess my sister thought she could cash in on the success that I had enjoyed in Italy and at the 1996 Olympics. She also knew that I had signed a professional modeling contract before the games in Atlanta. In 1995 Dawn Staley's friend Londell McMillan took me to New York City to see if any modeling agencies would be interested in me. One stop was at Wilhelmina Models Inc. where I met with Kevin Jones. He was six foot six, and when Kevin saw me, he said, "Oh my god. You are so tall. You are beautiful. This is great."

I did not have a professional portfolio, but he looked at the few pictures I had brought with me. There were a couple of shots from the Olympics, when my hair was in two French braids, and one photo of me with an ex-boyfriend. That was all I had to show, but Kevin saw something that he liked. "You could be used as a model in special situations," he told me. "You could open and close shows. You could do a variety of still shots. You have a nice face and a nice body. I could use you on athletic shoots or when we have a need for body-part models."

He thought that my unique look and height could bring something special and extraordinary to edgy designers. Usually, they want all their models to be about the same size, with the same look, so this gave me a chance to bring something different to the runway. Since I am much taller than the average model, he thought that he could also use me to model in shows where designers preferred to have celebrities wear their new line of clothing. That was his pitch. I thought it was cool. That would be fun. I was in New York City, and I was going to be a model!

When I was a youngster, the first career goal that I remember having was to be a weathercaster on television. The second was to be a model. Believe me, no one would have ever guessed that the shy, lanky young girl from Compton would one day get into modeling. I was still not the girl that people would pick out of a bunch of photos and say, "Oh, she is beautiful," but there was something about me.

I guess I caught the modeling bug when I was a young girl performing in Mom's mock runway shows at home. Each summer Dionne and I got four pairs of pants, two skirts, four tops, a sweater, a jacket, two pairs of shoes, socks, and underwear for the upcoming school year. We got most of it from the Compton swap meet or from Zody's (Compton's answer to Kmart), but we loved getting new clothes and could not wait to get home to model them. It did not matter if the pants cost five dollars or twenty dollars. The fact that they were brand new was exciting.

Dionne and I would come home from shopping, go to our rooms, lay our new clothes across our beds, and then try to decide what to model first. When I was all dressed and ready to show off my new clothes, I would call from my bedroom, "Okay, Mom. Here I come! Here I come!"

Dionne would sit with Mom while I strolled down the long hallway that led to her bedroom. That was the "runway." Mom would use her announcer voice and say, "And next on stage is Lisa. Look at her butterfly collar and jeans. And how about those new Jordache jeans!"

Dionne would go next, and I would sit next to Mom to watch. We would take turns going until all of our clothes had been modeled. Then, when our fashion show was over, we would hang up the new clothes in our closets. We were thrilled, proud, and so looking forward to wearing our new outfits when the school year began.

After the fashion extravaganza at our house, we would go over to visit Craigie and Braquel at Aunt J.C.'s house. Their closets were filled with new corduroy pants in brown, blue, and gray on one hanger, three pairs of jeans on another, four skirts on the third hanger, and lots more. But surprisingly, I did not feel any worse off than they were. I knew they had more of everything, but I was okay with that. They had their new school clothes, and I had mine. I knew Mom was doing the best she could, and I was really thankful and happy to have clothes to model every school year.

The summer before I started high school was the first time I got to do some real modeling. I had been playing basketball with the Miraleste team, and the coach's girlfriend got me to do a fashion show at Carson City Hall. I was really excited, and as the show got closer, I realized that I was not nervous. Instead, I was filled with confidence. I guess I figured, after all those years of modeling for my mom, how difficult could a real fashion show be?

In the Carson show, I was supposed to model with the kids, but I was so tall and I did so well in rehearsal that they wanted me to model with the adults. Some of the women were professional models. When the show began, I walked out, gave "the look," and then did the "fashion show turn." I modeled a blue dress with white trimming, and I had on white earrings. I also modeled some Capri pants with a white cotton shirt, and I draped a sweater around my shoulders. It was all very stylish, and I was really enjoying myself. I did everything that I thought real models might do, but I was way too serious. I so wanted to do well. I was trying to look professional, and I was working the "model attitude." When I walked off, people were clapping. I was in heaven. I loved modeling! It was better than basketball. I had such a great time, but I kept hearing people ask, "What was wrong with Lisa? Was she mad or upset? She looked beautiful, but the girl never smiled once."

The next time I modeled, I was attending USC. But I learned another hard lesson about trust. In the modeling world especially, you have to be very careful. Everybody tells you, "Oh, you are so beautiful. You should be a model. I can help you." I fell for that line from a woman who ran a modeling agency on Fairfax Avenue in Los Angeles. She promised to get my modeling career off to a great start and told me that photos would be taken and the best shots sent out to potential clients. Etiquette classes were also a part of the deal. I would be learning how to walk correctly and maintain proper posture, but none of these wonderful things could happen until I paid five hundred dollars up front.

What did I know? I scraped together what little money I had from my college stipend and made the payment. Now, do not get ahead of me here. The lady did not take the money and run. She really did set up a photo session. But it was horrible! They had me in this terrible hairdo. I looked like I had a Chiquita banana stack on my head. The make-up was hideous, and the outfits were sleazy. There were so-called "professionals" there to help me get dressed and ready for the shoot, but they had me too dolled up. I looked ridiculous, and my pictures were ugly. This lady had thrown me a line of garbage, and I had bought it, literally, for five hundred dollars. Her business was bogus, and she had robbed me of my money.

Young girls ask me all the time, "How do I get started in modeling?"

I tell them that it all begins with doing research into the agencies that they might be considering. My main advice is: do not pay any up-front money. That is absurd! There are some good, legitimate companies out there, like Willie West in Los Angeles and Elite Models Management, but there are a lot of small-time agencies that are nothing but trouble. The best way to start is by looking at their people. If you have not heard of any of their agents or clients, you might want to find another place to start your modeling career.

The truth is, when you get involved with a top-notch modeling agency, they will not ask you for money. You will go for an interview, and they will take a look at you. They might send you out to a photographer to get some shots taken. Then, the agency will make up a five-by-seven card for you. It will have some of your poses on one side and your contact information on the other. It is your instant mini-portfolio and business card. A lot of this is done electronically now, but that is the way it happened when I got to New York in 1996. Wilhelmina Models Inc. was the real deal, and I never had to pay them any money to get my modeling career off the ground.

Shortly after I signed with Wilhelmina in New York, they scheduled a photo shoot so I could get some high-quality pictures for my portfolio. Everything was first class. The photographer took shots of me in a linen dress and heels. I had my hair slicked back in a bun. He captured me posing in jeans and a T-shirt and then snapped some shots of me with a basketball so we would have the athletic angle covered. He finished with some stills of me with Leon, an actor who had been in *The Five Heart-beats* and *Waiting to Exhale*. By the time we were done, there were more than enough great shots from which to choose.

My modeling career was officially under way, and my portfolio was taking shape. I added some terrific pictures that had been taken for *Vogue* magazine by world-famous photographer Herb Ritts prior to the 1996 Olympics. He worked with a pretty impressive clientele, such as Calvin Klein, the Rolling Stones, Madonna, Tyra Banks, Naomi Campbell, and numerous other celebrities. Herb was known for his unique black-and-white photos, and on this shoot for *Vogue*, he was spotlighting some of the top Olympians leading up to the Games in Atlanta.

We did the photo shoot at a beach in Malibu. Herb and I got off to a great start. He told me that I reminded him of Naomi Campbell, and that flattered me. I have always been a big fan of hers. For the shoot, my hair was put in a ponytail and pulled all the way to the side so that I looked kind of like Pippi Longstocking. Herb started snapping pictures. He wanted me to laugh and show my teeth while I posed. It seemed unnatural to me, but it was so Herb! He loved the open-mouth look for his models, and it really worked. The *Vogue* spread was fantastic. From then on, when anyone looked at my portfolio, they saw the shots that Herb had taken—the ones that showed off my face and my body and my open mouth. Those photos were attention getters. Those are the kinds of photos that make potential clients take notice.

I also did an interesting photo shoot for *Newsweek* where I was in the sand. They put crimps all over my hair and blew it out with a fan. I wore a funky top and some Capri pants and heels. Sure, I was tall, but I wore a size 6, and I could fit into all the clothes that they had for me. If things were too long, we just rolled them up or scrunched them a bit. The shoot went very well, and I got lots of amazing pictures out of it. Wilhelmina took the best of my shots and added them to my portfolio.

I had been having so much fun in New York, but the time had

come to put myself out there like a real model. That was not easy for the woman that kids had called Olive Oyl back in Compton, but it was a real measuring stick for how far I had progressed in the confidence and self-esteem departments. I stayed at a hotel in SoHo to be close to all of my "go-sees." That is what models call it when they "go see" fashion designers in hopes of getting work in upcoming shows. Go-sees were really hard. I had eight go-sees scheduled in one day. It was not glamorous. At all! This was the working part of being a model, not the fun part everybody hears about. The physical and mental grind that went on behind the scenes was relentless.

I did not know my way around New York, so when Wilhelmina gave me an address to visit, I took cabs and spent way too much money just getting from place to place. When I did arrive at my destination, I would take my place in a line of about twenty to fifty girls of all colors, shapes, and sizes. There were many occasions when I would walk into a room of designers, and they would immediately say, "Oh no! You are too tall. Thank you. Next." That would be it. The cab ride took longer than the time I spent inside.

On the day I had eight go-sees, my first three said, "Go away." They were very direct.

"No, you are not right."

"No, you are too tall."

"No, not what we are looking for."

I had never experienced blatant rejection like that. It was different from missing the cut for a USA Basketball squad. At least with basketball, I got to show what I could do. I could battle against my competition and then leave it to the coaches to make their decision based on my performance and the needs of the team. In modeling, it was instant success or failure. You were either in or you were left out, and you never got to square off against your competition. You were competing against the concept of "the look" that the designers had in mind. It was totally subjective and potentially very damaging to my ego. I always thought I could talk my way into anything, and I knew I could schmooze with people if I got a chance, but in modeling, it did not matter how articulate I was. Success was all based on how I looked.

The clients were not bashful about detailing exactly what they did not like. "Too skinny! Too much hips! Crooked nose! Your ears are too big. No thanks." As a model, all you could do was stand there and try not to break down. That was not easy for me. I knew I was not supposed to take it personally, but the rejections hurt just the same. I found a phone booth and called my mom in California. I was crying when I told her, "Mom, I went on these go-sees, and the fashion people do not like me. They keep telling me that I am too tall and not what they need. They do not like me."

I was really upset and exceptionally whiney, but as usual, Mom put things in their proper perspective. She told me, "Lisa, you listen to me. Not everybody is going to like you. You're perfect, they just don't know it. You are a beautiful girl, and you have a certain look. Sometimes they want somebody short. Sometimes they may want somebody tall. They might want girls with long hair, dark hair, or blond hair. You know that you are beautiful on the inside and on the outside. If these people tell you no, just say, 'Okay,' and walk out. You are going places, Lisa. Don't ever get upset because a door closes. Just go around the corner, and you will find another door that is wide open for you."

Mom gave me every piece of positive affirmation she could think of, and she ultimately told me, "You just keep on going, and if, at the end of the day, you are still getting negative responses, just get on a plane and come on home. You have other things that you can do. If it is not your time right now, it is just not your time."

Mom made a lot of sense, and her long-distance pep talk was just the jolt that I needed. I told Mom that I loved her, and then

I hung up the phone and took a more positive attitude into my next go-see. When I walked in, the response was much better. The people said, "Wow! We would love to use you. You'd be awesome. We could use you to open our show."

I was so excited. Finally, somebody liked me. Unfortunately, they told me that the clothes for the show had already been selected and fitted for girls who were five foot eight or, at the most, six feet tall. The woman said, "I know we don't have anything here that would fit you. If we had only met you sooner, we could have had clothes custom made for you."

I went from delighted to deflated in an instant. I was bummed. The bad news was that I did not get the job. The good news was that these fashion people liked my look. Maybe I really could do this modeling thing. At the end of the day, I reported back to Kevin, and I told him there were four negative responses, two positives, and two maybes.

Kevin asked me point-blank, "So, how did you like it out there?"

"It was definitely different, and all those 'go sees' were truly a challenge," I said.

"Lisa, you do not have to do go-sees. We can find work for you, but you just experienced what it is really like to be a nine-to-five working model. That is what their lives are like."

I told Kevin that I would go out one more day and finish off my scheduled appointments. I was starting to understand that I was not cut out to do everybody's show. I was different, but that could actually work in my favor, and I felt as though I could find my special niche in the modeling world.

With Wilhelmina supporting me, it was not long before jobs started coming in, good jobs, too. The Anne Klein people saw my pictures and got in touch with me through the agency. That is how I got to work with Annie Leibovitz, one of America's greatest photographers. She used to be the chief photographer for *Rolling Stone* magazine. She had her own exhibit at the National Portrait Gallery, and it was Annie Leibovitz who, on the morning of December 8, 1980, snapped the famous shot of former Beattle John Lennon cuddling with Yoko Ono while nude. Several hours after that photo shoot in the Dakota Apartments in New York City, John Lennon was gunned down in front of that building and killed.

Annie Leibovitz had a wonderful reputation, and she was a truly creative professional. She took some amazing pictures of me with other celebrities on a shoot for the Anne Klein II ad "Celebrating the Signature of Women: Women of Substance and Style." It was a very classy ad. I met some amazing people and got to wear clothes that were very elegant and chic.

Other photographers expressed interest in working with me, too, and things were really picking up. I signed with Bruce Binkow, an agent with Management Plus Enterprises, and with him representing me, my workload multiplied. We did a deal with American Express that had me photographed under the Santa Monica pier. I wore jeans with a white button-down shirt that had the collar turned up, and I was holding a basketball. That photo wound up on huge billboard displays in the Los Angeles area. There was one on La Cienega Boulevard and another out at LAX, and a giant mural of that ad took up one entire side of a building on Highland Avenue. That was, literally, the biggest shoot that I did. It was incredible to see my image so much larger than life, and I must admit, Mom, Tiffany, and I practically lost our minds when we saw it. We screamed, laughed, and hugged. Then we took lots of pictures of the billboards. It was a big deal for us.

I also did shoots for *TV Guide* and *Sports Illustrated*, and photos of me from the Olympics started popping up and getting published. My name was becoming well known in the industry. I did a fashion show in New York City where I modeled for Tommy Hilfiger and another show for Giorgio Armani. I was working with top designers and wearing amazing new styles, and I loved it.

Modeling in fashion shows, however, can best be described as organized chaos. The girls have to look so calm and composed on the catwalk, but once they get backstage, it is pure pandemonium. I had to remove one outfit as quickly as possible and slide into the next one. It did not matter where I was or who was around. It was simply strip, dress, and get ready for the runway again. If you have seen the finale episodes of *America's Next Top Model*, then you know exactly what I am talking about. It got frantic. Models were tense, and everybody was in a hurry. That was why, prior to the shows, we rehearsed all the walks and the clothing changes. We had to. Each of us had four or five outfits to put on and pull off, and we could not afford to have any traffic jams backstage. Everything was rapid fire at the fashion shows, and by the time we finished one, we really knew the meaning of the term "working model."

My modeling career was going well, though, so well that the people at Wilhelmina threw a huge party for me in New York, at a place called the Cigar Room. I was in fashion heaven just getting ready for the evening. The agency brought in a make-up artist for me, and I got to pick through several racks of designers' clothing and borrow anything that I liked. I was doing what the big stars got to do! I picked out a very elegant, long white gown by Nicole Miller, which I really liked. Then they told me, "Take four or five dresses, Lisa. Just send them back when you are done with your events."

It was all so unreal. When I was dressed and ready to go, there was a limo waiting outside to drive me to the party in style. When I entered the Cigar Room, Lisa Leslie from Morningside High was mixing with some of the top people in the world of high fashion. Lots of other models showed up for the affair, too. It was a whirlwind for me. There were so many things going on and so many fascinating people. It was incredible fun. I do not know if I had ever felt so special or glamorous before. If only Aunt Pete and her "get your tall, skinny, lanky self and your big feet into this kitchen" could have seen me.

I enjoyed so many aspects of the modeling business, and for some reason, I really liked doing layouts. Those are the photo-shoot spreads that are often used in magazines, especially when a new color comes into season. Apparently, most models steered away from doing layouts, but I thought they were a lot of fun, and I knew that they were much more relaxing than basketball games.

I got to pose for *Elle*, *Shape*, and *Sports Illustrated for Women*, among others. Those were fun photo sessions because they were part hoops and part modeling, so I got to do two of the things that I enjoyed most in life.

Modeling in New York was a fabulous experience, but it did not take me long to realize that being a nine-to-five model was not for me. A lot of girls see the glamour and think, *Yeah, that is what I want to do!* Trust me. It is so much hard work. Just getting modeling work can be a full-time job all by itself. The business is highly competitive and much more cutthroat than basketball. I would stand in "go-see" waiting lines with lots of girls, and they would rarely talk with each other. There was no model-to-model chitchat, small talk, or anything. Nobody spoke, and everybody seemed to be in their own little world, doing their own little thing.

I tried to be friendly. My vibe was, "Hey, how are you guys doing?" I was used to being a team player. I would say, "Good luck," to the girls in line, or I might say, "Can you help me with this?" I was trying to communicate, and they seemed surprised. "Where are you from?" they would ask, with just a hint of atti-tude.

I usually got interesting looks and rolled eyes when I said I was from Los Angeles. To tell you the truth, the more isolated the other girls were, the more outgoing I became. My confidence soared because the other models were so quiet and timid. That was a switch for me.

Modeling was being very good to me. I was doing so many things, and as my notoriety picked up, my schedule got even busier. I did so much modeling in just a few months. I had several sponsors, and Bruce kept lining up more and more jobs. Life in the fashion world was so positive for me that I made a major career decision: my professional future was going to be as a celebrity model and not as a basketball player.

Chapter 10

We Got Next!

I was tired of basketball, and I was more than ready to start pursuing other goals. That was why I turned down offers of three hundred thousand to five hundred thousand dollars to play overseas. I had prepared myself to be so much more than just a basketball player, and now I wanted to focus on my modeling career. I was twenty-four years old—young enough to give modeling a shot and still go back to basketball if it did not work out. There was a chance my stock as an athlete would decrease the longer I stayed away from the game, but I was ready to take a chance on modeling. I put basketball on the back burner.

The new American Basketball League for women had just tipped off in the United States. Though they made me part of their core group, I opted not to play. As far as I was concerned, I was retired from basketball. I was a full-time model now.

But in January of 1997, Bruce Binkow told me that the National Basketball Association was starting a new league for women. It was going to be called the Women's National Basketball Association (WNBA), and the season was going to run from June through August. Ever since Team USA won Olympic gold in Atlanta, America had been buzzing about women's basketball as never before. The timing was right to start a new league. Sheryl Swoopes and Rebecca Lobo were the first players to sign with the WNBA, and Bruce told me that if I got involved in the new league, I could continue modeling in New York and could just play basketball during the summer. It sounded like an ideal situation to me, so I told him, "Okay, I'll do that."

I had played summer league basketball in Los Angeles before, so I figured the WNBA would be a bunch of small gyms, reversible jerseys, and very few fans. I thought they might sell a few boxes of popcorn to defray costs, and that was okay. I was on board, but I was not expecting anything big. After all, it was just a summer league. Just about every city in America had one of those.

I was already doing modeling shoots in New York when I signed a personal service contract with the WNBA, and then I started getting jobs promoting the new league with Rebecca and Sheryl. We were the face of the WNBA in its inaugural season, and I thought that was cool. We shot several commercials and promotional announcements. I did a Nike commercial, too, so I was doing a lot of work, but I was not playing any basketball. All I did was talk about basketball. I was so into the modeling and the commercial shoots that I never gave a thought to getting myself ready to get back on the court. I guess I figured, *Hey, I just played in the Olympics a few months ago*; and I was in the best shape of my life. Why wouldn't I be ready to play in the WNBA? Little did I know that I could be in incredible shape in the summer, yet be way out of basketball shape by the following spring.

The WNBA was going to have eight teams in its first season. Los Angeles, Phoenix, Sacramento, and Utah would make up the Western Conference, while New York, Houston, Cleveland, and Charlotte would comprise the Eastern Conference. The league wanted to do everything possible to ensure competitive balance, so WNBA officials determined its top sixteen players and assigned two of them to each of its teams. Those select players were placed in the cities and regions where they were best known, in hopes of drawing local fan support. For instance, the WNBA assigned Penny Toler and me to the Los Angeles Sparks. Penny had been a star at Long Beach State University, and I, of course, had been born in Southern California and had attended high school and college in the Los Angeles area. Playing for the Sparks seemed perfect for me. I could live at home in the summer and play in front of my family and friends. Sheryl Swoopes (Texas Tech) went to the Houston Comets, along with Cynthia Cooper, while Rebecca Lobo (UConn) was assigned to the New York Liberty with Teresa Weatherspoon.

I have to tell you, I was pleasantly surprised with how organized this new summer league seemed to be and by some of the people who had bought into the WNBA. Lakers owner Dr. Jerry Buss became the Sparks' owner, too, and his son, Johnny, got the job as team president. Our colors were going to be purple and gold, just like the Lakers, but with a touch of teal added. I was really surprised to find out that the Sparks' home court was going to be the Great Western Forum in Inglewood, the same building where the Lakers played. I had passed by their locker room a few times, but I had never thought I would actually have the opportunity to dress and shower in the same locker room that had been used by Wilt Chamberlain, Jerry West, Magic Johnson, Kareem Abdul-Jabbar, and James Worthy. I was also excited to hear that in New York City, we would be playing against the Liberty at historic Madison Square Garden. Right then, I knew that the WNBA was going to be much more than a little summer league. I thought, *Oh shoot! They are going to be selling tickets. This is big time!* It was only going to be a three-month season, but the WNBA was going first class.

By the time that realization sank in, it was already too late for me. I was not in shape and not prepared for what was to come. I was in big basketball trouble. It was already springtime, and I was just starting to pick up a basketball.

It was a little basketball, too, an orange and white one. They called it orange and oatmeal, but the important thing was that the WNBA basketball was one inch smaller in circumference than the ball that the NBA used. The idea was to make the ball easier to handle since women usually have smaller hands than men. I had not played with a small ball since I left USC after the 1994 season.

After the WNBA allocated its top sixteen players, the league held an elite draft, which placed, among others, Wendy Palmer with the Utah Starzz, Lynette Woodard in Cleveland, Nancy Lieberman-Cline with the Phoenix Mercury, and Daedra Charles and Haixia Zheng with me on the L.A. Sparks. International players, like Australia's Michelle Timms and Elena Baranova of Russia, were in the mix, too, so there were plenty of quality players to choose from.

Then, on April 28, 1997, the WNBA held its first draft of collegiate players. Nobody scouted college women the way that teams do now, and there was very little international scouting at all. Van Chancellor, the head coach and general manager for the Comets, probably did the best job of selecting players. Houston wound up with four Olympians on its squad that first year. Swoopes and Cooper were joined by Janeth Arcain from Brazil in the elite draft and Tammy Jackson in the second round of the college draft.

Chancellor used the very first pick in the very first WNBA draft to take Tina Thompson, my former Trojan teammate. She did not win a bunch of awards or accolades at USC, but in my opinion, Tina was a great player. I was mad that the Sparks could not get her. I am not sure that any other team in the league would have taken Tina with the overall number one pick, but Van knew what he was doing. I was hoping that Tina would join me in Los Angeles. Oh man, if the Sparks would have had Tina and me in the post, whoo-ee! We would have been awfully tough. I knew how she played, and I knew about her work ethic, but apparently, Van Chancellor knew about Tina, too. The Sacramento Monarchs used the second overall pick to take Pamela McGee from USC, and the Sparks got Jamila Wideman, a point guard from Stanford, with the third pick in the draft.

While all of the drafting and allocating was going on, the WNBA's promotional machine was revving into high gear to hype the inaugural season. The league's first slogan was "We Got Next," and Spike Lee filmed a commercial with that theme for Nike. It featured Swoopes, Dawn Staley, and me in New York City, playing against guys at a fenced-in outdoor basketball court. We played there all day long. I am serious. We played from morning until night on that shoot, and it turned out to be a great commercial.

At the beginning of the commercial, Spike Lee says, "Once upon a time there were three girls." The video shows Sheryl, Dawn, and me walking up to a court where several guys are playing a pickup game. I am wearing light blue sweats, a red top, and a dark jacket. I tell the boys, "Yo! We got next," and when we get onto the court with them, I hit a jump shot. Sheryl drives in for a layup. Dawn dishes out an assist and makes a strong defensive play. It is three girls against all guys, all day. At the end of the spot, you hear Spike Lee say, "And this isn't a fairy tale. They didn't beat every guy, but they beat enough to say that basketball is basketball and athletes are athletes."

That was what we were about. Girls were finally getting a chance to play. It was amazing how that spot opened the eyes of the American public to the fact that women could play basketball and play to win. That commercial aired numerous times during the 1997 NBA playoffs, and print ads for the WNBA popped up in several major magazines. NBA Commissioner David Stern made sure that the fans of his men's league got to

Smiling at my first track meet. I was seven years old. *(Photo by Christine Leslie-Espinoza)*

Mom and me bringing sexy back!
(Photo by Brenda Washington)

I took care of my little sister Tiffany from the moment we met. *(Photo by Christine Leslie-Espinoza)*

Me and my T-Bird. She's a little older here. *(Photo by Christine Leslie-Espinoza)*

Mom at 27 years old. Now you see why I wanted to be a model. *(Photo by Brenda Washington)*

Mom looking gorgeous, again. *(Photo by Brenda Washington)*

Grandmother Dear, the matriarch of the family, and Mom. Nothing would have been possible for me without them. *(Photo by Judy Carol Simpson)*

The real reason I play is to collect trophies! *(Photo by Tiffany Sanoguet)*

My letter of intent to USC. I was so excited to get four years of college paid.

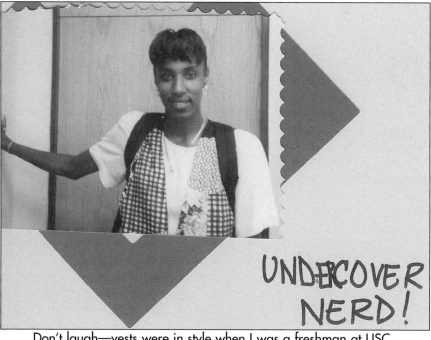

Don't laugh—vests were in style when I was a freshman at USC.
(Photo by Tammy Story)

I was the first player assigned to Los Angeles in the WNBA. Mom couldn't have been prouder.
(Photo courtesy of the WNBA)

Posing with my first WNBA Championship Trophy... but not my last.
(Photo courtesy of the WNBA)

Mom and Aunt J.C. are still my #1 fans! (And notice the Sparks earrings.)
(Photo courtesy of the WNBA)

Aunt J.C. likes this sign a lot.
(Photo courtesy of the WNBA)

Tiffany and Mom, still my
two favorite people.
(Photo by Tiffany Sanoguet)

The photo shoots I do for
the WNBA are always
pretty fun. This one was
taken at an All-Star game.
(Photo courtesy of the WNBA)

The love of my life,
Michael Lockwood.
*(Photo by Lisa Leslie
Lockwood)*

This was our second
date in Lake Tahoe.
*(Photo by Christine
Leslie-Espinoza)*

The Staples Center court was dedicated to me in 2006 on my thirty-fourth birthday.
(Photo by Michael Lockwood)

Broadcasting for ESPN. Michael proposed after this game.
(Photo by Michael Lockwood)

APR 4 2005

Moments before Michael proposed. *(Photo by Michael Lockwood)*

Standing on the beach in Maui as Mrs. Lockwood. *(www.amitymason.com)*

The first day of our honeymoon in Maui. *(Photo by Charles Smith)*

Hiking on our honeymoon. *(Photo by Michael Lockwood)*

Find the basketball in the picture.
Los Angeles Sparks' Media Day 2007.
(I was nine months!)
(Photo courtesy of WNBA)

Here is Coop excited about the
year 2029 draft pick.
(Photo courtesy of WNBA)

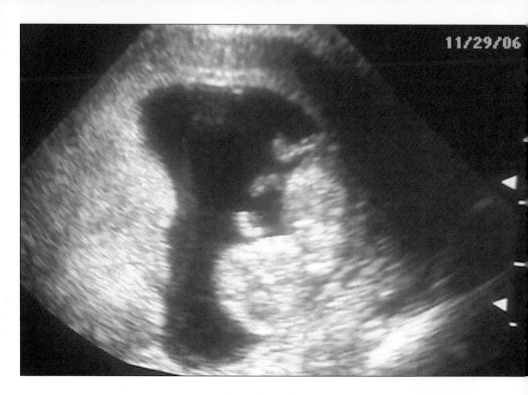

Lauren's first ultrasound.

Lauren getting a bath. *(Photo by Lisa Leslie Lockwood)*

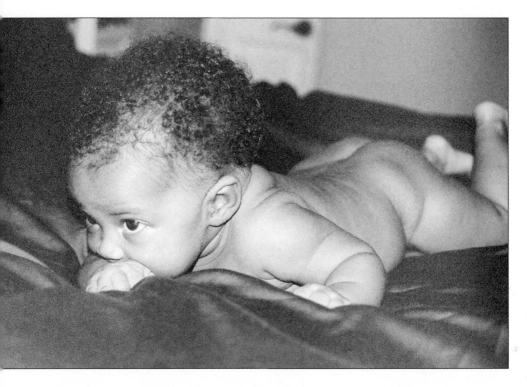

Lauren (baby got back) at three months old. *(Photo by Lisa Leslie Lockwood)*

With Gabrielle (age 14, left) and Mikaela (age 11, right). This was my very first day as a stepmom. *(Photo by Michael Lockwood)*

Our first family photo. *(Photo courtesy of the WNBA)*

hear all about the new women's league, and why not? The National Basketball Association was behind the WNBA financially and philosophically. It was in the NBA's best interest to do everything possible to make our league a success.

I cannot tell you what an awesome opportunity it was to be promoted and recognized as professional athletes. The WNBA was going to get exposure from its television deals with NBC, ESPN, and Lifetime. The league also had top-notch corporate sponsors, which were essential to it getting noticed and getting off to a solid start. Through their commercials, Nike allowed us to express ourselves as female basketball players, and they launched several signature women's shoe lines as well. Sheryl's Air Swoopes basketball shoe went on sale first. My shoe was called the L-9 to match the number on my jersey, and Dawn had her own shoe as well, the DS-5. With the exception of the Olympic years, women athletes had always struggled to get publicity and exposure, so it was important to the WNBA and all its players to have Nike and several other companies on board as corporate sponsors who were truly interested in marketing our sport.

The very first WNBA game was played on June 21, 1997. The Sparks hosted the Liberty in an L.A. vs. New York / East Coast vs. West Coast showdown at the Great Western Forum. Nobody knew for sure how it would go over, so we were happy to see the media come out in force to cover the historic event. The radio, television, and print reporters had access to all of the players prior to the game, and since our new league wanted as much publicity as possible, we tried to accommodate every media request, but it got pretty crazy. As game time got closer and closer, we were still taking pictures and doing interviews. The media kept swarming us. They asked me hundreds of questions about the Liberty. They wanted pictures of Rebecca and me face-to-face, almost nose to nose. The media wanted to create a rivalry out of our battle of the Olympic big girls. There were so many demands on our time, and so much to do, that when the madness finally subsided, it was time to play the game, and I was already worn-out.

More than fourteen thousand fans packed into the Forum for the opener. Tyra Banks, Arsenio Hall, Penny Marshall, and Magic Johnson were some of the stars who showed up for the event, and NBC was on hand to televise the WNBA's first game to a national audience. I remember doing a "photo opportunity" ceremonial jump ball with New York's Kym Hampton just before game time. League president Val Ackerman tossed the ball up between the two of us, and camera flashes went off all over the arena.

Penny Toler and Jamila Wideman were the Sparks' starting guards for that first game. I was in the middle, with Tamecka Dixon and Daedra Charles at the forward positions. New York had Rebecca Lobo and Vickie "V.J." Johnson at forward and Hampton at center, and the Liberty's starting backcourt featured Teresa "T-Spoon" Weatherspoon and Sophia Witherspoon. Once we finally got around to the real opening tip-off, the Women's National Basketball Association was officially under way. Fifty-nine seconds into the game, Penny put a move on Vickie Johnson, then pulled up and knocked down a jump shot from the right side. My teammate scored the very first basket in WNBA history.

The rest of the game did not go nearly that well. About ten minutes in, I tried to dunk. Actually, a better way to put it might be, an opportunity presented itself, and I thought about dunking. I can remember seeing the basket and thinking, *Lisa, get up.* Well, that was what my mind was saying, but my body was screaming, "No way!" I was psyched to dunk, but all that pregame media frenzy, adrenaline, and excitement had gotten to me. I had no legs. Nothing! I got up in the air, and I knew what I wanted to do, but I was totally exhausted. That orange- and oatmeal-colored basketball felt like mush, and I jammed it against the front of the rim. Okay, it barely hit the rim. It was just terrible! I could have broken my back. That was how bad it was!

I did manage to lead the Sparks with sixteen points and fourteen rebounds in that first game, but our team shot a horrible 31 percent from the field against New York, committed twenty-five turnovers, and made only one of eleven shots from outside the arc. Hampton and V.J. led the Liberty with thirteen points, and T-Spoon dished out ten assists as New York beat us in that historic opener 67–57.

The WNBA got off to a roaring start that weekend. Sixteen thousand fans showed up in Phoenix for the Mercury's game with Charlotte, and close to twelve thousand were at Gund Arena for Cleveland's game with the Comets. The ratings were pretty good, too.

Once the flash and excitement of the opener were out of the way, it was time to get down to the meat and potatoes of the regular season. The Sparks' first head coach was Linda Sharp. During her twelve seasons at USC, she coached Cheryl Miller and Cynthia Cooper and won two national championships, but in the WNBA, Coach Sharp had a lot of us scratching our heads. She wanted us to use some basketball techniques and styles that did not coincide with things that I had learned from Coach Stanley at USC or from Tara VanDerveer with the U.S. national team. Those were two coaches that I really respected and admired, but Coach Sharp's terminology was like nothing I had ever heard. She had us face-guarding the post with our backs to the ball on the block, and I had only played it facing the ball. It really threw me for a loop.

Haixia Zheng was on that first Sparks team. The four-time Olympian from China did not speak much English, but she kept saying, "No good! Coach no good!" Haixia did not even speak our language, but she knew that Coach Sharp was feeding us some questionable information.

Haixia and I were so different and yet so similar that it was amazing. Despite the language barrier, we were able to communicate. She was really fun. Unfortunately, Haixia was on the downside of her career. She was putting in an extra year or two just to get the experience of playing in the WNBA, playing in Los Angeles, and playing for the Sparks. She was not nearly at her best, but she was still a good shooter. Around the basket, she did not miss anything.

It was hard for Haixia because she had bad knees and was not accustomed to the quickness of the WNBA. They said the menisci in her knee were like chopped meat, and her legs were all knocked and turned. She limped and wore a knee brace, and most of the time, it was difficult just to watch her run. She worked out hard, though, and really tried, but she was in pain every day.

That made things tough for the Sparks. We did not know how to cover for Haixia's shortcomings the way the Chinese did. It was frustrating for me because I would get down court and find that I had to defend two post players, hers and mine, while we waited for Haixia to get back in position. While I was guarding Haixia's assignment, my player would score a basket. I would look to our bench and plead, "Please, get her out of here! I can't guard two people at once."

We definitely knew what Haixia could not do, but we made a big mistake in not cashing in on what she could do. There were so many other times when the Sparks just needed to get the ball to Haixia at the offensive end. The Chinese would run screens off of her. They would pop out, throw it to Haixia, and she was money. The Sparks were too busy dribbling between our legs to get the ball to our big threat in the paint, so Haixia would get frustrated. Her face would turn red, and she would say, "No good. This is not good."

Haixia Zheng wanted to win, and with a six-foot-eight, 285-pound highly talented player on our team, there was no reason for us not to be more successful. We should have won, but we did not know how to use her. Haixia hit 62 percent of her shots! All we had to do was throw the ball up high to her, and we knew that she would score. It was that simple. She cried because she wanted to do better. Like me, she was very emotional that first year, and like me, Haixia knew that she was not playing anywhere close to her best basketball.

Oh, man. That first Sparks team had so many issues. We had a lot of individuals who had a lot of talent but no idea how to play team basketball. Coach Sharp did not coach us in an organized way, and she did not teach us the things we needed to come together as a unit. It was a miserable feeling to have strong players like Penny, Tamecka, Mwadi Mabika, Linda Burgess, and Heidi Buerge (my OGDL foe) on our squad and still be losing.

The most shocking disappointment that first season was Daedra Charles, the Wade Trophy winner from the University of Tennessee. She was six foot three, but Daedra gained a lot of weight after college, and she was huge when she came into the Sparks' first training camp. Daedra was an All-American power forward who was strong and had some really nice post moves. She should have really helped us, but after that inaugural game, Daedra Charles never started another game for the L.A. Sparks.

Talk about disappointment. The Sparks lost eight of our first thirteen games that season, and Johnny Buss promptly dropped Coach Sharp. She was fired and replaced, on an interim basis, by assistant coach Julie Rousseau, who just a few months before had been coaching at George Washington Preparatory High School in Los Angeles.

I stumbled out of the gate that first season, the same way that the Sparks did. I was supposed to be the team's star player, but I really struggled. It literally took me most of the season to get in shape and to learn how to play with the WNBA basketball. The first balls were a mess. They were so slippery! I could not catch the ball. I could not focus on it or get accustomed to the fact that it was orange and sort of white. I started every game that season and averaged sixteen points and seven boards, but I shot only 43 percent from the field and under 60 percent from the free throw line. I was totally embarrassed.

Initially, the level of competition throughout the WNBA was mediocre, because so many of us came in unprepared. The better players were not ready to stand out right away, so most of us were pretty average that first year. The league was good, but nothing seemed really outstanding. Cynthia Cooper scored twenty-two points per game to snare the league's first scoring championship. Ruthie Bolton was next at nineteen points per game, and then there was me and everybody else in the WNBA, all averaging fewer than sixteen points per game. I never averaged so few points in any league at any level. It was horrible, but I never stopped trying to win. I was too competitive for that, but the Sparks finished at 14–14 in the WNBA's inaugural season, and we did not make the playoffs.

One of my biggest thrills of that start-up season was getting to play in the Great Western Forum. That was awesome! Every time I walked into that arena, I would see the purple and gold and all those Lakers NBA championship banners hanging from the rafters. I could almost feel the history. Just being on that court was an experience. I loved playing at the Forum. The seats were close to the court, so it was an intimate environment and just a great place to play. There are not too many better feelings in sports than the rush I got every time that I ran out of the tunnel and onto that Forum floor.

The WNBA averaged close to ten thousand fans per game in its first season, and the Sparks drew good numbers, too. Surprisingly, we were also very good draws on the road, and it did not take long to realize why: sports fans everywhere simply love to hate L.A., no matter the sport. I do not understand why. It must be genetic or ingrained in people. From the very first time that we stepped onto an opponent's court in that very first season, their fans *despised* the Sparks. And they did not like me in particular. Why? I did not do anything to them. I thought it was funny. People brought signs to the games and loved to shout, "BEAT L.A.! BEAT L.A.!" They could not stand us, but they loved to see the Sparks come to their town, and they came out to watch us play. I guess that is flattery in a backhanded sort of way.

Houston had the best record in the league that first season, despite the fact that Sheryl Swoopes only played nine games after giving birth to her son, Jordan. The Comets went 18–10 during the season, then knocked off New York in the finals to win the first WNBA championship. Cynthia Cooper was the league's first most valuable player, and Van Chancellor was the very first to win the WNBA's Coach of the Year award.

Prior to the 1998 season, the league added expansion teams in Detroit and Washington, D.C., while the Sparks removed the "interim" tag from Julie Rousseau. She was going to be our head coach for season number two, and former NBA player Orlando Woolridge was picked to be her assistant. Julie had great intensity, but she was not experienced enough to coach at the WNBA level. I love Julie! She did her best, but she was in over her head. Honestly, she was just too nice. She wanted to please everybody, and that did not work. It was an unfortunate situation for her, and we began the season with a 2–7 record. I thought that once management realized that we were in trouble, they should have done whatever they had to do to get us straightened out. Make a change, pay the money, cut your losses, and get us the best coach available. Finally, when the team was 7–13, Julie was let go and replaced by Woolridge. We finished 5–5 under Orlando, but we missed the playoffs again.

That 1998–99 off-season turned out to be a very interesting one for me for several reasons. In October I dedicated the Lisa Leslie Sports Complex at Morningside High School. It was forty-two thousand square feet of court space, with twelve baskets. Nike was behind me all the way on the project. The company allowed me to give back to my high school, and that was a great feeling. We could not have achieved our goal without the help of Raye Pond, Nike's representative for women's professional basketball. Raye bent over backwards to provide whatever support Nike could give, and she is the person I thank most for making the Lisa Leslie Sports Complex a reality.

And then, in November, Mom detected a lump on her breast during a self-examination. She found it on Tom's birthday and did not want to spoil his big day, so she kept the news to herself. The next morning, she phoned her doctor. She was very secretive when she made the call and spoke in hushed tones as she told the nurse about the lump. Mom knew that Tom was in the next room.

An ultrasound was performed, and two lumps were found. One of them burst before a biopsy could be performed, and thankfully, the second lump was benign, but it still had to be removed, and surgery worried Mom. When she returned home, she told Tom the good news about the benign tumor and the worrisome news about the invasive surgery. Tom was supportive and told her, "God did not finally give me the right woman just to take her away. You are going to be fine."

Mom took our love and prayers into surgery with her, and everything went fine. Well, almost everything. While the doctor was sewing Mom up, he cut himself and bled into her incision. Do you know what a scare that would be today, not to mention the lawsuit! But at the time, all the nurses did was tell her that they wanted to do a blood test to make sure that everything was okay. Mom told us, "They wanted to charge me three hundred fifty dollars, plus tax, for the blood test. I told them no thank you."

Needless to say, breast cancer awareness and prevention became a big concern of mine. Shortly after Mom's ordeal, I was honored to become the spokesperson for the National Breast Cancer Foundation. As a spokesperson for breast cancer awareness, I wore the classic pink ribbons to spread the word, but I was not truly knowledgeable about the disease, so I got more educated about it. Mom and I shot a public service announcement that ran on television and on many jumbo screens at sporting events. It told women how to educate themselves, and it urged them to see past the myths that surround the disease. For example, breast cancer is not solely hereditary. Anyone with breasts—male or female—is susceptible to the disease. And early detection is key. It saved Mom's life, so she encouraged women to administer self-examinations once a month, and she strongly recommended mammograms for women who were forty and over. I liked that my position as a spokesperson brought attention to an issue that touched my family directly. It was nice to do something really positive with my notoriety.

While I faced important issues at home, the off-season for the Sparks proved full of pivotal decisions. The league expanded to a dozen teams with the additions of the Minnesota Lynx and the Orlando Miracle. The Sparks had Orlando news, too: they hired Orlando Woolridge to be our head coach for the upcoming 1999 season and picked Michael Cooper, the former Laker, to be his assistant.

There were other changes, too. Haixia decided to stay in China, and after just one season with the Sparks, Pam McGee retired. The American Basketball League drew its last breath, and that meant that some high-quality talent, like Katie Smith, Shannon Johnson, Yolanda Griffith, and Natalie Williams, were going to be available in the WNBA draft. The Sparks cashed in and took DeLisha Milton with the fourth pick and also grabbed Clarisse Machanguana, Ukari Figgs, La'Keshia Frett, and Gordana Grubin on draft day.

Despite all the new faces, our squad came together pretty

quickly in 1999 for the WNBA's third season. Everybody was contributing, and we felt good. By the time the very first All-Star Game rolled around, we were 10–5.

The stellar affair was held on July 14 at Madison Square Garden. It was East vs. West, and the game definitely brought out the stars. Julius "Dr. J" Erving was there, along with Tipper Gore, Liza Minnelli, Tom Brokaw, Tina Louise (Ginger from *Gilligan's Island*), LL Cool J, Katie Couric, and Leon (the same Leon from my New York photo shoot).

Whitney Houston sang the national anthem, and then, just as we did in the WNBA's inaugural game, Kym Hampton and I squared off for the opening jump ball. Sheryl Swoopes, Tina Thompson, Michelle Timms, and Cynthia Cooper started with me on the West squad, while Kym was joined on the East team by Vickie Bullett and Chamique Holdsclaw at the forward spots and Teresa Weatherspoon and my old running buddy Nikki McCray in the backcourt.

New York always has great fans that enjoy quality basketball, and they were out in force at the Garden as our West squad jumped out to a big lead. We outscored the East 50–22 on points in the paint and won the game 79–61. I was awarded the most valuable player trophy based on my thirteen points and five rebounds. Playing on our Western Conference All-Star team felt a lot like playing on the 1996 U.S. Olympic team. I was comfortable with my teammates, and any one of us could have won the MVP award. I would be lying if I said I was not thrilled, though. It was awesome to win the inaugural WNBA All-Star Game, and it was a tremendous honor to take home the very first All-Star Game Most Valuable Player award.

After the game, I took a cross-country flight back home, and it was back to regular-season play. The Sparks won six of our next seven games after the break, and we led the WNBA in scoring. Offense was Coach Woolridge's strength. During his thirteen-year NBA career, he had averaged better than twenty-two points per game and had shot 51 percent from the field. Defense, however, was not. He rarely emphasized it; therefore, the Sparks did not excel at it. Coach Woolridge also made some major lineup changes that bruised a couple of egos and left many of us confused. He benched Penny Toler, our starting point guard, in favor of a Grubin/Figgs combination, and Orlando sent Tamecka Dixon, the Sparks' top shooting guard, to the bench as well. Those moves created conflict in our team. None of us knew the reasons behind the changes, and nobody thought it was important enough to explain them to us. Some players lost their respect for Coach Woolridge. Once that happens, respect is rarely recovered, but we persevered and finished the 1999 regular season with a 20–12 record, the most wins in franchise history. We made it to the Western Conference finals and split the first two games of that best-of-three series with the Comets. That set up the deciding third game on August 30 at the Summit in Houston.

That game is probably best remembered for the altercation that took place between me and Tina Thompson. That is right. I got into it with my former USC teammate. DeLisha Milton and I had come up with our "salute," which we used to encourage each other and to celebrate. DeLisha had three nicknames. She was called Sunshine for her happy personality and D-Nasty for the aggressive way that she played the game, and sometimes she was just D. Before some games, D would get on the court and be so hyper and so anxious to play that she would be way too aggressive. Keep in mind, DeLisha had an eighty-four-inch wingspan. That is seven feet from fingertip to fingertip. Her arms were so long that there were times when she could not control them. That would get D really frustrated, and then, if a ref called a foul that she did not like, she overreacted. She was not satisfied with her lack of discipline or self-control and wanted to get away from that "D-Nasty" image.

Our salute was supposed to help her get through those stressful moments. If she was fussing with an official, I would yell,

"Hey," and I would shape my hands in the form of a cup. That was to let her know, "Jesus has got you. You are right here in his hands. Relax." Sometimes that was the only way to calm her down. If I yelled, "D, don't fuss at the referee," it might look like I was scolding her, and that was definitely not my intention.

One night during the season, I was watching *The Maury Povich Show* on television, and this man sang a song called "A Soldier for Jesus." DeLisha and I are very spiritual people. We would hold Bible study meetings with the Sparks' team chaplain. I later said, "D, why don't we use a salute as our sign, like we are soldiers for Jesus?" She liked the idea and thought it would help, so from that point on, whenever we stepped on the court to start a game, D and I would slap hands and then salute each other. When we played, we would cheer for and encourage each other. If D made a good play at the other end of the court, we would make eye contact and salute. Those were happy times. The salute had special meaning for us, and we had a special bond.

The salute was our thing throughout the season. Sparks' fans caught on and started to do it, too. If anyone asked us about it, we used it as an opportunity to spread the good word. People knew. Our team started to pray before games, and we would huddle and pray after games. We saw it as a spiritual movement that would bring us closer to God and closer together as a team.

DeLisha and I never, ever saluted in another player's face or used it in a derogatory way. There was nothing negative about it. When a time-out was called, we might salute and give each other high fives and a hug and then walk to the bench. It was that type of connection, total positive reinforcement for us, and sometimes, when things were going bad, I would salute D and say, "C'mon, you gotta be strong. Get with it."

From the very start of the WNBA, the Sparks and the Comets developed a strong rivalry. When we met in those 1999 conference finals, Houston was the back-to-back league champion defending its crown, and we were the first-time team in the playoffs, trying to gain some respectability. The Sparks and the Comets always played hard against each other, but we never exchanged foul words. We just played ball. We respected each other.

The Sparks had come a long way, and going into Game Three of the Western Conference finals, we were just one win away from eliminating the Comets and earning our first berth in the WNBA finals. The two teams played it close in that critical third game, but Houston eventually took control and pulled away. It was obvious in the closing minutes that the Comets were going to beat us. That was when Tina struck a raw nerve with me. She started talking trash and shouting profane things.

Now, Tina and I are two people who do not really curse much. Even when we hung out, we would say, "Let's try not to curse." I am proud of the fact that I do not swear a lot. She is, too, or at least she was. So, it was totally disrespectful for Tina to start cursing near the end of that game. I kept thinking, *What? That's not even you, Tina. What are you talking about? What are you doing?*

She was disrespecting our team, and then she started saluting and telling us to "go home." That threw me over the edge! It was one thing for her to talk trash, but when she started saluting and cursing, that was too much. The salute was something so positive for us as Christians. For her to twist its message really sent me into a rage. I snapped.

Losing control like that is the worst feeling for me. It is a misrepresentation of who I am. It is very embarrassing, and it is not the message that I want to send to anybody, but that was what happened in the final minutes of game #3. I was running down court, and Tina was facing me as she backpedaled on defense. I kept telling myself, *It's okay, Lisa. Just stay calm!* Tina kept talking, though, and looking at me. She was taunting me! She had made it personal, and that pushed me past my limit. The fact that we had been teammates in college made it worse than if it had been some woman that I had no history with. Tina's taunting hit home, and it hit me really hard.

I knew that by the time that I reached Tina, I was going to hit her. I *had* to hit her. In a split second, I thrust my arms out to shove her. My hands went all the way to her throat. I made contact, but then I quickly stepped back. The only thing that saved her was the fact that I knew Tina and I had a love for her. That was why I decided, at the last second, not to sock her. I just shoved Tina really hard. When I looked at my friend, I could not hit her the way that I really wanted to. I knew it was not right. But I was so angry and frustrated that then I started cursing. I felt like Tina had turned on me.

Looking back, I guess that was Tina's way of celebrating and feeling liberated. Her team had dodged a bullet. After losing that first game to us in Los Angeles, the Comets came back to win the next two games on their home floor, to earn another trip back to the WNBA finals. That was a great accomplishment under pressure. I can understand that now. I understand the emotion of it, but not the personal level to which Tina took it. We both got ejected from the game. My season was over, but Tina and Houston went on to beat New York in the finals, to win their third consecutive WNBA championship. I love playing with Tina, she still has a special place in my heart, and to this day I would still pick her to be on my team.

At the end of the 1999 season, the Sparks' revolving coaching door twirled again. Orlando Woolridge got into a contract squabble with Johnny Buss and got fired, so Michael Cooper was promoted to head coach. The L.A. Sparks had been in existence for only three seasons, and already we were on our fourth head coach.

I was actually happy that Coach Cooper got the job, even though we did not hit it off well the first time we met. When I was attending USC, I worked as a counselor at Coop's summer camp in Pasadena, and he was a real jerk to me. The man called me out in front of all the kids and was very mean to me. Coop challenged me to a dunk contest, and I did dunk, but the man was so difficult. I thought he should have been nicer. Michael Cooper loved kids, but he was really tough on his camp counselors. At that time, I did not like him, but once Coop became an assistant coach with the Sparks, I learned to appreciate and respect him. The man never really talked much as an assistant coach, though, so I wondered if he was going to be able to handle the Sparks' head coaching job for the upcoming 2000 season.

That was the year that the WNBA increased to sixteen teams by awarding expansion franchises to the Indiana Fever, the Seattle Storm, the Miami Sol, and the Portland Fire. For some of us, it was going to be a very busy summer, because the WNBA season was scheduled to end in late August, and the Olympics in Sydney, Australia, were scheduled to begin mid-September.

The Sparks lost point guard Gordana Grubin to Indiana in the expansion draft, but we gained a point guard when my former USC teammate Nicky McCrimmon was taken with a fourth-round pick. Michael Cooper was under the microscope because he had never been a head coach before getting the Sparks' job. He had worked briefly as an assistant coach under Magic Johnson and then for two years under Lakers head coach Del Harris, but Coop was best known as a defensive specialist and top-notch three-point shooter on the Lakers' "Showtime" championship teams of the 1980s. He is still the only Lakers player to ever win the NBA's Defensive Player of the Year Award, so as you might expect, Mr. Cooper emphasized defense from the first day of training camp. He also made it quite clear that we were all there to win the WNBA championship. Anything less was unacceptable.

I met with Coach Cooper to find out exactly what he expected from me and what he wanted me to improve on. Coop was really good at helping me to understand the game. I loved to learn, so we had a good rapport. The man owned five NBA championship rings from his days with the Lakers. Why would I not listen to him?

Coach Cooper gave me the nickname Smooth because he thought my game was smooth, like that of his former Lakers' teammate Kareem Abdul-Jabbar. That was high praise when you consider that Kareem is one of the best basketball players of all time. To be compared to Kareem, in any way, was a tremendous compliment, and Smooth sounded kind of special.

In Coop's first season as head coach, the Sparks worked more on defense than in any year in our history, and it paid off. We held our opponents to sixty-eight points per game, four points less than our defensive average in the Sparks' first three seasons. We were getting better, and part of the reason was that Coach Cooper let everyone on our squad know exactly what her role was. He would stand in front of the entire team and tell each player why she was there, what her responsibilities were, and what he expected. Everybody knew her job and what everybody else's role was, too. That really helped our team. Coop would say, "The ball goes through Smooth," so I knew that 50 percent of the time I was going to touch the ball on offense, and the play was going to go through me. I knew that I was expected to score when possible, but I also had to be a good passer and find my teammates when I was double- or triple-teamed. Coach Cooper was straightforward with all of us, but he would pick his spots, too. Sometimes, he would be bold and get in our faces as a team, and other times he would handle matters privately. I totally respected that.

Coach Woolridge used to curse me out in front of the squad when he was upset with me, or he would say, "The superstar needs to step up." But Coop would say, "Smooth! Come outside so we can talk." When we got outside, he might say, "I don't ever want to see you do that again," or he would tell me, "You need to get yourself together."

I liked that Coach Cooper was usually calm and handled things in a professional manner. Anyone who knows me knows that I do not need someone cursing me out to get me motivated. All a coach has to do is tell me that I am not working hard enough, or that I am not doing something right. I may not always like what the coach has to say, but I will try to fix things and make them better. Coop understood that. He also knew how to push my buttons to get the most out of me. A lot of times, Coach Cooper would use reverse psychology on me. He might say, "That's okay, Smooth. You probably couldn't have accomplished that, anyway." Or he would try to make me think that another player was better than me. "Did you see how she did that?" Coop would ask me. "That is what you need to do. She is really good, isn't she?" He was constantly trying to make me better. He knew that I would strive to get his praise without ever asking him for it.

At first, I did not know if I could trust Coach Cooper, but through his words and his actions, I found that I could. I would write down my goals, such as winning the WNBA championship and earning the league's most valuable player awards, and I would let Coop look at them. It was strange because, initially, I did not feel as though he believed that I could attain my goals. At the same time, I was hesitant to believe him when he said that I could achieve them. It was confusing until I realized that Coop and I were on the very same page.

The Sparks began that 2000 season with four straight wins, followed by two losses. Then we won twenty-four of our next twenty-five games. Coach Cooper's defensive schemes really worked for us, and that year the Sparks were the only WNBA team to hold its opponents under 40 percent in field goal shooting. In our first season under Coop, we finished with the best record in the L.A. Sparks' history and the best record in the WNBA. We went 28–4 but got bounced from the conference finals by our annual nemesis, Houston. The Comets ousted us and then did the same thing to New York in the WNBA finals. Van Chancellor's team maintained its stranglehold on the league championship. Their victory over the Liberty gave the Comets four titles in the league's first four seasons.

I did not win the Most Valuable Player award that season, but I was named to the All-WNBA First Team. It hurt to get eliminated again, but I felt good about the Sparks' direction. For the first time in franchise history, we seemed to be on the right track. When Michael Cooper took over as head coach, the L.A. Sparks finally had the leader who could bring out the best in each player and put the players together as a team. Coop gave us that swagger, attitude, and confidence that we had been missing. We were a team in every sense of the word, and it was time for us to start playing like champions.

Chapter 11

Bridging Adversity with Maturity

When the Sparks' season ended in mid-August, I joined the U.S. national team that was preparing for the 2000 Summer Olympic Games. The opening ceremony in Sydney, Australia, was less than one month away, so we had a lot of work to do, but this was not our first time together as a team. Our Team USA squad went 38–2 on a tour that started in September of 1999 and finished in late March of 2000. Then it was time to close up shop for a while on the U.S. team and get down to the business of the WNBA season. As the summer rolled on and our respective teams got eliminated from the league's championship race, the U.S. national team slowly began to regroup and get ready for the Olympics. We got in some workouts and then went 8–0 on a mini-tour that took us to Canada, Hawaii, and Australia. We capped it off by beating the Australian national team in Melbourne just six nights before the opening of the Olympics.

Nell Fortner was Team USA's head coach. She had enjoyed great success with the Purdue Boilermakers and had put off starting her new job as head coach of the Indiana Fever so that she could guide the U.S. women's team through the 2000 Olympics. Geno Auriemma and Peggie Gillom were Nell's assistants. We had six players back from the squad that won the gold medal in the 1996 Olympics, including Dawn, Ruthie, Sheryl, Teresa, Nikki, and me, but there were several newcomers as well. Katie Smith, DeLisha Milton, Yolanda Griffith, Natalie Williams, Kara Wolters, and Chamique Holdsclaw had all earned spots on our Olympic roster.

Sydney, Australia, was super safety conscious for the 2000 Summer Games. The bombing at the Atlanta Olympics was fresh in everyone's mind, so security was tight and highly visible. Fortunately, there were no explosions or tragedies at the Australian Olympics, but the games were not without incident. We had demonstrators outside of our Team USA hotel in Melbourne. There had been large, and sometimes violent, protests in Melbourne against the World Economic Forum (WEF) that had been held in the city in the days leading up to the Olympics. The WEF was comprised of many of the world's business and government leaders whose focus was corporate globalization. The organization counted Exxon, Ford, Microsoft, Coca-Cola, and Nike among its numerous members. I endorse Nike and was told that the company had sent staff members and athletes to Australia ahead of time to make sure that the situation in Melbourne was safe. Nike was being accused of alleged unfair labor practices, so the company's representatives had given us a lot of information on Nike and how its products were produced. We had even gone on a tour in China to visit the so-called "sweatshops" to reassure us that the workers were being well provided for. Quite frankly, the whole protest thing was a little scary, but I did not have time to deal with anything but basketball. I was trying to get acclimated and ready for our first game, against South Korea.

The demonstrators did not make that easy for us. Our Monday morning practice had to be canceled when we were left waiting in the hotel casino while our bus tried unsuccessfully to get to us through a mass of demonstrators. The activists were everywhere, and they were chanting and shouting. Security put up a fence around the hotel, but after what happened in Atlanta in 1996, there were still plenty of reasons for concern. The situation was so bad that the U.S. men's basketball team canceled its practice, but eventually, Nell Fortner's attitude was, "We are the USA. It is a peaceful demonstration. We are just going to go to practice. I don't care if we have to take a boat."

It might have looked like a peaceful protest, but those people were very passionate about their cause. Who knew what they might be thinking? It seemed very dangerous, but Nell still sent us out of the hotel to walk through the demonstrators. They were chanting, "No Nike! No Nike!" and some of us, like me, were wearing Nike gear. Why would we walk into a situation like that? It was an incident waiting to happen. We were told, "Put your heads down and walk. Do not look at anybody. Do not say anything." To me, that was just too much. Nell was adamant, though, so we cut through the demonstrators and eventually made it to the bus. The demonstrators were peaceful, considering that we walked right through their protest. But it was still quite an ordeal, and as Allen Iverson might say, "We were talking about *practice!*"

Once Team USA had completed that all-important practice session, we had to figure out a way to get past the demonstrators and back into our hotel. Several streets had been closed because of the protests, but there was a river that ran right behind the hotel, so we loaded the team into boats and started down the waterway. It was a great idea, but we were not able to avoid all of the demonstrators. Some of them were lined up along the banks, and when they saw our boats coming, they started yelling at us, mooning us, and flipping us the finger. I guess you do not earn points if you are a classy demonstrator. The whole thing was nerve-wracking, but I guess it could have been worse. When you think about it, we were sitting ducks out there on those boats. If someone had wanted to harm us, they could have done it very easily.

The aggravation did not end when we arrived at the hotel, either. Our entire team had to sneak back into the building in order to get to our rooms. The demonstrators had gotten more aggressive, and we did not want to take any chances. From that day on, both the U.S. women's and men's basketball teams had to try to outsmart the demonstrators if we wanted to get to practice. We started leaving the hotel around 5:00 AM to avoid the demonstrators, and then we would board our bus and get out of Melbourne as fast as we could. One day, the activists sent a representative from their group, a man with a big Mohawk hairdo, onto our bus to make sure that we were not sneaking Microsoft's Bill Gates, or some other WEF big shot, out of the hotel. Little did I know that this bizarre experience would mark the start of two of the most exciting years of my basketball career.

Team USA went into the Olympic competition shorthanded because Chamique Holdsclaw had a stress fracture in her right foot and could not play. That left only eleven players on our roster, but we still managed to blitz through our first seven opponents. That earned us a spot in the gold medal game against the host team, Australia. The Aussies were also undefeated, and they dearly wanted to grab the gold in front of their countrymen. The Australian team had improved greatly, and in 2000 they were planning to make a name for themselves at our expense. We knew that beating the Aussies on their home court in Sydney would be our toughest challenge in the Olympics.

The Australian roster was jam-packed with WNBA players Sandy Brondello, Michelle Griffiths, Kristi Harrower, and Michelle Timms, plus they had two nineteen-year-olds, Lauren Jackson and Penny Taylor, who would become future WNBA stars. Going into those Olympic Games, there was already a ton of hype about Lauren and me. There was already a rivalry brewing in the media, and basketball fans were arguing about which of us was the better player.

Team USA wore our white uniforms with the red and blue

trim for the deciding game. The Aussies wore their green and yellow one-piece unis, which they call unitards. Kevin Garnett, Vince Carter, and several other U.S. men's team players were on hand at the Sydney SuperDome to watch the game and cheer us on. Vince wore an American flag, and K.G. was a great cheerleader. It made our team feel great to know that the guys were there to support us. We had emotional inspiration as well. The gold medal game would be the final Olympic appearance for Teresa Edwards, who was retiring from international competition after representing the United States so well, and with so much class, through twenty years of worldwide basketball.

The Aussie fans were really loud when the gold medal game began. They had their flags and signs, but there were also a lot of Americans in the crowd, and they got something to cheer about when Team USA jumped out to a quick lead. We were too strong and too deep on the inside for Australia, and that helped us to a thirteen-point advantage at halftime.

Our squad took care of business in the second half, too, but there was controversy coming for Lauren Jackson and me before this game would end. We did not guard each other very much during the game. Our coaches knew that things always seemed to escalate when we matched up, and they were concerned that we might get into foul trouble or worse. We did have some battles, however, and Lauren would curse at me a lot. She was always talking trash and calling me the "B" word. She kept saying, "Get off me, B." Dawn kept telling me, "Don't get involved, Lisa. Just play." I never said one word to Lauren, but she would constantly talk and curse. I did not know what her deal was. I kept wondering, *What is wrong with this girl?*

Late in the game, it was pretty obvious that Team USA was going to win the gold medal. I was not completely certain, but when we lined up for a free throw attempt, I thought I saw one of the Australian players tell Lauren to pull my hair. I had been wearing French braids throughout the Olympics. It took about four to six hours to get my hair done in French braids and about two hours to take them down. Since our team was going to fly home after the gold medal game, Nikki McCray and I decided that we would take our braids down prior to Team USA's showdown with Australia. Once the braids were down, we got some hairpins and attached fake ponytails to our hair. It was simple, and we were ready for the game. Postgame would be more convenient for us as well, because we would not have any hair issues to deal with while we were preparing to leave Sydney.

Everything was good in the hair department until Lauren Jackson and I started mixing it up late in the game. A long rebound bounced out that neither of us could get to, and as I turned to run up court, Lauren grabbed my ponytail from behind and yanked it right off of my head. How was I supposed to deal with that? The girl had deliberately ripped my hair off. Did I have another Tina Thompson incident on my hands? Would I snap once again and go after Lauren? The answer to all those questions had to be no.

It was more than a little embarrassing, but I leaned over, picked up my ponytail, tossed it toward the baseline where the photographers sat, and ran down the court. I had learned from the incident with Tina in Houston that I had to be more in control of myself when people were baiting me or talking about me. That was why when Lauren Jackson pulled my ponytail, I was finally at a point where I could say, "It's okay. I can deal with this!"

Lauren said afterwards that her fingers got caught in my hair, and when she tried to free them, my ponytail came off. The Australian press made the incident sound as if it was a funny accident. I knew in my heart, however, that Lauren had purposely ripped the hair off my head. I am positive. Lauren Jackson knows that. Her teammates know that, and my teammates know that. There is no doubt in my mind.

I went back to playing and ran up and down the court a few times before Nell called a time-out. A cameraman brought the ponytail over to the sideline, and the Australian players got a good laugh out of it. When I came back in the game after the time-out, I told myself, *Lisa, don't do anything*, but my alter ego was saying, *I am going to get you back, Lauren.*

I was on the court, but my head was not in the game, and I could not focus on playing basketball. I don't think I contributed much down the stretch, because I was thinking a lot more about controlling myself than I was about scoring points. If I had not had that experience with Tina during the summer, I probably would have tried to beat up Lauren while the world watched on TV. It would have been worse than my fight with Tina, because of the global spotlight. It would have been horrible for me, my career, USA Basketball, and the Olympics. I was still seething inside, but I was able to smile at my adversity. I was able to talk my way through it. If I had gone after Lauren Jackson, it would have been really ugly for everyone.

I was pleased with the way I handled things, and I was really happy just a few minutes later, when Dawn Staley dribbled out the clock, and we had a 76–54 victory and another Olympic gold medal for the United States. Dawn grabbed an American flag, and so did I. DeLisha was doing a celebration dance, and Team USA was feeling pretty good. We had a lot to be proud of. We beat the home team in the gold medal game, plus we helped Teresa Edwards close out her Olympic career with her fourth gold medal.

We had an opportunity to go back to our locker room before the medal ceremony, so I used that time to put my ponytail back on. I just wrapped it around my bun to make a bigger bun on my head. I put on my lipstick, earrings, and my cute little blue sweat suit, and then I headed back to the court, where Team USA received its gold medals. It was just as sweet as the gold we'd won in Atlanta.

I went over to my mom, but people kept trying to pull me away to do media interviews. Mom was crying and hugging me and telling me I looked beautiful and played well. She also wanted to make sure I was okay after the hair incident.

I started crying, put my gold medal around Mom's neck, and told her, "I won this gold medal for you. I'm fine. I'll see you back at the hotel."

As my mom headed for the exit, our Team USA publicity people almost went into cardiac arrest about me not having my gold medal. They said, "No, Lisa, you have to have your gold medal for the pictures and the media interviews." They had to track down my mom and get my gold medal back so I could wear it to the press conference.

When I got to the media area, they sat me at a table, next to Robin Roberts, and Lauren Jackson was seated on the other side. I told the reporters how excited I was to win my second Olympic gold medal and how rewarding it was to win the gold by beating Australia on their own home court. When I was asked about the hair-pulling incident, I told the media members, "I know in my heart that Lauren pulled my hair on purpose. She can have the hair. I congratulate her on winning the silver medal, but I got the gold." I was very satisfied with the outcome, hair or no hair.

Team USA had gone undefeated in Olympic competition once again, and shortly after we got back to the States, the L.A. Sparks were pulling the trigger on some major moves during the WNBA's off-season. The team needed strength and depth on the front line, so Penny Toler, our General Manager, traded Allison Feaster and Clarisse Machanguana to Charlotte for Rhonda Mapp, a six-foot-two center who was big, burly, and tough in the paint. The very next day, Penny traded La'Keshia Frett to the Sacramento Monarchs for Latasha Byears, a five-foot-eleven forward who played a physical inside game and had always been a thorn in the side of the L.A. Sparks.

I had mixed it up with both of those players in the WNBA's

early years. Rhonda Mapp used to try to muscle me when she was with the Sting, and she talked a lot of trash, too. She would always say, "Get some," after she tried to score, but I used to block her shots and say, "Get this!"

Latasha was nicknamed Tot by her grandmother and had the name tattooed on her arm. She quickly became known as Toto (pronounced Tott-oh, and not like Dorothy's dog in *The Wizard of Oz*). Toto was a *real* piece of work. When she played for Sacramento, she liked to talk a lot of trash. Many players talked trash, but Toto took it further than everybody else. She would call me the most vulgar names, many of which involved body parts. The "B" word was one of her favorites, but nothing was out of bounds. Crude, over the top, it did not matter. Toto was relentless.

In one of my more memorable moments playing against her, she was still with the Monarchs. We were lined up next to each other for a jump ball, and Toto kept trying to place her foot over mine to get better position. I knew she was trying to intimidate me, but I was not going to back down. Until this moment, I had ignored all the comments she had made to me on the court. But not this time. I took a good look at her and said, "Don't let this lipstick fool you! I will knock you out!"

Early in my career, the knock on me was that I was soft, not physical enough, and could be muscled out of my game. I never really believed that, but my coaches told me, "Lisa, they are going to try to be physical with you. Just keep playing strong." I was labeled as a finesse player who did not like contact from the day I started playing basketball. I did not consider it an insult. I was used to it. I knew my opponents were going to be physical, so I had to focus on emphasizing my assets. I was faster, so I could outrun them and get layups. I had better footwork, and I could step outside and shoot, or drive around them, to score.

To me, physical play is just one aspect of the game. If I have to be down low in the post, I know it is going to get rough, but I can handle it. I like doing what people say I cannot do on the court. Moving past their narrow expectations is great motivation for me. It makes me work harder. It is weird how that happens, but it is true. When I am on the court, I do not notice the physical play. I guess my body has become accustomed to the bumping and pushing and vying for better position under the basket; it feels natural. And throughout my career, I have never felt as though I have been pushed around or beat up, though that is what a lot of people think.

Another thing that I hear all the time is, "Lisa, I love how feminine you are on the court, but you be ballin'! You work hard, but you are so feminine!" I have no idea what they see. What is feminine? I am just being me, on the court and off. I do not put any extra swish in my walk. I am not prissy. I do not run around looking in a mirror all the time, saying, "Don't mess up my hair," but I am perceived as feminine, and that is not a bad thing. It has been used against me in my athletic career, but in general, I feel like a woman, and I like that I can bring that quality to my athleticism without either one having to suffer. I like wearing feminine clothes, but I am not consciously trying to be girly. Even as a kid, I did not go to the gym in big, baggy shorts and a long T-shirt, though that was what the boys around me wore. I am no less feminine now than I was then. I am just more visible.

Back when I first started playing, I wore two pairs of socks, which I pulled up and kept very neat. I would put on my shoes and tie my laces so that they would not drag on the ground and get dirty. Short shorts were in style, and that was fine with me. Longer shorts got in the way and made me hot.

In high school, I used to make sure that my shoestrings matched my clothes. It was a girl thing. Normally, I wore stud earrings. Those were things that my mom always checked before we left the house. She would say, "Go put your earrings on, and make sure you brush your teeth. Let me check your mouth before you go. And do not even think about walking out that door with that scarf on your head."

I also started wearing a little red lipstick before every game. It became part of my pregame routine, no matter who we played or where we played. To me, it seemed natural. My mom wore lipstick when she drove her truck. And if my aunts were in a room and someone wanted to snap a picture, they would all yell, "Wait, wait, wait," so that they could reach into their bras and pull out a tube of lipstick. And they *all* had lipstick!

On the basketball court, my uniform is always neat. When I tuck it into my jersey, it rarely comes out unless one of my opponents yanks it out. I still wear lipstick for each game, and now I wear mascara and sometimes blush. But really, my appearance has more to do with presenting myself well and having pride in who I am, how I look, what I do, and what I represent than with being feminine. I know that every time I step on the court, I am going to be watched and judged by thousands of people, so I work hard to showcase myself and the game in the best way that I know how. I know that I cannot please everybody, but I maintain my standard of how I want to represent myself. Hopefully, that is pleasing to about 90 percent of the people. I cannot waste time on the other 10 percent. Life is just too short.

I have heard people say that success happens when preparation meets opportunity. That is where I am today, sitting at that intersection, so to speak. But to stay there, I have to focus on the things that have worked for me: training hard, playing hard, and being myself. It is the only way I know how to be. And I would hate to miss my next opportunity because I am preoccupied with other people's ideas of how I should or should not be. It is not worth it.

So I guess you could say that I am different.

I know that my teammates talk about me. They always have, but it does not bother me. I respect them for who they are. All I ask is that they respect me for who I am. I tell them, "You don't have to like me, but you are gonna respect me." As long as we can meet each other halfway, I am fine.

With this in mind, I knew that my issues with trusting other people were keeping me from some potentially rewarding relationships with my teammates, and I wanted to be more open. That was my outlook when Latasha "Toto" Byears and Rhonda Mapp joined the Sparks for the 2001 season. We had been bitter opponents, but now we were teammates, and everybody needed to start over with a clean slate. All I cared about was what Toto and Rhonda did at work. And I knew they would bring much-needed attitude and strength to our team.

Once Toto got to L.A., I was not judgmental. I did not try to impress her. I just showed her respect. I would go hard at her and Rhonda. They did not see the lipstick chick or the girly girl who was on the posters. They saw somebody who brought her best game every day and worked very hard. They had to respect my game. And with the level of respect there and everybody working hard, we were fine.

Every day Toto and Rhonda proved how important they could be to the Sparks and to me. Rhonda was a very physical player. Coach Cooper made her believe that the paint was her territory, so in practices, she was supposed to keep me out of her area. My job was to get past her and do my thing. My mind-set was, *That is my house. Rhonda is not going to keep me out of my house!* We had some amazing battles.

Toto had fast hands, and she knew that her defensive strength was getting the ball out of my hands before I could bring it up to take a shot. She forced me to protect the ball, because if I did not grab it with authority, she was going to take the basketball away from me. Toto was strong, too. She was not tall, but she would body up on me and would not give an inch. I knew that I was in for a physical practice every day, so I had to become a more physical player.

We still had DeLisha "D" Milton up front as well. She was physical and extremely quick. D brought a different dimension to the game for me. I had to slow down, be patient, and play smart basketball against her. She forced me to outthink her, because I knew that D was quick and could steal the ball.

D, Toto, and Rhonda all gave me different looks and styles to deal with, and that made me a better player. I was challenged over and over on the practice floor. One of them might get the ball from me, but they all knew that I would be coming right back at them on my next trip down the floor. We were all relentless in our efforts, and because of that, we all became better basketball players.

The 2001 season was the Sparks' first in our new home, Staples Center, in downtown Los Angeles. It was an incredibly modern facility that seated almost nineteen thousand people, and it was completely different than the Great Western Forum. This arena had purple seats, luxury boxes, a restaurant, and so much more. Unfortunately, when the season began, we did not spend much time in our new building, because nine of our first thirteen games were played on the road, but when we did get to play in L.A., we took a quick liking to our new arena. And it was a nice complement to the strong season we were having. At the All-Star break we were 17–3 overall and 8–0 at our new home.

The All-Star Game was in Orlando that year, and I was a little surprised to find out that the WNBA's fans did not vote me to start for the West All-Stars. It was not really an issue initially. I did not look at it as though I had some God-given right to start in the All-Star Game. The fans did the voting, and I did not have an attitude about that, but a lot of people, including several commentators, interpreted the snub as a slap in the face for me, and they let me know about it. That made me think. Was it really an insult? I mean, the fans voted in some good players. It was not like the league, the coaches, or the players had picked the starters. But the more I thought about it, the more unfair it seemed. I started to wonder if I should go to the All-Star Game at all.

It was crazy. Normally, a player would expect the hometown fans to vote her in, but for some reason, the All-Star balloting was not a big deal to the Sparks' management. It was different for the Monarchs and the Comets. Their franchises really got into it. Game after game, they would make announcements in the arenas, hand out ballots, and then have workers go through the stands to gather up the forms and stuff them into the ballot boxes. Sacramento and Houston really worked at it, and in 2001 each of those teams had multiple players on the starting squad for the West.

I did not think the Sparks did a good job of promoting the All-Star balloting. In fact, I can remember only one home game in which the ballots were put on the seats in the arena. Most nights, the ballots were available in the lobby, but there was no publicity or fanfare about it. The fans were expected to find the ballots on their own, fill them out, and then deposit the paper-work in the little boxes that bore the All-Star logo. We did not do any promos on the big scoreboard or anything. I did not know about the voting, and I never saw one thing that said VOTE FOR LISA or VOTE FOR TAMECKA. I do not even think that I voted for myself. Tamecka and I were both lucky that the coaches added us to the All-Star roster as reserves. It was not a priority in L.A.

Now I try not to meddle in front-office business, but on this occasion, I let the Sparks' management know that I thought our organization had dropped the ball and should not make that same mistake again. It would be one thing to have our fans vote for the All-Star starters and get outvoted by other WNBA fans, but it was ridiculous for the Sparks' players to get left out be-cause our fans were not made aware of the balloting process.

After a lot of thought, I decided that I should go to the game.

I figured, *Okay, if I can't start in the All-Star Game, then I will just be the MVP off the bench. That is my goal.* I looked at the situation and tried to find the positive in it. In my mind, the plus was that the starters would only be playing about five or six minutes, and then I would come off the bench with some of the other reserves. I would still have the same opportunity and playing time that the starters got. It would be up to me to get in there and play.

So I headed to Orlando right after my final Sparks game before the All-Star break, and I was happy to see Van Chancellor, the head coach for the West's All-Star team. He was fun and my teammates were cool, even though one of them was Seattle rookie Lauren Jackson, the Australian player who had pulled my ponytail off at the previous Olympics. This marked the first time that we had ever played on the same team. Our interaction was limited. Lauren did not really know me, and I did not know her, but I was not a person who carried a grudge. I spoke. She spoke. That was pretty much it. We practiced, enjoyed the festivities, and got ready for the game.

It was a little weird for me when the pregame introductions took place inside the TD Waterhouse Centre. In the two previous WNBA All-Star Games, I had been introduced with the starters, but this time I was not a part of all the noise, the pyrotechnics, and the excitement that accompanied the entrance of each starting player. This was a new and different feeling, but I was already focused on what I was there for and what I wanted to do.

The East team was really pumped up for the game. The New York Liberty had three starters on the squad: Teresa Weatherspoon, Vickie Johnson, and Tari Phillips. Orlando's Taj McWilliams-Franklin and Washington's Nikki McRay joined them in the lineup. Our West team had won the first two All-Star Games, and the East was tired of losing. They were talking about kicking our butts.

197

I sat on the bench and watched as the game got under way. Orlando Magic star Tracy McGrady was sitting courtside. He kept telling me, "Lisa, when you get in there, BALL!!" Coming off the bench was definitely motivation for me. I had found out that Glen Rice was the only player in NBA or WNBA history to win the MVP award as a nonstarter, and that was back in 1997.

When I heard Coach Chancellor call my name, I went into the game, along with my Sparks teammate Tamecka Dixon. Tamecka was a first-time All-Star, and she was very excited to be there. I was happy for her, too. We got rolling with some nice passes, layups, jump shots, and three-pointers. Everything was clicking. I blocked a shot in the area near T-Mac, and I yelled, "Get that outta here!"

He yelled, "Yeah! Yeah!" Tracy was going crazy. I love it when guys are into the women's game. It shows that they appreciate our skills. They understand what it is like to play, so it is a huge compliment when NBA players come out and enjoy a WNBA game. I think it is great that they support women's basketball.

It was already set in my mind to win the MVP trophy, so during the game, I was thinking, *Have fun and put on a show.* I was excited. I hit a three-pointer and held up my fingers to count one, two, three. I drove and kicked the ball to Lauren Jackson. She hit a three-point shot from the corner. We slapped five and ran back down court.

What I really wanted to do was dunk in that game, but a good opportunity never came up. I was focused on jamming one down, and the East was focused on making sure that I did not get a dunk and embarrass them. Tamecka tried to set me up with a pass, but it just did not happen, and I did not want to force it.

When the final buzzer sounded in Orlando, the West had an 80–72 victory, and I was the unanimous choice as the All-Star Game's most valuable player. I had scored twenty points, grabbed nine rebounds, and blocked three shots in just twenty-three minutes of play. I had accomplished what I had set out to do, even though the fans had not voted me in. That had been my motivation, and I think Coach Chancellor knew it. After the game he said, "See, you went and pissed Leslie off, so she came down here and got the MVP. She was on a mission." He said it jokingly, but he was right. I thought that if nothing else, I needed to make the statement that I deserved to be an All-Star starter.

The All-Star Weekend had interrupted the Sparks' eight-game winning streak, but after the break, we got right back on track and won ten more games in a row. We finished the season with a 28–4 record, exactly the same as the year before, but this time we led the league in scoring, rebounding, and assists, and we closed out the regular season undefeated at home, earning home-court advantage for the playoffs.

Our first-round foe was the Houston Comets, who had managed to work their way into the playoffs, despite playing the entire season with Sheryl Swoopes sidelined due to an ACL surgery. We had taken two out of three games from Houston during the regular season, but our playoff history with them was not favorable. We had never been able to get past the Comets in the postseason.

Every time that the Comets eliminated us, it forced us to reexamine ourselves and strive to improve. We just had to get over the hump. We had to be hungrier during the playoffs. We had to play more like champions and not leave the results up to chance. Houston knew how to go to that next level. They were a veteran team that had learned about maturity and intensity from their early years in the playoffs. As far as we knew, the Sparks did not have another level. What we learned from losing to the Comets was that we needed to have better focus and play with unrelenting intensity. We had to understand that the regular season was just that—the regular season. You want to play well during it, but you do not want to burn out your team. What you really want to do is create good habits and put yourself in the best position to be successful in the postseason. In previous years, we had played the regular season to get a great record. But, like my teammate Tamecka Dixon said at the time, "The regular season don't mean anything. It's just a good time for us to tune up for what we need to do in the postseason."

She was right. By the time the L.A. Sparks got to that first-round series with Houston, we were already in shape. Our shots and our moves were pretty much in place. We knew our offense, we knew where our teammates would be on the court, and our defensive principles were ingrained in our minds. The big difference in the playoffs is mental, not physical. The team that is best able to stay focused and limit mistakes usually wins.

We took that philosophy into our series against Houston and won handily. The win gave us seventeen consecutive victories at home, and it set up a showdown with the Sacramento Monarchs for the Western Conference championship. After the final game, Lakers guard Derek Fisher, who had been sitting courtside and wearing my number nine Sparks jersey, started to chant, "MVP! MVP!" I felt a twinge of excitement, but I knew I had to keep my cool; we still had to beat Sacramento before getting to the finals.

The Western Conference championship was a roller coaster. The Sparks and Monarchs had developed a very bitter, very physical rivalry over the years, and the Monarchs' arena was always a raucous place to play. The fans really got behind their team and were extremely loud with their taunts and their cowbells. As a result, Sacramento was awfully tough to beat in their own building.

Game One went down to the wire in Sacramento. We led by one point with two seconds left on the clock and managed to hang on. In Game Two, we were back in L.A., and I was awarded the WNBA's Most Valuable Player trophy in a pregame ceremony at center court. I was very honored and grateful. The award meant a lot to me because the voters had recognized my talent, my hard work, and my value to the Sparks. We had a game to play, though, so the MVP trophy was carted off, and the playoff stage was set. But that is not the only reason I have such vivid memories of this game. It was also one of the most physical games of my entire career.

The Sparks needed just one victory to move on to the WNBA finals for the very first time, and the way the game started out, our chances looked pretty good. The Monarchs missed their first six shots. We had them down by eleven points in the first half, but they got physical and stormed back. And I do mean *physical*.

In diving after a loose ball, an opponent's head crashed into my eye. Another Sacramento player swung her elbow and hit me in the same eye. And then, later on, I was elbowed in the face. I walked away from the game with a busted lip, rattled teeth, a black eye, and one very sore nose (which, thankfully, was not broken). I had been worked over and beaten up all game long. Coach Cooper later said to me, "Smooth, you feel like you got your butt whipped, don't you?" All I could do was nod.

We got beaten on the scoreboard, too. Sacramento won by twenty points, and our seventeen-game winning streak at home was over. This set up a major showdown for the final game of the series. The winner would advance to the WNBA finals.

As I sat in our locker room after that loss in Game Two, the thought that would not leave my head was, *I am not going to be the one crying tomorrow.* That was my biggest motivation to get the job done in Game Three. The Sparks, as a team, had to decide if we were going to dig in for that game, play hard, and fight back, or let the conference championship slip through our fingers.

Coach Cooper took me aside before Game Three and said, "Smooth, I need for you to show up. We need to see the MVP in this one." I understood the challenge and the stakes. My teammates and I were determined to win, and we jumped out early.

We beat Sacramento in the paint, time after time, and by half-time, we were up fifteen points. The second half was more of the same. I wound up with a career high of thirty-five points, plus sixteen rebounds and seven blocked shots. The L.A. Sparks were Western Conference champions for the first time, and we had earned our first ticket to the WNBA finals.

Chapter 12

To the Victor Go the Spoils

It was August 30, 2001, and the L.A. Sparks were in North Carolina for Game One of the WNBA finals against the Charlotte Sting. My girl Dawn Staley was the starting point guard for Charlotte, and we met on the court before the game and hit hands. It was time to play. If this had been a regular-season game, we would have been out there stretching, joking, and laughing. Dawn and I were very close, and normally, I would have talked with her during warm-ups. But this was the WNBA finals. Not one word was said. We looked at each other, and we both knew that this was it.

The first time I met Dawn was in the summer of 1989. I had just finished my junior year at Morningside High School, and she was a freshman at the University of Virginia. We were both in Colorado Springs, trying out for the U.S. junior national team, and we wound up being roommates. I had no idea who this short girl was, but I could see right away that she could really play. I was in awe of her talent. Dawn was exceptionally fast and a terrific passer, too. She called me Big Girl, and I thought that was the best thing since apple pie. She would yell, "Get down on the block, Big Girl," and I would get to my spot in a hurry. Dawn fired me up when she called me that name, because whenever I heard it, I knew I was getting ready to score, and somebody on the opposing team was in for some trouble. "Big Girl, come on. We need one," she would say. "Come here. It's me and you. Pick and roll. Two-man game." Dawn had an intensity level that made me want to be my very best every second that I was on the floor with her. Magic Johnson is like that, too. When I practice with him, I never want to mess up. I always want to be on top of my game, because I know that he will. Dawn was the same way.

Both Dawn and I made the junior national team, and over the next fifteen years, we would go on to be teammates for numerous USA Basketball adventures. Every time we made a team, we roomed together and laughed and giggled all summer long. It was as if we had a routine: play basketball, win games, earn medals, and go back to our respective homes. We played all over the world together, earning gold medals at the Olympics, world championships, and Goodwill Games. I guess you could call us the Golden Girls. In any regard, that is a lot to accomplish with the same teammate.

Dawn and I played so well together because we clicked in our understanding of basketball, and we could really communicate with each other. Dawn knew how I played, and she was confident about my skills. I knew that she was always the floor general. Whatever she wanted, whatever play she called, that is what Dawn Staley got from me. There was never a question about who was in charge. Dawn was always the captain, and I was her center. There would be no mutiny on our ship. I think that kind of respect made our relationship work. If Dawn did not throw me the ball, I knew there was a good reason. You could not find a stitch of selfishness in her, so there was never any doubt about her motives and never any room for thoughts of jealousy.

But all the good memories and warm sentiment had to be put behind us when our teams squared off for the 2001 WNBA championship. Dawn was steering Charlotte's ship, but now I was the opposing center, and we both wanted what only one of us could have.

The Sting had stumbled out of the gate in the regular season. They slumped to a 1–10 start, but Dawn kept telling me, "Don't sleep on Charlotte. We're coming."

I would tell her, "Y'all ain't doing nothing!"

Dawn and I were always talking trash to each other about our teams. I would say, "Y'all can't get past New York, so I'm not worried about Charlotte."

She'd come back with, "Yeah, but you've got to see Houston."

We always got a good laugh out of it, but Dawn turned out to be right about her team. The Sting got their act together under head coach Anne Donovan, and they pulled off an amazing turnaround.

Dawn and I had teased each other all season long, but once we hit the playoffs, all the kidding stopped. Everything got very serious, and Dawn and I never communicated again during the postseason. That was difficult for us. We had constantly joked about meeting in the finals, but when our Sparks-Sting matchup became a reality, there was no room for friendship, though there was no love lost. That was just the way it had to be. I could not let her spoil my chance to win a championship ring, and Dawn was not about to give up her big opportunity for me.

Game One of the WNBA finals was at the Charlotte Coliseum, and we knew the Sting would be psyched to grab a win in front of their home fans. Dawn was Charlotte's floor leader, and she had some excellent players to work with. Andrea Stinson was a solid frontline player. Tammy Sutton–Brown was a highly touted rookie playing the center position, and two of my former L.A. Sparks teammates, Allison Feaster and Clarisse Machanguana, were key contributors for Charlotte as well.

The game was played pretty evenly through the first half, but Stinson canned a buzzer beater just before intermission, and the

Sting took a four-point lead to the locker room. In the second half, Charlotte stretched its advantage to eleven points before the Sparks finally mounted a comeback. Our defense set the tone by holding the Sting scoreless for over seven minutes. I finished with twenty-four points, eight rebounds, and two blocked shots. DeLisha and Tamecka hit for double-digit points as well, and the L.A. Sparks took the first game of the WNBA finals by a score of 75–66.

Dawn had ten points and three rebounds in the game, but she also had an uncharacteristically low two assists and an unusually high six turnovers. During the postgame media interviews, I reminded everyone what a tremendous competitor Dawn Staley was and how tough the Sting could be. Charlotte had gone on the road to New York and had won back-to-back games against the Liberty just to get to the finals, so we knew we would have our work cut out for us in Game Two. The Sparks needed just one more win in the best-of-three series to capture our first WNBA championship. When the finals shifted back to Los Angeles, our job was to put away the Charlotte Sting as quickly as possible.

On Saturday, September 1, Staples Center was packed for Game Two, and the stars had come out for the event. Lakers general manager Jerry West was there. Penny Marshall was courtside, along with Michael Clarke Duncan, Vivica A. Fox, and Tyrese, but it was the Sparks who were putting on a show. We were hitting on all cylinders, and although Charlotte outshot us in the first half, the Sparks led 38–30 at the halftime break.

The second half turned into a blowout. We outscored the Sting by twenty points and won the game 82–54. It was the largest margin of victory in any WNBA finals series, and the win made the L.A. Sparks the first team, other than Houston, to capture a WNBA championship. The Comets had won the first four crowns, but now Los Angeles had one, as well. In a nice note of symmetry, the Lakers had won the NBA championship just a few months before, so things were twice as nice for L.A. hoop fans that year.

Finally winning the WNBA championship was a tremendous accomplishment for us, but when the game ended, I knew we had to go hit hands with our opponents. I was okay with that until I saw Dawn. When I saw her, I just broke down. It was so difficult because I was used to winning with her. We had been through a lot together.

When I got to Dawn after the game, I told her that I was sorry. I know that sounds kind of weird, and I know that everybody cannot win, but for the two of us, the feelings ran so much deeper than just winning and losing. I knew how bad Dawn's knees were, but she had never stopped fighting. She had pushed herself the way that true leaders do. She had brought so much to the game. I felt bad at a time when I should have felt wonderful. It was a "chokey" moment for me. My heart was in my throat. Dawn was very strong and usually hid her emotions well, but she started crying, too. She told me, "I haven't cried in ten years, and now you've got me going." Dawn gave me a big hug and then walked off.

I was not sure what to feel. There were so many negatives for Dawn and her team, yet so many positives for the Sparks and me. I was standing there as a WNBA champion, and individually, I had had a terrific postseason run—so good in fact that I won the Most Valuable Player Award for the WNBA playoffs. League President Val Ackerman handed the trophy to me, and I raised it high for every Sparks fan in the building to see. I did not know it at the time, but winning that award made me the first woman to capture the WNBA's All-Star MVP, regular-season MVP, and playoff MVP trophies in the same season. It also put me in some very elite basketball company, with Willis Reed, Michael Jordan, and Shaq. They were the only players who had accomplished the MVP trifecta in a single NBA season.

I was really excited and happy for my team. I was also somewhat relieved, thinking, "Wow! We made it. It was so much fun!" The stands were jam-packed with Sparks fans, who were cheering, applauding, and celebrating. I spotted my family, which always sits in the exact same section each game. They were cheering and waving and egging me on. What a great feeling! I started working my way around the arena, smiling and giving the thumbs-up to our crowd. I was ecstatic. My heart was pounding, and I could not have wiped the smile off my face if I had wanted to. I really love our Sparks fans and their continued support. Those great people stuck with us when we were losing, cheered us to victory, and earned their right to celebrate.

I stepped up on the scorer's table and started throwing T-shirts to the fans. Wouldn't you know it? On one of the most incredible days of my life, I could barely throw a shirt more than a few feet. I guess they needed to be balled up tighter to be more aerodynamic so I could launch them to our enthusiastic fans that were way up in the stands, but these shirts did not travel well. They were loose and floppy, so even when I tossed one with all my might, the T-shirt would flutter to the floor about three feet away from me. How weak! I was so disappointed, and I am sure that the people in the upper levels of Staples Center were saying, "She may be the MVP, but she sucks at throwing shirts!"

Except for the throwing thing, I was having a terrific time, and the fans were having fun celebrating in the arena. I had security and PR people yelling at me. "Lisa, Lisa, come on. You gotta go. You gotta get out of here!"

I yelled back, "Give me more shirts for the fans!" I wanted every fan to get one, because I could not stop thinking about how much they had done to help and support us on our way to the title. I did not want to leave. The energy, electricity, and excitement in that building were absolutely amazing!

When they finally pulled me down from the table, I kept laughing and waving to the crowd as I jogged to the Sparks' locker room. I was the last player to get there, and when I walked inside, I saw black plastic covering our lockers. Then it hit me. *Oh God, champagne!* In my mind, I knew what a victorious locker room should look like. I had seen teams celebrating their championships, but it never registered in my mind that it was going to happen for the L.A. Sparks. I had never won a WNBA title before, and I did not know if the celebration would be the same for the women champions as it was for the men.

Before I knew it, a wall of teammates came at me. They were shaking bottles and squirting champagne in my face, my hair, everywhere. My eyes were burning. They messed me up so badly. I was rubbing my eyes, straining to see, and saying, "Give me a towel." Then I thought, *Hiding your face in a towel to avoid the spray of champagne? That's a wimpy thing to do in a champion's locker room.* The champagne was everywhere, though. It was dripping from my hair and down my face, and my uniform was completely soaked. I was so excited.

When I could finally see again, I grabbed a bottle of champagne, shook it, and started spraying my teammates. We were playing like little kids, and then this swarm of people stormed into the locker room. All we could see were lights. The masses of media were coming in to record our celebration. There were so many cameras, lights, microphones, and reporters. We just kept dancing around, jumping, laughing, and singing. Why shouldn't we? The Sparks had accomplished what we had set out to do way back in May, in training camp. Our 34–5 record was the best in the league. We went undefeated in the playoffs, and in our first season at Staples Center, we went 19–1 at home and brought our fans their first WNBA championship. It was an amazing season.

The Sparks had enjoyed good team chemistry throughout the 2001 season, but in that championship locker room, it was *great* team chemistry. We had so many different personalities and lifestyles on our squad, but we always respected each other. You could hug anybody. It did not matter. We had all worked together to achieve our goal, and that was a wonderful feeling. Our team started singing that song that goes, "It's over. It's over now. Sorry, we can't be stopped!" It was the perfect song for the Sparks because there had been so many doubters who did not believe that we could be champions.

The truth is, our 2001 team would not have been successful without the solid foundation that had been laid the year before. Our squad had great talent, which had finally blossomed in Coach Cooper's second season. We had learned how to win, and that had made our confidence grow. The team had found its personality, too, whether it was me counting three fingers every time I made a three-point shot, or Tamecka Dixon looking in the stands, putting her hand behind her ear, and letting the crowd know that she wanted more noise. We had really come into our own.

Toto always worked like a warrior for the Sparks, too. She brought us an attitude that we did not have before. Mwadi Mabika was our silent assassin from three-point range. DeLisha would slap me a hard high five before each game, which sent the message "Man, it is on!" to our opponents. I think all of that inspired us, brought us closer, and made us a better team. We stood there in that championship locker room, laughing, dancing, hugging, spraying champagne, and singing, "It's over. It's over now. Sorry, we can't be stopped!" For that moment, for that day, we were on top of the world. The L.A. Sparks were WNBA champions.

It would have been easy for me to kick back, enjoy the off-season, and savor success, but I knew it was going to be difficult for the Sparks to defend our title. So I spent a lot of the winter trying to make my game even better. I worked hard on my hook shot, my passing, and my ball-handling skills so I would have a more complete arsenal for the WNBA wars that I knew would be coming in the 2002 season.

It also would have been just as easy for the Sparks' front office to rest on its laurels and stand back during the off-season, but that was not the way that our general manager operated. Penny Toler had a keen eye for talent, and she was always looking for ways to improve the team. When draft day rolled around on April 19, 2002, Penny shocked a lot of people. She traded Ukari Figgs, who had been the starting point guard on our championship team, to the Portland Fire to get Nikki Teasley, a six-foot guard out of the University of North Carolina, who had been Portland's choice with the number five pick in the WNBA draft.

It was a gutsy move to trade a proven commodity for a rookie with potential, but the deal paid off immediately. Nikki T. moved right into our starting lineup, and the Sparks ran off to a 12–1 record to start the 2002 WNBA season. Coach Cooper called Nikki Lady Magic, because she reminded him of his former Lakers teammate Earvin "Magic" Johnson. That was high praise, but we could see early on that Nikki had great court awareness. She knew how to read each and every player on the floor. She also knew where they wanted the ball and when they should have it. On top of that, Nikki was a clutch three-point shooter.

I think there was a lot of pressure on Nikki, coming in as a rookie and being handed the reins of a veteran, championship squad. There was pressure on Coop and his assistant coaches, Karleen Thompson and Ryan Weisenberg, too. Once you win a championship, people expect you to keep winning. If you do not, the coach usually takes the heat. But Coop did a great job of keeping our team focused and loose. One of the things that I loved about him was the way that he gave us options as to how we would guard our opponents and handle different things on the court. We liked that because he made us feel like we were part of the process and not just pawns in it.

There was pressure on us as players for the upcoming season, too. Once a team tasted success, it either got hungrier or lazier. In 2002 the Sparks developed a serious appetite. We really wanted to defend our championship, and we had top-notch talent, playoff experience, and a will to win. All the ingredients were there, and when the league broke for the All-Star Weekend in mid-July, the Sparks owned a 15–3 record. Things were looking good.

That year's All-Star Game was played on a Monday night in Washington, D.C., and this time, the fans voted me onto the West's starting lineup. Houston's Sheryl Swoopes and Tina Thompson were alongside me, and our starting guards were Ticha Penicheiro from Sacramento and Sue Bird, the Seattle Storm rookie who had been the number one overall pick in the 2002 draft. I was happy to have my Sparks teammates Mwadi Mabika and Tamecka Dixon on the stellar squad as well.

The Eastern Conference All-Stars featured a front line of New York's Tari Phillips, Charlotte's Andrea Stinson, and Indiana's Tamika Catchings. The Liberty's Teresa Weatherspoon was in the backcourt for the East, along with my friend Dawn Staley, the point guard for Charlotte.

A lot of the media talk leading up to that All-Star Game had centered on a perceived "changing of the guard" in the WNBA. The thinking was that young players, like Sue Bird, Lauren Jackson, and Tamika Catchings, were ready to take the torch of league leadership from the "old-school" veterans, such as Sheryl, Tina, and myself, who had been there when the WNBA began back in 1997. I was already motivated to play, but when I heard that, I was really ready.

The game turned out to be the tightest one in the league's brief All-Star history. The West squeezed by the East by a score of 81–76, and I was fortunate enough to win my third All-Star MVP trophy. There had only been four WNBA All-Star Games, and this was probably the most physical of them all.

Once again, the fans and the media had been hoping to see a dunk in the All-Star Game, but it did not happen. The East played us really tough and did not give up many fast breaks. I was disappointed, too, but I made it clear at the postgame press conference that dunking was one of my goals and that I would be working hard to make it happen before the end of the 2002 season.

I had dunked in practice and in warm-ups when I was at Morningside High School and at USC. I had dunked in a summer league regulation game called the Say No Classic, and I had dunked in Sparks practices, but I had never dunked a basketball in a WNBA game. Nobody had. My trainer, Adam Friedman, told me that I should start thinking seriously about including dunking in a game as one of my goals. I wrote down, "Dunk in a WNBA game this season," as a goal that I really wanted to achieve.

Seven nights after the All-Star Game, I became the first WNBA player to reach three thousand career points, and eight nights after that, on July 30, I got a chance to achieve my goal. The Sparks were hosting the Miami Sol, and we were trailing 36–25 with 4:44 remaining in the first half. I was angry because we were playing terrible defense and losing to an expansion team. Miami had moved the ball around effectively, and they seemed to be making just about every shot that they put up, so when Betty Lennox launched a three-point shot, we were all a bit surprised to see the ball clang off of the iron and into the hands of my teammate Toto.

I just reacted and started sprinting down court, and Toto turned and tossed the ball. I was just barely across midcourt when I caught the pass. Lennox was chasing me, but there was nobody between me and the basket. I knew that I needed only two or three dribbles to get there. I was going for it. I was going to dunk! My steps were right, just as they were that rainy day at Morningside when high jump practice was moved into the gym and I dunked that tennis ball. On this night, I went up and I dunked it HARD! I was so happy that it was not some wimpy "I just barely pushed it in" kind of dunk. It was not like my fingernail just barely made it over the rim. There was no question about this one. It was a quality dunk. People were not sitting there, wondering, *Did she try to dunk?* They knew and I knew that I had clearly dunked the ball. The rim had snapped down and popped back. Everybody had seen it!

My reaction was pure amazement. I threw my hands up in the air and started running back down the court. I was thinking, *I did it!* Usually during a game, I was so focused that I did not hear much crowd reaction, but after I dunked, the noise was incredible. There was a collective "Ahhhhhhhhhhhhhhhhhh!" Everybody in the arena was up. They had seen a little piece of history, and I could hear them cheering. The fans were in shock. The Sparks were in shock, and so was the Miami Sol.

Betty Lennox was the closest one to me when I dunked it. She had the best view and was in all the photos. She later told me that she saw the dunk coming and knew she could not stop it, so she was going to grab my foot. The only thing that kept her from doing it was not wanting to get thrown out of the game.

Coach Cooper was jumping up and down when he saw the dunk. Coop had seen his share of great dunks during his days with the Lakers, but he was really excited to see me slam one down and make history.

Later, people walked up to me and told me they had watched my dunk on the highlights on ESPN. It was replayed over and over, and the next morning it was listed as one of the top ten moments in sports. It even made international front-page news. The accolades were wonderful but the terrible thing was that we lost the game 82–73, and to an expansion team at that.

The dunk brought with it a burning question: *When are you going to do it again?* The ball had barely dropped through the net, but I could not escape this question. People also speculated about what the dunk might mean for the future of women's basketball. Would there be more interest? Would there be more respect? Those questions were not easily answered. Even after the dunk, it seemed like women still had to do so much to feel validated on the court. And the dunk did little to quiet the talk about differences between men's and women's style of play. It is an ongoing battle.

Sometimes I hear people say great things about me, or about past legends, like Cheryl Miller and Ann Meyers. But in the general scheme of things, we still get overlooked. Maybe it just takes time. Maybe when the WNBA reaches its fiftieth year, our players will be treated like Bill Russell, Kareem, and the many elite players of the NBA.

I think as the WNBA matures as a league, more women will dunk, and that may bring more attention. We realize how appealing that is to fans of the sport. Maybe sometime soon we will be able to name ten players in the WNBA who can dunk and create that kind of excitement. We are not there yet, but that time is coming. Younger players, like Candace Parker, Sylvia Fowles, Mya Moore, Deanna Nolan, Margo Dydek, and Michelle Snow, are doing it. And hopefully, I can put down a few more before I retire. But I am happy to have been the first. Fans, in fact, voted my dunk as the "Greatest Milestone" in the WNBA's first decade. It is nice to go down in the history books.

It was difficult to pull away from all the hoopla that surrounded my dunk, but the Sparks still had games to play and a WNBA title to defend. The remainder of the season was just as tough as the previous one.

We opened the 2002 playoffs in Seattle, against Lauren Jackson, Sue Bird, and company. They had beaten us in our last two meetings, and they had been effective sending double, and triple, coverage at me. But not this time. The Sparks' playoff experience paid off, and our defense took hold. We swept Seattle in a two-out-of-three game series, and Lauren Jackson scored just four points in the second game.

The Utah Starzz were our next opponents, but we crushed them in a sweep and celebrated our return to the finals for the second time in as many years. And this time, it was a showdown: the L.A. Sparks vs. the New York Liberty. L.A. against New York was the championship matchup that people had been anticipating ever since the league tipped off in 1997. It had all the makings of a sensational series, because we were big-time rivals, and each team had a powerhouse lineup.

New York had been to the finals three times, and they had lost to the Houston Comets every time. They knew this was their chance finally to win it all. Teresa Weatherspoon was the leader of their team, and she gave New York a lot of energy and emotion. Coach Cooper would always tell us that a team can ride on emotion only for so long, and then winning comes down to talent and intelligence. As a team, we felt that we were smarter than New York, but we also knew that New York was extremely talented and very physical.

On the day of Game One, it was raining in Manhattan. When our bus pulled up to Madison Square Garden for the shootaround, security would not let it it drive in. I do not know if it was a legitimate safety precaution, gamesmanship, or the home team trying to take us out of our routine, but security made us get off of the bus outside in the rain, and we were not happy about it. Every other time that we had been to MSG, our bus had pulled right up to the loading dock that led us to the elevator and our locker room.

The door to our bus had been opened and closed several times as our driver tried to get clearance to drive into the building, so the bus steps got wet and slick from the rain. As our team began to unload, Tamecka Dixon stepped down, slipped, and fell to the pavement. She injured her ankle badly, and with the start of the WNBA finals just hours away, she was lying in pain outside of Madison Square Garden.

It was one of those things that did not have to happen. If we had been allowed to unload in the tunnel, the way that we always did, there would never have been a problem. This was a major blow. We knew we needed all of our big-time players to win in New York, but before the finals had even begun, we had lost a starter. Coach Cooper reminded us that the Sparks were so deep in talent that we had starters backing up starters. And he was right. Toto took Tamecka's place in the starting lineup, and the duel with the Liberty was back on.

I was matched up against Tari Phillips, a six-foot-one, two-hundred-pound center, who was in great shape and on top of her game. She was the most physical, and most active, post player that I had ever played against, and she probably played defense against me as well as any big player in the WNBA. I knew if I was going to be successful, I had to go at her and play my most physical game, and I could not complain about hard hits. I really had a lot of respect for Tari Phillips. She had quick hands and was adept at forcing steals, so I had to protect the basketball on my drives to the hoop. She was a big challenge for me, but I was mentally prepared, and it was time to roll up my sleeves, get in there, and match her intensity.

The score was tied at halftime, but the Sparks pulled away in the final minutes to win Game One. It was a total team effort and a huge win, because we beat the Liberty in their own house, and we did it without Tamecka.

The next two games were scheduled for Staples Center, and the Sparks knew that we needed only one win to earn our second straight championship, but we also knew that New York was not going to roll over. The Sparks really wanted to end the series with New York in Game Two. Coach Cooper had our squad well prepared, and our fans packed Staples Center in hopes of seeing us close it out and finish the season on top. The Sparks roared out to an early lead, but the Liberty chipped away and tied the score with just eighteen seconds on the clock.

Coop called a time-out, and he diagrammed a final play for

us. I think everybody in the arena assumed that the ball would come inside to me for the potential game-winning shot, because I had already scored seventeen points in the game and because the Sparks had enjoyed great success running that play for me all season long. The way it was designed, Nikki was supposed to dribble to the wing and pass the ball to me as I made my move to the basket, but New York was familiar with that play, too, and they were ready for it. We got the ball inbounds, and as Nikki worked her way to the wing, I moved to the block on the left side. Weatherspoon dropped down from her guard spot to double-team me, so there was no way to get the ball in my hands. The clock was winding down, I was completely covered, and our team was running out of options.

Nikki picked up her dribble and looked inside, but she could not find a way to get the ball to me. We were in trouble. The game clock was ticking down to the final seconds. The fans were on their feet and going crazy. The play that we wanted to run had busted, and Nikki knew that she had to make something happen in a hurry, so with 2.4 seconds left to play, she launched a three-point shot. The ball went up and seemed to hang in the air forever, but when it came down, that orange and oatmeal sphere swished right through the net. Staples Center went crazy, and when Teresa Weatherspoon missed a desperation shot at the buzzer, the game was over. The L.A. Sparks won the game 69–66, and we were back-to-back WNBA champions.

It was an awesome finish and a tremendous accomplishment for Nikki, our rookie, to help us win the title in such dramatic fashion. She never panicked under the pressure, and her heroics made our GM, Penny Toler, look like a genius for pulling off that draft day deal with Portland. It was amazing how things had fallen into place for us. We had worked our tails off to get our second straight title, and for the second consecutive year, I had been named MVP of the finals. Life was so good.

Chapter 13

Third Time's a Charm

I really believe that with true champions, the more you win and the more rings that you get, the more your desire grows to gain even more success. After finishing on top, anything less than a championship leaves you disappointed. I was now the proud winner of back-to-back WNBA championships and back-to-back WNBA playoff MVP awards, but I was not satisfied. Winning had become a habit that I really loved, and I did not want it to stop. So in September of 2002, I joined the USA Basketball squad for the world championships in China. The competition internationally was getting stronger every year, and I wanted to get in on the action.

Anne Donovan was our head coach this time, and the U.S. national team knocked off our first seven opponents by no less than thirty-four points per game. In the semifinals, we got an Olympic rematch with Australia, and we had a fantastic game. Our defense held Lauren Jackson to just nine points, and we went on to beat the Aussies and advanced to the gold-medal round against Russia.

We had steamrolled the Russians in our opening game of the championships, but they were better prepared the second time around, and the game stayed close. With less than ninety seconds to play, our lead was only three points, but in the final minute, I grabbed a rebound at one end of the court and scored a bucket at the other end. Sheryl Swoopes hit some big free throws, and our U.S. national team picked up a 79–74 victory and our seventh gold medal in World championship competition.

It seemed like our team was unbeatable, and I felt the same way. On the heels of two very successful WNBA seasons, I was playing well internationally, too. The U.S. team went undefeated in China, and I was named the tournament's most valuable player. In the process, I eclipsed the Team USA records for games played, points scored, and rebounds in world championship play. Things just kept going my way. Two months later, I was named the 2002 USA Basketball Female Athlete of the Year. It was my third time earning that honor.

The Christmas holiday season gave me a brief break to catch my breath, and then it was time to turn my thoughts to WNBA basketball once again. Going into the 2003 season, the L.A. Sparks were the two-time defending champs, and we definitely felt as though we had the makings of a dynasty. Every position was filled with strong players. Nikki was the best point guard in the league. Tamecka's jump shot was money. Mwadi could drive to the hoop and nail the three-point shot. DeLisha could play down low and step outside, and she could guard any player that our opponents put on the court. And Toto was tough and ornery; she enforced the concept that Staples Center was Sparks territory, and no opponent was allowed to come into our house and do as they pleased. If somebody was messing with me, Toto would say, "Smooth, don't worry. I got 'em!" And that would be the end of it.

Our squad was honest and open, and we shared a strong team bond. With Coach Cooper running the show, we felt really good about going into the 2003 WNBA season. We were a confident, winning unit; we never had to question our coach or his staff; and we never had to worry about our game plan, because Coop and his assistants, Karleen Thompson and Ryan Weisenberg, were the best at communicating and keeping us on top of our game. We always knew what we were supposed to do. That liberated us just to play.

But not everything worked out the way we had hoped it would. A few WNBA franchises went under. Then Toto, our big post player, who gave the team its swagger, was accused of sexual assault and was released by management. We were all shocked. The player who had been such a huge part of our championship success was no longer a part of our team. In our first game after Toto's dismissal, we stumbled to a one-point win, but her presence was missed on the court. (No charges were ever filed against Toto, and in 2006 her wrongful termination suit against the team was settled.)

At the All-Star Game, I was again happy to start for the Western Conference, but my teammate Lauren Jackson went up to block a shot by Swin Cash, and Swin fell on my right knee. I was down, and I was hurting badly. There was no way I could stand up. I cried, clutched my knee, and knew right away that something was very wrong. I had to be helped to the locker room. I worried that surgery would be necessary, and I wondered if my career was in jeopardy.

I was also going through a painful breakup with Todd, my boyfriend of five years and my second fiancé. I should have known something was not quite clicking when after he asked for my hand in marriage, I said, "I can handle that." But Todd was a really good guy. I just think I was at that stage where I thought I could really fix him up, change him, make him *better*. Todd was my "potential" guy. Over time I realized that you cannot change a guy into what you want him to be. He has to be that already. But it hurt to end that relationship, and it made it tougher to deal with a potentially career-ending injury.

An MRI showed that I had bruised the bone in my right knee. It was not as bad as it could have been, but it was the most serious injury I had ever had. I had to wear a brace and use crutches. As it turned out, I did not play again for almost a month. Not long after this, the Sparks took another direct hit: Rhonda Mapp became the first player dismissed from the WNBA for violating the league's antidrug policy. We were slowly losing the pieces of the puzzle that had previously made our team unstoppable. But somehow we made it to the playoffs again and to the Western Conference championships for the third straight year. Despite all of the difficult player adjustments, we were getting to defend our back-to-back titles.

The team that wanted to get between us and a three-peat was Detroit, the Eastern Conference champs, who were coached by NBA great Bill Laimbeer. Bill and Coach Cooper knew each other very well from their playing days in the NBA, and there was little love between the two. Coop's Lakers had beaten Laimbeer's Pistons to win the 1988 NBA championship, and the next year Detroit's "Bad Boys" had turned the tables to win the first of their back-to-back titles. Coop had been the WNBA's Coach of the Year in 2000. Laimbeer had won the award for his team's "worst to first" turnaround in 2003. They had a bit of a rivalry themselves. So we really wanted to win—for the three-peat and for Coach Cooper.

The Sparks hosted Game One of the WNBA finals at Staples Center, and things could not have gone much better for us or much worse for Detroit. We enjoyed a twenty-one point lead at intermission, the Shock missed fifty of their seventy shot attempts in the game, and we won by double digits.

Game Two was at the Palace in Auburn Hills, Michigan, and this time the Shock had everything going their way. They pulled out to a nineteen-point advantage and limited me to just two points before halftime. I did manage to score sixteen more in the second half, and the Sparks came all the way back to take the lead with slightly more than a minute to play. But Detroit pulled away from us in the final moments. The series was all tied up.

The Palace was packed for Game Three with a WNBA record crowd of more than twenty-two thousand fans. Derek Fisher from the Lakers made the long trip from L.A. to lend his support to the Sparks, and Detroit had a celebrity cheering section of its own. Pistons greats Joe Dumars and Vinnie "The Microwave" Johnson were courtside, and so was former welterweight champ Thomas "Hit Man" Hearns.

The key to the game was Ruth Riley at center. She had been a decent player in the WNBA, but Ruth played the game of her life against us in the championship game. Detroit led most of the way, but with twenty-four seconds left in the season, DeLisha dialed long distance with a jumper and put the Sparks in front by two. But that was the last time we were able to score. Detroit won its first WNBA championship against us, 82–80.

For the first time in three seasons, the Sparks were not the ones hoisting the trophy or tasting champagne, and I was not holding the league's playoff MVP award. Ruth Riley had it. But not one player on our team cried, because we knew that we had given it our all. It just was not our year. But that just made us hungrier; we knew we needed to retool and regroup before the 2004 season began. But there was a lot to think about before then. We were, after all, approaching an Olympic year.

I was a member of the U.S. national team, and we trained to compete, sometimes internationally, each spring. The WNBA season conveniently runs from May through the end of the summer. The timing is great, and I have not had much trouble playing for both organizations. In fact, the U.S. national team has been a great way for me to play quality basketball before the WNBA season gears up each year, and it is a nice boost before the Olympics, too.

In 2004, however, there was an overlap. The WNBA decided to shut down for the entire month of August so that its athletes could play in the Olympics and then pick up again when the Games were over. It made a lot of sense.

Before the WNBA went on hiatus, we got dramatic news: Michael Cooper had stepped down as head coach to take an assistant coaching position with the Denver Nuggets of the NBA. Coach Cooper had been such a huge part of the Sparks' success, and he had worked so well with me. Coop had turned down a few assistant coaching offers from NBA teams before in hopes of landing a head coaching job in the NBA, but when the Nuggets called, he obviously felt the time and the situation were right for him. Our team was devastated.

I cannot blame Coop for doing what he felt was best for himself, his family, and his career, but it was difficult to lose the man who had pulled the Sparks together and had taught us how to play like champions. Karleen Thompson and Ryan Weisenberg were promoted to co-head coaches, and all things considered, we played exceptionally well. I felt a nice momentum as I headed to my third Olympics.

The Olympic team gathered in New York, at Radio City Music Hall, to practice for two days and to square off against a team of WNBA All-Stars—the top players in the league who were not playing in the Olympics. This event gave the fans an All-Star Game, and the added bonus was that it was great training for the national team. After the All-Star Game, it was off to Europe for tune-up games against France and Spain, and then, finally, to Athens for the Games.

Greece was incredibly beautiful! During the opening ceremony at Athens Olympic Stadium, there were fireworks and music and dancing and a reflecting pool in the center of everything, which was ignited to form the five Olympic rings in a fire. The ceremony was filled with pageantry, a presentation of Greek culture, and a parade of floats. Thousands of Olympic athletes marched into the stadium in the parade of nations, and as usual, the countries were introduced in alphabetical order. The twist at the Athens Olympics was that the teams entered according to the Greek alphabet.

I was especially excited when all the U.S. athletes walked into the stadium because one of our smallest athletes was carrying the large American flag and leading our delegation. The U.S. Olympic teams' various event captains had voted five-foot-six-inch Dawn Staley to be our country's flag bearer. It was a tremendous honor for Dawn, who had announced that she would be retiring from international competition after the Games in Greece. I thought Dawn was the perfect choice to carry our flag. She was nervous and eager as the opening ceremony drew closer, and I made sure to tell her playfully, "Whatever you do, don't trip. You know how your knees knock sometimes." Of course, everything went off without a hitch, and I was so proud of her. Watching her was a reminder of how far she and I had both come since those days with the junior national team.

The women's and men's Dream Teams stayed on the Queen Mary 2 during the Olympics. The ship was docked in the Athens harbor, and with the world still reeling over the 9/11 attacks, global terrorism, and the bombing at the Atlanta Games, I have to admit, I felt a lot safer living on the cruise ship. It was a great place for our athletes to get together and party, too. There was a great club on board called G-32. We had some fun times there, and WNBA standout Diana Taurasi still jokes when she sees me, "I'll meet you at G-32."

The U.S. athletes all ate in the same area on the ship, so that gave us opportunities to sit down, talk, and get to know each other. That is where I met Dwyane Wade, the point guard for the Miami Heat. I talked a lot with him, and I also spent some time with LeBron James and Lamar Odom. Lamar had just been traded from Miami to the Lakers in the Shaquille O'Neal deal, so it was exciting to talk with him, because we were sure to be seeing a lot of each other back in Los Angeles. I met a lot of interesting people on the Queen Mary 2, and because we were on a ship and could not go out very much, we developed a camaraderie that was very special.

That made it all the more odd that this Team USA had a different chemistry than the squads at the two previous Olympics. As each year passed, there was less and less certainty that we would win the gold. Maybe it was because the players were changing. Things had obviously changed for me. In 1996 Dawn and I were the youngsters joining a veteran group of players that had already tasted international competition and was on track to win Olympic gold. In 2004 we were the veteran players who had two gold medals under our belts. We knew what we could do, but we had some questions about the experience level and dedication of the younger players who joined us. I guess, at the end of the day, we were not sure just how good Team USA was going to be, though we knew our team was incredibly talented. Tamika Catchings started every game for us in the summer games, and Diana Taurasi, Sue Bird, and Swin Cash came in and really played well. Dawn did a great job of being the veteran leader who kept us all focused and together as a team. But I would be lying if I said there were no lingering doubts. In the meantime, I wanted to enjoy the Games and the experience.

One of the best things about the Olympics in Greece was the atmosphere. The entire time that we were there, things were peaceful, calm, and close to perfect. Everybody had talked about how terrible the traffic was going to be and how congested the city might be, but neither was a problem. Getting around was fairly easy, and our team buses could pull right up to where the Queen Mary 2 was docked. All we had to do was hop on board and drive off to our practice sessions or games. There were not many hassles at all. Apparently, a lot of people stayed away from Athens out of fear that there might be a terrorist incident. I know that several American athletes pulled out of the Olympics because they did not want to put themselves in harm's way. They did not think it was worth the risk, and you cannot really blame them for making a personal choice like that. It was just a shame that terrorism had made fear a part of the Olympic experience.

I tend to believe that wherever the Olympics are held is probably the safest place in the world to be for those few weeks. I know I felt safe in Athens because we had the U.S. Navy, Air Force, and Marines protecting us. They were in the waters off of Greece the entire time, and we could feel their presence when we were on the Queen Mary 2. U.S. jets would occasionally fly over to assure everybody that we were protected. So that gave me the peace of mind to enjoy myself.

One of my funniest experiences happened on an off day in Athens, at the spa on the ship. My cousin Braquel was with me on the trip, so we decided to go relax in the spa, just as we had done many times at spas in California. We went into Canyon Ranch, got completely undressed, hung our clothes in a locker, and put on a robe so that we could hang out by the pool, get in the sauna, then have a massage, just the way we did in the good old USA. When Braquel and I came out of the locker room, our first stop was the pool. We started swimming around, and there was a large spout that was pouring water back into the pool. It was like a faucet, but it was really ornate and grand. With my height, I could stand in the pool, reach over my head, and hang off of the spout. Once I got my hands around it, I yelled, "Look, Braquel," and then I pulled my legs up and fell back into the water before surfacing again.

My cousin was laughing, but she warned me, "Girl, you better stay off that faucet before somebody catches you." I told her, "Okay," and went back to playing in the water. But when we looked up, there was a man walking by the pool. He did not see us, but we definitely saw him. I glanced at the man, and then I looked at Braquel. We were both like, "A guy just walked by! Wait a minute. We are naked. That was a guy. Was that a guy?"

All of a sudden, it dawned on us that the pool was coed. Nobody had ever said anything. There weren't any signs, but we came to find out that not only was the spa coed, but we were supposed to be wearing swimsuits. We were there just falling out. It was so embarrassing.

We needed to get to our robes pronto, but they were all the way across the pool. One of us was going to have to get out of the water to retrieve them, so I told Braquel, "You go get the robes," but she wanted me to go. Eventually, my cousin got out of the water very quickly and picked up our robes and towels. She brought mine over to me, and we put them on and walked toward the steam room. I could not believe that I had been hanging off of a giant waterspout, buck naked, in a coed facility. In hindsight, we probably should have figured that since we were on a ship, bathing suits would have been a good idea. But we were in Europe, and we just were not thinking.

Then mild paranoia crept in. We asked each other, "Do you think there are cameras in there?" From then on, whenever we ran into people, we would ask, "Are there cameras in the spa?" One person told us that there were cameras in one area only. "Do they have them by the pool?" we asked. Mercifully, the answer was no. All I could think about was someone sitting back, with feet up, watching my cousin and me on a television monitor while we frolicked in the pool.

So by the time we got to the steam room, my mind was a thousand miles away. You can imagine my surprise when I pulled the door open and saw Greg Popovich, the U.S. men's basketball coach, there with his assistant coaches. Apparently, they did not know that the spa was coed, either! When Braquel and I walked in, they looked up with surprise, reached to cover up quickly, averted their eyes, and managed to mumble, "Oh! Ladies." Everyone was in a slight state of shock and embarrassment. Coach Popovich turned a bright red. Obviously, he and his assistants thought that the steam room was for men only. All of the guys tucked their towels around their waists and walked out.

When we saw Coach Popovich a few days later, he told us, "I am so sorry. We did not mean to be rude when we rushed out of the sauna that day. We did not realize that the place was coed." I knew exactly how he felt, so I let him off the hook and told him the story of our pool experience. We all got a good laugh out of it, and now, whenever I see Greg Popovich or his coaches, I always say hi, but I cannot help but smile inside just a bit.

Going into the early games in the Athens Olympics, I was very relaxed. Van Chancellor was the head coach of our women's team again, and he and his staff did a great job of getting us prepared for the Olympics in a short amount of time. Honestly, we did not face a whole lot of competition in the early rounds. We beat New Zealand by fifty-two points in our opener and then reeled off six straight victories before getting a test from Russia in the semifinals. We survived with a four-point win, which put us back in the gold-medal game to face Australia again.

Both Australia and Team USA entered the gold-medal match undefeated, and more than ten thousand fans filled OAKA, also known as the Olympic Indoor Hall. This was a rematch of the gold-medal game that Team USA had won in Sydney in 2000. Lauren Jackson and Penny Taylor were, once again, Australia's mainstays, and they got plenty of help from WNBA players Kristi Harrower, Rachel Sporn, and Suzy Batkovic. It was going to be a fantastic game.

Coach Chancellor asked me to guard Lauren, and that was fine with me. She had been talking a lot about how Australia wanted to face the United States in the gold-medal game, and here was her opportunity. Now, she had to deal with *me*. My job was to get in her face, contest her shots, and get her out of her comfort zone. As the game got going, though, neither of us seemed very comfortable, and neither of us seemed to be on top of our game. I was making some baskets, and Lauren was scoring at her end of the floor, but we were both missing shots, too.

The game went back and forth, and Team USA had the lead at halftime, but then Penny Taylor heated up, and the Aussies moved on top in the third quarter. That was when Dawn stepped up for us. Every time we got in a jam in that game, Dawn did something to get us out of it. She scored five points in a flash, and the United States was back on top. Dawn huddled us at the free throw line and said, "Tina has the mismatch, and that's where we are going to get the ball." Dawn sent Tina down on the block and got her scoring so well inside that she led our squad in scoring.

Dawn was our smallest player, but she had the biggest heart, and she was a great leader. She took control of that gold-medal game when she started penetrating and going to the basket, and her energy spread throughout our team. Tina hit some buckets, and I scored some points toward the end, but there was no question in my mind that Dawn was the one keeping us in the game. She hit four free throws and scored on a driving layup in the final two minutes. Appropriately, she had the ball in her hands when time expired on the game clock. We beat Australia 74–63, and that gave the U.S. women's basketball program its third straight Olympic gold medal and its twenty-fifth consecutive win in Olympic competition. We danced and cheered and waved the Stars and Stripes, and there were a lot of hugs and smiles when we received our gold medals. It was a great way for Dawn to end her Olympic career.

I led our Olympic squad in scoring in the Athens Olympics, and when the Games were over, I had become Team USA's all-time leading scorer, rebounder, and shot blocker. I was feeling good, playing well, and having fun, so I did not see any reason not to look ahead to playing in the 2008 Summer Olympics in Beijing, China. The only problem was that I could not imagine what it would be like to suit up for international competition without Dawn Staley. I have so much respect for her. She is all about the *team*, and that is just the kind of attitude needed to win. Our Olympic squad won the gold-medal game in Athens because we were unselfish, had balanced scoring, played team defense, and got contributions from several players. That is the only way to do it. But if there is one quality I see fading from USA Basketball, it is the concept of teamwork.

The individual, "me first" approach just does not work. It is one of the reasons the U.S. men's national team has difficulty when they play internationally. They settled for the bronze medal in Athens after finishing sixth in the 2002 world championships. In both cases, they were defeated by squads that had less individual talent but better team skills. The same fate could easily be in store for our U.S. women's side if we don't get smart in a hurry.

But for the moment, the women's game is pretty phenomenal and wildly successful. We have achieved amazing success internationally, and the WNBA as a league is doing well. And yet the recognition that women's basketball gets in our country is virtually nonexistent. We keep winning gold medals, but it does not seem to matter. Nobody seems to pay attention, and that is really hard for me to digest. The only time I feel certain that we will make big news is if we lose a gold-medal match. Then all the cameras and microphones are pointed at the players, with reporters asking, "What happened?" while sports and news programs show highlights of our shocking loss. But for now, the women's game is much more team oriented than the men's. And I think that has been a big part of our success so far.

As I look ahead to 2008, I hope that I can help our young Olympians understand how important it is to keep putting self second. There is nothing wrong with averaging six points per game in the Olympics if your team wins gold. It is not okay to average thirty points individually while you watch your team lose. That is not to say that individual goals should not be sought after and recognized. I understand the desire to put up the highest numbers, but it cannot come at the expense of the team. Winning as a team is what is most important, and the U.S. basketball teams might lose our edge in this area if we don't shape up.

With the 2004 Olympics over—and with another gold medal for the women's team—it was time to get back to the second half of the WNBA season. The Sparks were still adjusting to life without Coach Cooper, but our new head coaches, Karleen Thompson and Ryan Weisenberg, were doing their best to keep the team on track.

Karleen had gone from being my teammate at USC to working for the Sparks as our equipment manager. She was the one who did all the dirty work and washed all the team's laundry, but she was around basketball, and she worked hard while raising two great kids. She was eventually signed on to be one of Coop's assistants. That was the same year that Ryan joined the staff, and his story was just as unbelievable. He had gone from high school coach to video coordinator for the Lakers to Sparks assistant coach, and now, he and Karleen were the two-headed coaching partnership that would guide the L.A. Sparks through the rest of the 2004 season.

It was such a tough year. Emotionally, the team was spent. We lost Coop. And the Olympics had drawn out the season, so we were tired. But the good early run we had before the Olympics continued, and we finished with the best record in the WNBA and were the top seed in the Western Conference. I was so proud of Karleen and Ryan, because they worked their butts off coaching us and did everything within their power to make sure that we did not miss a beat after Coop left.

Round One of the playoffs pitted us against our old friends, the Sacramento Monarchs. The first game of that series was in Sacramento, and again, the fans were as loud and raucous as ever. The Monarchs really came ready to play and blasted into us. We lost by twenty points. Though the Sparks came back to salvage a win in Game Two at Staples Center, Sacramento stuck it to us in Game Three. It was so frustrating and disappointing. It hurt to have the Monarchs move us out in the very first round of the playoffs, but what was worse was letting them do it in our own building and then watching them celebrate on our home floor. That was totally unacceptable. The loss was difficult to accept, but we had no excuses. The only thing we could do was find a way to regain our home-court advantage for the next season.

Chapter 14

Michael, Maui, and Marriage

Basketball had been a big part of my life for a long time, but do not get the wrong idea; I always had other things going on, too. In 1997 I got my bachelor's degree in communications from USC, and five years later, I decided to go after my master's of business administration (MBA) at the University of Phoenix.

By the end of the 2004 WNBA season, I had not been in a romantic relationship in close to three years. I had dated Marcus in college and Todd afterwards, but then it became important to me to focus on just myself for a little while. For a long time, I was a serial monogamist. I had not given myself enough time in between relationships to grow and recognize what I really wanted and needed; I had not given myself time to see what God wanted for me. I knew that I needed to enforce my values and standards to get what I really wanted, yet I kept acting on impulse. So I stopped. In the past, I had compromised too much on the wrong things. I had tried to keep myself grounded by not making it a prerequisite that a man had to be as successful as me. I had not wanted to be overly picky, but on some issues, you need to be. Going back to school to get my MBA turned out to be one of the best decisions I ever made.

I was hoping to learn how to better manage and invest my earnings. I wanted to understand how to prepare a business plan and do the proper research prior to investing. And most importantly, I wanted to learn how to be my own boss. The University of Phoenix has a Gardena campus, and I went to classes there every Monday night, even during the Sparks' season. In a little more than two years, I graduated with a 4.0 grade point average. I had achieved another one of my goals, and I was chosen to be the keynote speaker for our graduation ceremony, which, coincidentally, was held at the Forum in Inglewood. Wasn't it interesting that after so many years, my life path would lead me back to Inglewood and back to that building, which held so many great memories for me?

Learning at the University of Phoenix was a great experience for me, and being single made it easy to focus. I did not know it then, but that focus was about to shift in another direction. I guess it is true that sometimes the best things do happen to you when you are not looking for them.

Every year I go to Alabama to spend Thanksgiving with Braquel's father, my Uncle Craig and his new wife, my Aunt Melba. As usual, I had a great time with them in November of 2004, but the time went by too quickly. Before I knew it, Braquel and I were at the airport, getting ready to fly back to Los Angeles. While we were in the main terminal, I noticed a pilot nearby. He was about five foot ten, had a dark complexion, and was wearing brown slacks. I kept telling Braquel, "Hey! There you go. There's a guy for you."

My cousin was single at the time, but she summed up her feelings on the matter with her favorite one-word answer: whatever.

It was very early in the morning, around 6:30 AM or so. I said,

"That's okay. Don't worry about it. He's got a wedding ring on, anyway."

I figured that was the end of that, so we went through the security check and then found some seats near our departure gate. I went over to the counter and asked the lady what time our plane would be taking off, and she told me it was going to be a little bit late. As I turned to walk away, that pilot I had noticed before came up to me and said, "Excuse me. You're Lisa Leslie, right?"

I told him that I was.

"Oh, cool!" he replied. "My wife and I are really big fans of yours. My wife's name is Lisa, and she played basketball in California, too."

He told me his wife's name, but unfortunately, I did not recognize it. I just smiled and tried to be friendly.

"Wow! You are so shy!" he said.

"Not really," I said. "I'm just answering your questions."

What he said next really shocked me. "I've got a really good friend. You guys would make a great couple. Are you married? Do you have a boyfriend?"

Even today I cannot tell you why I answered this complete stranger's questions about my personal life. But I did; I answered no to both questions.

"You should give him a call. He's a good brother. He's tall, like six foot six. He works out, and he enjoys outdoor sports, like boating and skiing."

"Nah, I really don't think I want to do that," I replied.

This guy was persistent, though. "Why don't you give me your number, and I'll have him call you?"

I was still pretty leery. After all, I had just met this man, and here he was, in the middle of the airport, asking for my phone number. I looked for Braquel, who was still sitting on the other side of the gate area, not paying the conversation any attention. I knew the right thing to say, and I said it. "No, I don't think so."

"Then why don't I give you his number, and you can call him?"

"No. I probably wouldn't call him. I don't make it a habit to call men. Besides, everyone always tells me that they know a guy who is really tall, and then I find out later that he is maybe six foot two, while I'm a full six foot five."

"No. I am positive. He is at least six foot six. He's taller than you, and he is a really good guy."

I do not know if I was intrigued or just trying to get rid of this man. But I still cannot believe what came next. I swallowed hard and said, "How about if you give him my number?"

No kidding, I gave my phone number to this absolute stranger. I guess I figured that he would give it to his friend and that would be the end of it.

So I flew back to L.A., and about three days later, the pilot's friend called me and left a message on my answering machine. "Hi. This is Michael. My friend Rod told me to give you a call. Give me a call back when you get a chance. I look forward to talking with you."

I was at my mom's house, and I said, "Mom. Mom. Listen. This guy called me."

My mom listened to the message. "Call him back!" she said right away.

I did not call him back. But the next day, Michael called again from his home in Miami. I saw his ID on the phone but did not answer. He left me another message. "Girl! I've called you twice now. You better give me a call back! No. I'm just kidding. I hope you have a good day. Call me when you get a chance."

I let my mom listen to that message, too, and again, she told me to call him. I still was not swayed.

On the third day, Michael called me and left another message. "Look, girl. Don't make me come out there and get you. You better give a brother a call back." He seemed really down-to-earth, and even through the answering machine, he made me laugh. I let my mom listen to this message, too, and she said, "Lisa, this is not right. You should really call him back."

I did finally call Michael back, and we talked on the phone for about three hours. By the time the day was done, we had been chatting on the telephone together for close to eight hours. No joke. Those were my first conversations with Michael Lockwood, and I think the beautiful thing about our talks was that we were just being ourselves. There was no façade, no trying to be something that we were not. We were just keeping it real.

Michael told me about himself, and I told him about myself. We talked about what we liked and disliked, and the main thing that we seemed to have in common was that we were both a little old-fashioned in our thinking, kind of old school. You know, "the man works and the woman stays home" kind of people. It is not easy to make that concept a reality, however, when both people in the relationship have very nontraditional jobs, the way that we do.

Michael works as a pilot for UPS. He captains a 767 aircraft and flies all over the world. Years ago he played basketball at the Air Force Academy, and he later flew jets in the Middle East as part of Operation Desert Storm. He delivered Patriot missiles to Israel when that country was the target of Scud missile attacks from Iraq, and in 1993 Michael piloted the C-5 Galaxy cargo plane that flew into Somalia, under fire, and flew out with the bodies of the U.S. Marines who had been killed when their helicopter was downed by enemy fire. That scenario was the basis for the Hollywood film *Black Hawk Down*.

After that first conversation, Michael Lockwood and I talked every single day. I am not a real phone person, but I could talk to him for hours. He kept calling, and we kept talking. Michael would say, "I have never been on the phone this much with anybody in my life." I was the same way. It was just amazing how strong our chemistry was from day one. After a few weeks of cross-country long distance, he finally asked me out on a date. Michael called on a Friday and asked, "What are you doing tomorrow?"

I told him that I had no real plans, just probably a massage or something like that.

"Would you like to go out?" he asked.

"Sure, but you're in Florida."

"Hey, hey, hey, I'm a pilot. I will be there tomorrow."

So, Michael flew to California and checked into the Sheraton Hotel near LAX. He was going to rent a car, but I told him that would not be necessary. I wanted to pick him up. As I drove up to the hotel, I kept looking in my rearview mirror to see if I could spot him, but before I could, my phone rang. It was Michael. I told him that I had arrived, and he said, "I have too. You better get out of your car and give a brother a hug." His voice was so nice, but he said so many things that sounded country to me. It was kind of cute.

Before I got off the phone and out of the car, I caught a glance of Michael standing there, and when I looked at his face for the very first time, I said to myself, *That is my husband.*

He came over to me, and I hugged him like he had asked me to on the phone. I noticed right away that Michael had this incredible smile and pretty white teeth. His dark skin looked so beautiful. He had big dark eyes and dark hair, and I loved his long eyelashes. He was very handsome and clean-cut. I was already interested in the man that I knew Michael to be from our phone conversations, and seeing him in person made him even more intriguing to me. I was impressed with his style, his smell, his stature, and those big, broad shoulders. I just loved the way he carried himself, like a real man. Michael Lockwood seemed just right for me.

When we got in my car, he just stared at me. I could be a little shy at times, and I could not help smiling. Michael said,

"Girl, you better say something to me." He was playing with me. I asked him if he was going to stare at me the whole time, and he told me, "Yes! You are beautiful!"

We drove to my house, and I fixed breakfast for him: biscuits, sausage, eggs, and home fries. Michael came in and sat down. He was impressed. "Wow! You cook too?"

"Yeah, I like to cook," I said. We had breakfast, and everything went really well.

After breakfast, we went to the Westfield Mall near my house. In one of our phone conversations, Michael had talked about how difficult it was for him, at six foot six, to find tall clothes that fit. I told him that I knew a great place where a lot of the NBA players got their clothes, so we went to the mall, and I picked out several different outfits for him to try on. It was fun. Michael went into the dressing room, and I stayed nearby in case he needed anything. One of the advantages of being so tall was that I could see right over the top of the dressing-room door and into the mirror. I was kind of peeking at him and thinking, *Oh wow. He's got nice legs and nice arms.*

Then Michael would come out wearing a shirt and some nice slacks. I could really see his physique. He had a great body, and that was a big plus! An intelligent man with a really nice body. What woman wouldn't like that?

Michael tried on several outfits, and he looked so cute in his XXL-tall Sean John jeans and shirts. He was excited. "I can't believe these shirts are long enough," he would tell me. "I've never had clothes that were really long enough for me after one wash unless they were custom made."

Somehow, fittingly, we shared our very first kiss in that Big & Tall shop. It was kind of cute, because I went up to the dressing-room door again, and I was looking at something that Michael was trying on. He asked me what I was thinking, and I told him, "I like it."

He said, "What? The pants or me?"

I told him, "Both!"

I do not really remember the moments that led up to the kiss. I know it was just a peck, but we had our first kiss that day at the Westfield Mall. Michael must have bought three or four pairs of pants and shirts that day. It was kind of cool, because he was really happy, and I was, too.

We went from the mall to the beach, where the weather was perfect. It might have been the most beautiful December day in the history of Southern California. The temperature was about eighty-five degrees, and it was absolutely gorgeous! There was even a nice breeze, and the sky was cloudless. Michael commented on the beautiful Southern California weather, and we sat on the beach, dug our feet in the sand, watched the ocean, and talked. The setting was really pleasant, and our conversation was, too. I remember looking at him and thinking, *Mmmm. He has really nice teeth. His skin is really beautiful, and he has great legs.* I was trying to see his toes, but he had them buried in the sand.

It was an excellent day. Michael was a true gentleman and very kind. I was really feeling him, and I was comfortable talking with him. It started to get a little cool at the beach, so Michael helped me up, and I drove him back to his hotel. He wanted to take a shower and change into some different clothes before dinner, so while he was in the shower, I decided to write him a letter on the hotel stationery. I wrote about what a perfect day it had been and how great it was to finally meet him. I told Michael that it was God's plan for us to meet and that I was so thankful that we had gotten some quality time together. I left the letter on the bed.

Michael came out after taking a shower, and my eyes immediately went to the ugly, washed-out black jeans he had put on. I cannot stand black jeans that are washed out! But now I knew why he had really needed some new clothes. (Sorry, babe, but it was true.)

We had a nice, romantic dinner at a jazz restaurant named Vibrato, and then we fed each other strawberries and whipped cream. Afterwards, I drove Michael back to his hotel, and our first official date was over.

Shortly after that, we had our second date, when Michael flew out to see me in Lake Tahoe. That was pretty cool. My family and I had gone there right after Christmas to bring in the New Year. Michael stayed for three days. He played games with us and did some snowboarding. We had a really, really good time just hanging out. It was huge for him to meet my family, but I was already sure about him, and I think he became sure about me. The way that Michael describes it, though, he was sure about me a long time before Tahoe . . . but I will let him explain.

Michael's Version:

Okay. Let's start at the beginning, when my friend Rod gave me Lisa's telephone number. I already knew that she was a basketball player, but I will never forget telling him, "Man, I don't know. Those girls can be kind of rough." I was not so sure that this was a good idea.

He said, "No, trust me. You really want to meet her. She is feminine. She is nice and really, really sweet."

I was a little nervous, but I figured, You know what, let me get on the computer and Google this girl. *A ton of pictures and articles came up, so I started clicking through all the material.* She is really pretty, *I thought to myself. But pictures, of course, can't let you know who a person is.*

After three weeks of talking on the phone with Lisa, we finally made a date to meet in Los Angeles. As I was flying from Miami to L.A., I thought, This girl is awesome. She is so sweet and nice. We have the same perspective on life. I have got to see her. I have got to be able to put all these pieces together.

I knew she was smart, tall, and athletic, but I needed to know if she was FINE. I needed to know what she was working with. God is my witness, I was in the airplane, and I said, "God, just let her have a little bit of booty, too." I knew that if she had just a little bit, I would be done. It would be all over!

When I got to Los Angeles, she came to pick me up at the Sheraton Hotel. I still wasn't sure. I thought, I wonder if she is going to get out of the car? I hope so, because I just have to see what she has going on.

Lisa ended up getting out of the car and walking toward me. I was walking toward her. She was smiling, and I was smiling. I said, "Come on. Gimme a hug." She was still facing me, though, so I could not see what I really wanted to see. I was trying to be tactful, trying to steal little peeks over her shoulder, but it just did not work.

We got in her car and started talking, but she seemed very shy. When we got to her house and went inside, I decided I would eventually get this figured out. Lisa had already made breakfast for me. She said, "Go ahead and take a seat. I have got most of the breakfast cooked already. I just need to warm it up."

I was just thrilled. I thought, A woman like that and she cooks, too! *I was sitting at the bar. Lisa was looking at me, and then she turned around to the sink. I finally got the view that I had been waiting for. I got my look and said to myself,* YES! YES! YES! It is over, Michael Lockwood. She has got it all, and you are done! *Let's face it; a man has to have a visual. A woman might be the greatest in the world, but she still has to have something going on. That is my story, and I am sticking to it.*

* * *

After that Christmas visit, Michael and I tried to be together every day that we possibly could. We both traveled so much, but we talked to each other on the phone all the time. That was where our relationship had started, and it never got dull. Sometimes, we just checked in with each other, compared our schedules, and prayed for each other. We enjoyed talking to each other, and we enjoyed each other's company. Michael told me about his two teenage daughters, Mikaela and Gabrielle. He loves them so much, and I think they are wonderful. I have always loved kids. Michael and I have so many things in common, but we also have enough things not in common to keep life truly interesting.

Michael loves to travel and go. He is very social, very outgoing. I am more of an introvert. I guess opposites do attract, because he will talk to women, men, boys, girls, and anybody who will listen. That is cool, but it is definitely not me. I think the one thing that we agreed on right away is that relationships are not about trying to change people into what you want them to be. The motto "You be you and let me be me" works for us. We are totally compatible.

I had always found dating to be difficult because it was so hard to find a man that I could follow, someone who trusted in the Lord and stood for something. He did not have to make a ton of money, but he did need to have morals and values. Michael has so much integrity, and he is a man of his word. When he knows something, he speaks on it. When he does not know, he says, "Babe, I have no idea." I like that.

Michael and I are both Christians, and we love the Lord together. Michael is also always caring and considerate, and that is very important to me. From the very beginning, he wanted to take care of me. I had never had that before, and I found it to be very sweet.

We lived in different places, but we made time for each other. I remember working as a commentator for ESPN's women's college basketball Final Four coverage in Indianapolis and him flying in to surprise me. Unbeknownst to me, he had talked with my boss about proposing to me on live television, during the game on ESPN. That idea got shot down, but during halftime, he delivered a little basket with a honey bun to me. Apparently, everybody thought that I had expected an engagement ring to be in the basket, but that thought had never crossed my mind. I was happy about the honey bun.

After the game, Michael walked me from the television studio to my hotel room. When we got to the room, the lights were off, but there were candles glowing.

"What's going on here?" I asked. I still had no clue.

There were lots of chocolate Hershey's Kisses on the bed. They were in the shape of a heart that spelled "I love you!"

I looked at Michael and said, "Oh, babe! Thank you so much!" I was really impressed by what he had done, but I was also exhausted, and I was losing my voice. I had worked a lot during the Final Four weekend. "Thank you so much! This is so sweet!" I added.

Then I noticed that there was champagne on ice. "Whew! You went all out, didn't you?" I said. I was excited, but I was really tired.

"Come here, babe," Michael said. He was going to kiss me.

I still had on the heavy make-up that I had worn for the television broadcast and needed to get it off. I said, "Please, babe. Just let me go wash my face. At least let me take this lipstick off." I wiped off the lip gloss and leaned over to Michael for our kiss.

"I just wanted to tell you that I asked God and I asked your mom and now I am asking you . . ."

He started getting down on one knee, and then it finally hit me. I gasped loudly and could not speak.

"I was wondering if you would marry me?"

"YES!!!! OF COURSE!!" I couldn't say yes fast enough.

I was really excited. I never had any doubt, any second thoughts, none of that. I did not even cry. You know how you always wonder what you might do if somebody proposes? Well, I had been proposed to twice before, but neither of those compared to what Michael had done. This was the real deal. It was just awesome. We were officially engaged to be married.

With the previous proposals I had received, I always knew in my heart that that man was not the one God had sent for me. But when Michael asked me, I knew at that moment that he was it, and I heard my heart say yes.

Now there were wedding plans to make, but there was also a WNBA season coming up soon. During the off-season, the Sparks had hired Henry Bibby, the former NBA player and USC men's basketball coach, to be our new head coach for the 2005 season. Penny Toler had also pulled off a blockbuster trade that sent DeLisha "D" Milton and a first-round pick to Washington in exchange for Chamique Holdsclaw, who had been the WNBA's overall number one pick in the 1999 draft.

I was shocked. D and I had been so close, and she had been a tremendous contributor to the Sparks' success. There had been rumblings, though, that some of our players were unhappy and wanted bigger roles on the team. There had been a lot of complaints, and some of my teammates had taken those complaints to Penny. I know that one of those players was D, but I will never understand why she got traded. No offense to Chamique, but D is the type of player that I would take into battle any time, any day. I was never really sure if she asked to be traded or if Penny had just had enough of her, but the Sparks lost a lot when D went to Washington.

Chamique Holdsclaw came to us with great credentials. She had won three NCAA championships under Pat Summitt at the University of Tennessee. She had been the WNBA's rookie of the year in 1999, she had led the league in scoring in 2002, and she had been a three-time All-Star with the Mystics. The media wanted to know if the Sparks would have enough basketballs to keep Chamique and me satisfied, but that was never a problem. We played well together.

The problem was that the Sparks did not play well together under Coach Bibby. In 1996 USC had hired him to coach their men's team and to bring some discipline to the program. His squads posted two twenty-four-win seasons at the start of the new millennium, but they followed that with two sub-.500 seasons. Only four games into the Trojans' 2004–05 season, Coach Bibby got fired, reportedly because several of his players complained that he had brought too much discipline to the program.

The situation was similar when Coach Bibby took over as Sparks head coach. We were a team in need of direction. Coach Bibby was a hard man to read, though, and I think some people questioned if he was in the WNBA for the right reasons or just there to get some exposure that might lead to another college coaching job or a job in the NBA. Obviously, we all wanted to win, but when you had major changes like the Sparks had, everything was going to be different because everything was new. We knew we had talent on our squad. Coach Bibby had the task of molding our individual skills into team talent in a very short period of time.

With D gone and a new coach in place, the highly touted team chemistry of the Sparks took a major hit. We needed time to develop team unity, but time was a luxury that the Sparks did not have in 2005, and that intangible bond never seemed to materialize. On top of that, I started the season with a strained groin. It was a nagging injury that affected my ability to jump more than anything else. I got all kinds of treatments for it, and the injury improved, but rest was the only way to get back to 100 percent, and I did not have time for that. We had games to play, so I just fought through it and kept working hard.

Chamique and I were fortunate to make the Western Conference All-Star team as reserves. We were both putting up decent numbers, but I was hobbling, and our team was only 9–7 when the WNBA broke for its All-Star Game. We had seven losses at the break! That was only two fewer defeats than the Sparks had in the entire 2004 season.

That All-Star Game, I got a clear path to the basket and dunked the ball. The fans and the media had finally got the All-Star dunk that they had been waiting for. It was nice to get the first one, but it was not nearly as dramatic or exciting as my dunk against the Miami Sol back in 2002. It did give the fans something to talk about, though.

But there were lots of other things to talk about, too. The Sparks were losing under Coach Bibby, and his assistant coach, Joe "Jellybean" Bryant (Kobe's dad), was chosen to guide our team through the rest of the season. Another coach fired and another coach hired. I remember crying that night in the locker room, because I was so upset. Our players and coaches thought that I was mad because Coach Bibby was gone, but it was not about him at all. I was sad that my career was being wasted and that the Sparks kept getting further and further away from winning another championship. That season, I posted some of the lowest numbers of my career, and even my Uncle Brainard told me, "Lisa, if you play next year like you played this year, it is time for you to retire!"

With so much basketball stuff going on, I was not sure when Michael and I would squeeze in the wedding. The best time seemed to be between the end of the WNBA season and the start of the Thanksgiving and Christmas holidays. We chose November 5, 2005. I did not like the idea of having the wedding in one place, spending my wedding night in a hotel, and then leaving all our friends and family behind the next day, when we went off on our honeymoon. I wanted a one-stop wedding and honeymoon site.

We both really enjoy the outdoors, so we looked into Santa Barbara and some other areas where there was sun, water, and a beach. We love to be outside in warm weather. I thought, *Let's go to Maui.* I had been there and thought it was really romantic. We could invite some select family and friends (Dionne was invited but did not attend), have the wedding and the reception there, and then stay on the island for ten days and live it up.

I had to prepare our entire wedding in about two months. I put together a guest list, mailed out invitations, and figured out all of the other details, including picking out dresses for my maid of honor (Tiffany) and two bridesmaids (Braquel and Karleen Thompson). And, of course, I had to find a wedding dress.

Michael had two groomsmen, and his stepfather was his best man. Since the wedding was in Maui, we thought it would be a great idea for everyone in the wedding to wear all white. Michael wore a white linen suit, and my dress was white chiffon. It was a really nice material that moved well and did not wrinkle easily. I found the dress that I liked in a magazine and then had Jhoanna of Élevée make it for me. She had done most of the clothes that I had worn for red-carpet events.

When the sun came up on the morning of the wedding, it was about as close to a perfect day as you could ask for. Michael asked only one thing of me. "Babe, just promise me that you won't get stressed out. Whatever happens, just don't get stressed out," he pleaded. "If there is a problem or if something goes wrong, don't worry about it. Just keep moving. We are going to have a great time."

Thankfully, I was totally stress free throughout the entire wedding. The bridesmaids were on time. There were no "wardrobe malfunctions." And our make-up and hair looked great. I did not have any problems. It was great. The wedding started about fifteen minutes late, but only because once I was all made up and in my gown, I had to hop into a golf cart to take me from my dressing area to the wedding site. That must have been quite a sight to see—a six-foot-five bride-to-be all dressed up and riding to her wedding in a golf cart.

When the wedding party was ready, a man blew a conch shell to announce our arrival. Tiki torches were lit, and Hawaiian dancers escorted us into the ceremony. Karleen walked in first, followed by Braquel and then Tiffany. Uncle Brainard walked me down the grassy aisle. He was the one that I had picked to give me away on behalf of all of my family. We had about eighty people there, and the ceremony was beautiful, the weather, too. It can get really hot in Maui, but we were very comfortable because there were a few clouds, which kept the sun from beating directly down on us.

As I started down the aisle, I spotted my husband-to-be. He was so tall that I could see him over the heads of all the people. Michael looked so handsome. Once I locked my eyes on him, I never stopped looking at him.

We had a wonderful pastor, who blessed us and read 1 Corinthians 13:13, which talks about faith, hope, and love, with love being the greatest of them all. Michael and I had read that scripture many times before, so it was significant that the pastor chose those very words to describe our love on our wedding day.

About a month before the wedding, I had given my engagement ring back to Michael because he needed it to get my wedding band. I felt weird without it, and I never saw the ring again until my wedding day, so when Michael put the ring on my finger, it was like seeing it for the first time. I loved it and even turned to give the crowd an approving look after Michael put it on my finger.

Michael had designed my ring, and I was thrilled with it. The ring was perfect. The ceremony went perfectly, and everything was perfect on our wedding day. Once Michael and I were officially declared husband and wife, his daughters—now our daughters—

released doves. It was a wonderful sight to see, and then we walked off.

Our reception was terrific. People would ask me about my new husband, and I would tell them, "Michael is like me, but he's a boy." Seriously, at times it seems as though we are the same person. He is what I would be if I were a boy, and we are kind of like brother and sister. You may not always agree with your brother or sister, but you love them just the same. I think the great thing about my relationship with Michael is that we met at an ideal time for both of us. We both had been in and out of relationships before, but we were single when we met, and we were really comfortable with ourselves. We were past the point of trying to impress. We each realized that we had to be ourselves. I also knew that our morals and values were also truly in line, so that made things much easier.

Our honeymoon was fabulous, and we were so glad that we had planned to have the wedding and the honeymoon in the same place. That way there were no hassles, no packing, and no flights to catch. We were very happy right where we were. Michael and I had a good time spoiling one another. For example, he knew that I loved to take baths, so he made sure that there were rose petals in the bathtub every night. It was a really nice touch and so thoughtful.

For the next several days, we rode bikes, drove around and explored the island, swam, and ate. We stopped at about ten different waterfalls and hiked several miles through rain forests. Michael would pick up a stick and take off all of the branches for me so that I would have a weapon just in case we saw some critters along the way. I felt like Moses with that huge stick in my hand.

On the other side of the island, we stayed at a bed-and-breakfast place that Michael had found online. It was a cute little cabin on a black sand beach. The coolest part about driving around Maui was that one side of it was so tropical and green, while the other side was completely dry. One side of the island was like Florida, and the other side was like Arizona. We were in awe of our surroundings and of each other. And we took pictures of just about everything we saw. But here is the thing about honeymoons and pictures: the great part is that there are just the two of you, and the bad part is that there are just the two of you. Michael and I wound up taking a lot of pictures of each other and holding the camera at arm's length to snap a picture that we hoped would have both of us in the frame. But I could not complain. I finally had the man of my dreams all to myself.

Chapter 15

Retirement or Russia?

My family life was going really well now, but I knew that after my disappointing 2005 WNBA season I needed to find a way to get back on top of my game. I thought if I went overseas, it would really give me time to focus on my skills, so I signed to play for Spartak, a team that played in Moscow during the winter as part of the Russian Basketball Federation. I had not played overseas professionally since Italy in 1995. That had been a very lonely experience for me, so I had vowed at that time not to play pro ball outside the United States again unless I could take a husband with me. Well, I had a husband now, and Michael was happy to come along. He took a leave of absence from flying so in January of 2006, he and I made the trip from LAX to Moscow.

You already know how much this California girl dislikes cold weather. I was really concerned about the frigid temperatures in Russia, so I took a lot of thermals with me. When we arrived in Moscow, the ground was covered with snow, but my new team had flowers waiting for me, and a driver was there to take Michael and me to our home. In fact, we had a driver for our entire stay in Moscow, and that was great. Whenever I had to go anywhere, I could stay nice and warm in the car and then dash into the gym or the store, so I never had to be outside in the cold for more than thirty to forty seconds at a time.

The most surprising thing to me about Russia was how much it had changed since I had been in St. Petersburg with USA Basketball back in 1994. At that time, Russia was under Communist rule, and the hammer was really down. The city was all gray. The people did not smile, and they did not seem happy at all. On this trip, though, there were all kinds of colors in Moscow. I know it sounds weird, but color was the thing that stood out the most to me. The buildings had color, and people were wearing bright shades of pink, orange, and green.

The other huge change was in our gym facility. I was surprised at how nice Spartak's gym was, and it actually had heat! Our home court was DS Vidnoe. It was comparable to one of the small college or high school gyms in America. The arena seated about two thousand people, but it was a quality facility, and it was warm. I was surprised and happy about that, because it meant that I did not have to practice in sweats, a scarf, a headband, and a beanie. I could warm up for practice in my sweats and then take them off as the workout progressed.

My accommodations were much improved from my first trip to Russia as well. Spartak had set me up in a two-story house that was nice and warm. When I was there for the Goodwill Games in 1994, it was so cold that we had to sleep in our clothes. They would not turn on the heat until 5 PM, and then they turned it off at midnight. So, it was really nice to be in Moscow in 2006 and to have a really nice home and a new, warm arena to play in.

My new teammates were very welcoming, and there were some familiar faces from the WNBA on the Spartak team. Ticha Penicheiro, whose Sacramento Monarchs had knocked the Sparks out of the playoffs the past two years, was on my team, and so were Crystal Robinson and Linda Froehlich from the New York Liberty. When Tamika Catchings, of the Indiana Fever, and my former Sparks teammate Gordana Grubin joined us along the way, I had several English-speaking teammates, and that was a real plus.

I liked Spartak's team president, Shabtai Kalmanovic. He was a unique man and very wealthy. He also loved women and liked to touch and caress his players. I gave him a nickname: Papa san. I was the only person that called him Papa san; I wanted something with "Papa" in it to make it doubly clear that I did not want him to touch me or be disrespectful to me. The "san" part sounded a little exotic and reminded me of what younger people sometimes call their wiser elders. I told Papa san that I wanted to be treated as if I were his own daughter. After that, he was very respectful, and we got along great. Papa san was extremely intelligent, so I talked with him about buying and selling gold and silver, investing in the stock market, and opening a European bank account. I learned a lot from him, but I never forgot what I was there to do: improve my game.

I had four things to work on in Russia: my turnaround jump shot, field goal percentage, offensive rebounding, and free throw shooting. Working on those skills proved an interesting task because of the unusual practice sessions that we had with Spartak. We practiced twice a day, and the first session was called Tac, Tac, Tac!! We would get a ladder, lay it across the floor, and work on quick foot movements. We would run in and out of the ladder, and that was pretty much all that we did through the hour-long practice. We would go through all the foot drills, then lift weights and work on agility. When that was done, we would go home for a while and then return to the gym around five or six o'clock for our second workout of the day. That session lasted about sixty to ninety minutes, so we only got very limited time to actually practice on the basketball court.

Spartak had a trainer named Virgus who loved to be in control of the girls. After each practice he would tell everyone to take off their shoes and run two laps in their socks. I was thinking, *Dude! We don't really do this in the United States. Why are we barefoot?* He seemed to think that this was good for our feet, so I tried it the very first day and decided right away that I would never do it again. I ran only in my Nikes from then on.

I thought our practices were way too short, too. Our team would run up and down the court about three times, and then everything else we did was half-court. I worried that as a team, we were not in great shape, so when our workouts were over, I put in extra time running wind sprints or the stairs. I felt that I had to do what was best for me. It was very important for me to get in better shape.

The Russians did not work nearly as hard as we did in the WNBA, and their rules were a little different, but they were very skilled in offensive play. Overall, the league was extremely physical, especially away from the ball. For example, when the ball came off the rim, you could go over another player's back to get the rebound. You can climb on your opponent, slap the ball out, or tip the ball over your opponent's head. The Russians also did a whole lot of reaching, grabbing, and touching in their game. It was a real adjustment for me, and I got into a lot of foul trouble in my first few games over there. I could not get the opponents off of me, and I could not get free to rebound when I played it my way, so I made some adjustments. I got more physical, and I learned how to tap the ball out and rebound with two hands. I came to understand that I really had to go after the ball, because if I did not, my opponents would just go over my back and take it away.

Trying to learn the language was difficult, too. Michael and I bought Russian vocabulary books and started to learn the alphabet. Every time that we rode in the car, we would try to say words that we would see on the signs along the way. I learned some words and some phrases, but learning the Russian language was like solving a puzzle.

When I was not playing basketball, I spent a lot of time at a place called the Ramstore (in English). It was an Internet café, and Michael and I would go there to check our mail and pay our bills. There was also a Kentucky Fried Chicken, a McDonald's, a Sbarro Italian restaurant, and a Pizza Hut. I really enjoyed eating at those places, but I also got into doing some serious cooking of my own while we were in Russia. I had always liked to cook, but had never had the time. In Moscow, it was painfully cold outside, so I decided to pick up my old hobby again. I called home and got a lot of my mom's and my grandma's recipes and cooked up a storm. Macaroni and cheese, cabbage, sweet potatoes, fried chicken, hot wings with different sauces, cake—these were some of the foods that I had always wanted to make, and now I was able to. The dish that I was most proud of making was gumbo, my husband's favorite. In fact, I called Michael's mom to get the recipe so that I could fix it just the way he liked it.

To keep ourselves entertained, we watched DVDs of a few television series. TV was good company for the Lockwoods in Russia. We always looked forward to movie night, and believe me when I tell you that it was the most television that either of us had watched in years.

Michael and I also set some business goals while we were abroad. We read a lot about real estate and commercial real estate, and we decided that we would like to buy property, things like apartment buildings and strip malls. Basically, we set goals regarding how much money we wanted to make in the next ten years. Our focus right now as a couple is to be diligent with God's money, to replenish it, and to make it grow tenfold. Our "alone" time in Russia turned out to be very productive, and it provided a nice balance to the new style of basketball that I was learning.

My Spartak head coach was Nedelko Lazic, and he was okay. His assistant, Rafi, was from Israel, and he took me through a lot of the drills that I had done with Michael before we left Los Angeles. Rafi taught me different things about facing up, reading defenses, and feeling a player against me and then reacting to

257

that. He helped me with my turnaround jump shot and along with Michael, was one of the primary people who helped me improve my free throw shooting. I really enjoyed spending time with Rafi, and I liked the way he helped my game.

But the Russian league seemed so strange to me. For some games, Papa san would say, "No, daughter. You stay home. I don't want you to travel."

"What? You don't want me to play?" I would ask in surprise.

"No. You rest."

Sometimes, the top players did not have to participate. I do not know why. But there were so many things in the Russian league that boggled my mind that when Papa san told me not to play, I just didn't play.

In February 2006, I took a break from Russia and returned to the States for the NBA's All-Star Weekend in Houston. I competed alongside Kobe Bryant and Magic Johnson in the Shooting Stars competition, but Team Los Angeles got edged out by Tony Parker, Steve Kerr, and Kendra Wecker of Team San Antonio.

After the All-Star Weekend, I returned to Russia for EuroCup play. Spartak had a big game against the Anda Ramat Hasharon team from Israel, which featured Detroit Shock stars Deanna Nolan and Cheryl Ford. Their team was talking a lot of trash in the newspapers about how they were going to beat us, and their coach was calling her squad the Dream Team. She even mentioned that Anda had two players on its roster that she thought were better than Lisa Leslie.

When people started to ask me about it, I said that Deanna Nolan and Cheryl Ford were two of the WNBA's great young players, and Anda was fortunate to have them on the roster. I knew that they were very strong players, and I told everyone that we hoped to play our best against them. I wanted to take the high road.

When Spartak finally played Anda, there was a lot of anticipation. It was a home game for Spartak, and before each of our home games, we always gave the opposing team's players and coaches huge bouquets of flowers. It was a nice gesture, but when we were beating Anda in the final minutes, they shredded the bouquets and threw the flowers all over our gym. To this day, it is one of the most unsportsmanlike displays I have ever seen.

When we flew into Tel Aviv for the rematch, the people there were pretty confident that Anda was not only going to win, but win big. In EuroCup play, it is all about the combined numbers. Spartak had defeated Anda by seven points in Russia, so they had to beat us by more than seven points in Israel, because the team with the highest combined score from the two games would be the squad that advanced to the semifinal round.

For some reason, when we first got to Israel, we were not allowed to practice on Anda's home court. The next day, when we got on their court, there were maintenance people working on the floor, and the opposing coach kept coming in out of the gym while we were practicing. There was way too much drama, but we beat them, anyway, and got to move into the next round of the EuroCup.

In the semifinals, we got past Halcon Avenida of Spain, even though the second game of that series ended in a 61–61 tie. That was how they did it over there. Since Spartak had won convincingly in the first game of the series, there was no need to have a winner in Game Two. The Spanish team did not equal or surpass our combined point total in regulation play, so we advanced to the finals with a 132–116 advantage in the two-game series.

We were set to face le Pays d'Aix from France when the Euro-Cup finals began on March 2006. We took the lead fourteen seconds into Game One, never relinquished it, and defeated our opponents on their home court. Le Pays d'Aix would have to beat us by sixteen points in Moscow in order to keep us from winning the championship, but they did not even come close. Instead, I put up twenty points and grabbed fourteen boards to help Spartak capture the 2006 EuroCup Championship.

I was picked as the league's best center. What more could I ask for? I had a coach who appreciated me, and a professional championship in Europe to go with the two WNBA titles that I had won in the States. My experience in Russia was a good one. I think the people there appreciate women's basketball much more than Americans do.

Another great thing about Moscow was that I never felt a hint of racism. The people were always friendly when Michael and I walked down the streets, and no one ever said a word about the color of our skin—at least not in English.

Back in America, the WNBA celebrated its tenth anniversary in 2006 by adding the Chicago Sky as its latest expansion team. The league also announced its All-Decade team, which honored the ten best and most influential players from its first ten years of play. I was very pleased to be named to that All-Decade team. Sheryl Swoopes, Tina Thompson, and I were the only original players from the WNBA's inaugural season to receive the honor, and Houston's Van Chancellor was named the league's Coach of the Decade.

After playing in Russia, I felt really good about coming back to play with the Sparks. It was time for me to see if I could give Uncle Brainard enough good reasons not to push me into retirement. But, as had become the trend in recent seasons, I was not coming back to a team that I totally recognized. Nikki Teasley had been traded to Washington in exchange for former WNBA rookie of the year Temeka Johnson and veteran forward Muriel Page. And Joe Bryant had gotten the full-time job as the Sparks' head coach.

To start the 2006 season, the Sparks split six consecutive road games, followed by eight straight wins. In the last game of that streak, I nailed a jump shot that made me the first player in WNBA history to score five thousand career points. It was another exciting accomplishment.

My overall game was stronger than in the previous season, but more importantly, I felt good. Chamique was playing well, and Temeka Johnson was running the show for us and dishing the basketball. Our record was 14–5 as the Sparks got ready to face Indiana on July 7 in Los Angeles, and I made a note of that date for two reasons: it was my thirty-fourth birthday, and the Sparks' president, Johnny Buss, had a very special birthday present for me.

Our team broadcaster, Larry Burnett, emceed a pregame ceremony at the corner of the Staples Center basketball court. We were right near the Sparks' bench when he told the crowd, "Usually when you go to court, it is not a good thing, but from now on, when you come to this court, it is going to be a very special thing. The Buss family and the Sparks understand that when you have greatness in your midst, you enjoy it, you nurture it, and you acknowledge it. Tonight, Lisa Leslie's greatness is going to be acknowledged right here, and, Lisa, this is a very special night. Usually, you have to be retired or dead before something like this happens, so enjoy it. The president of the Los Angeles Sparks, Johnny Buss, is here with a very special announcement."

Johnny was all smiles when he took the microphone. He said, "Oh my God. This is so much fun for me. This is a special night. Obviously, it is Lisa's birthday, so it is a great night to begin with. I couldn't think of anything to get her for her birthday, so I thought this city, the Buss family, and the Sparks owe this woman a debt of gratitude for ten seasons of incredible basketball and a ton of accolades. Without any further ado, Lisa, I want to dedicate this Sparks court to you on your birthday in this tenth anniversary season of the WNBA. If you can just help me lift this carpet up."

We both reached down and removed a piece of carpet that

had been covering the corner of the court. It revealed a brand-new stencil on the floor, which read, LISA LESLIE COURT. My number nine was there, as well as a large facsimile of my signature. Johnny said, "There it is, the Lisa Leslie Court. Lisa, thank you so much. I love you to death."

I was literally stunned, but I got a brief chance to collect my thoughts as the song "Simply the Best" blared through the Staples Center sound system. Then, it was my turn to talk, so I addressed the crowd and said, "I am just humbled because you know I give all the glory to God. I am just so thankful for the life that I have and the blessings I have been blessed with to play a sport that I love and to have the family that I have. I just thank God, because I am from Compton, California, the inner city. My mom was a single parent with three girls. We worked hard. Thank you, Mom, for everything you have given me: my morals and my values.

"I just try to come out every day and represent my family and my city and my country the best that I can, because I am grateful to be able to play this sport, not just to play basketball, but also to be able to represent God as a Christian. I'm just thankful to have a court named after me. I don't know what to say. I am just thankful and for all the little girls out there and the little boys, write down your goals and keep working hard. You can do, and achieve, anything that you want to do. I am an example for you. I just thank you. Continued blessings to you guys. God bless you, and to my husband, I love you, babe. Thank you."

It was one of my most special and unforgettable birthdays.

I made my sixth All-Star squad that season, and for the first time, the Eastern Conference won. The Sparks had a tough schedule after the break. Most of our games were on the road, but we played well, and Coach Bryant was fun to play for. He always seemed to see the bright side of things, he always had a smile, and he had a laugh that could be heard in the next county. He gave our squad a lot of freedom, and the Sparks responded. I knew I was making Uncle Brainard proud, and I was voted most valuable player again. That honor put me in great company with Sheryl Swoopes as the only WNBA players to own three regular-season MVP trophies.

The Sparks were back on track to be a serious threat for the finals. We faced the Seattle Storm in Round One, and after losing Game One, we came back strong in the next two games to advance. Next up was Sacramento.

The Monarchs once again had the crazy, loud fans that made it tough to play them on the road. In Game One, I missed shot after shot after shot, and as a team, we just could not dig out a win. Game Two was back in L.A., which was great, because we always played well at Staples Center. But Staples Center was booked for an *American Idol* concert, and neither *American Idol* nor the WNBA would change their dates. We were forced to play our "home" game at the Arrowhead Pond in Anaheim, which was deemed a neutral court.

It is awfully hard to have home-court advantage when you are playing in someone else's building. We had not played at the Pond all season long, and we were not familiar with the court, the backboards, or the rims. We did not even know where the locker rooms were located, and we never found our comfort zone in Game Two against the Monarchs. They jumped on us early and never let up. It was horrible. We scored only eight points in the second quarter, and we trailed by twenty-four at intermission. I finished with ten points and had another rough shooting game. Sacramento grabbed the win, 72–58; won the conference crown; and eliminated us from the playoffs for the third consecutive season. I might have been the league's MVP, but that did not mean very much to me when our 2006 season came to that abrupt ending in Anaheim.

Once my WNBA season had ended, I was supposed to report to USA Basketball to prepare for the world championships that would begin in Brazil in September, but the day after the Sparks got eliminated, I got word that my Uncle Ed Shaw had been in a car accident. His Chevy Suburban had been hit by another vehicle and had wound up wrapped around a tree. When they got Uncle Ed to the intensive care unit at Harbor U.C.L.A. Medical Center, he had no feeling from his chest down.

As days turned into weeks, he started to improve a bit, and we were hoping that he would regain all of his feeling. I kept getting calls from USA Basketball. They wanted to know when I was going to get to camp, so I explained my situation and told them that I felt it would be best that I withdraw from the team. Believe me, that was a very difficult decision for me, but Uncle Ed was not like some relative that I talked to only once a year. We were very close. He was only a few years older than me, so we actually grew up together, and he had supported my basketball development from early on, and he was critical to all of the success that I had achieved. He was an essential part of my life. I was not comfortable leaving him and taking off for Brazil to play basketball.

So for the first time since the eleventh grade, I was not going to be part of the USA Basketball team. It was a strange feeling, but my teammates understood and sent me their good wishes. Unfortunately, the U.S. team could only manage a bronze medal in the world championships. More troubling, though, was that Uncle Ed's physical progress had become limited, and his hospital stay was extended. Weeks became months, and he was still paralyzed. I spent a lot of time with Uncle Ed, and I tried to motivate him the same way that he had encouraged me on the basketball court. I said, "Come on, Uncle Ed! Be strong! You gotta fight!"

Hopefully, Uncle Ed's condition will take a turn for the better, but he was hospitalized in August of 2006, and as I write this, he still is.

A lot of people thought I had bowed out of the world championships because I was pregnant. That was not the case at the time, but it was not for lack of trying. Michael and I were looking forward to starting a family. He said he had always thought that he would not have any more kids after Gabrielle and Mikaela. But he thought I would be an awesome mom and was open to having more children. I really appreciated that. The problem was that I was not sure that I wanted to bring a child into an uncertain world full of war, poverty, homelessness, sickness, and other big issues. Then I realized that the world had its share of problems back when my mom had me and when Mom's mother gave birth to her. Things change, but kids continue to survive and flourish and grow up to make more kids. It is life, and that is part of what we are here for. There is still a lot of good in this world, too, and I wanted to contribute to it. Michael and I were ready to take that big step.

The first time that we thought that I was pregnant, we bought the little home pregnancy test kit and followed the instructions. No pink stripe showed up, but the sad face did. I was not pregnant, but we went back to practicing, and we started using an ovulations indicator, which would display a happy face to let me know when I was ovulating. When the happy face showed up, I would give Michael a sly smile and say, "Now." I was pregnant in no time.

The first month of my pregnancy went smoothly. I did not have any morning sickness. From time to time, I did get a terrible metallic taste in my mouth, so the doctor told me to do whatever I could to stabilize myself and be happy. I ate candy to try to get the taste out of my mouth. Lots of candy. I probably munched on more Skittles, Starburst, and mints while I was pregnant than at any time in my entire life.

Once we got to the second month and were certain that I was pregnant, we had to start letting people know. Ironically, two days before we were going to spread the news, my agent called to tell me that the L.A. Sparks had been sold by the Buss family to Kathy Goodman and Carla Christofferson, two avid Sparks fans who were also very savvy Los Angeles businesswomen.

Besides my surprise, all I could think about was how I was going to tell the new owners that I was pregnant. The Sparks' sale talks had been very hush-hush, very confidential, but as soon as I found out about the sale, I called Kathy and Carla and informed them that I was expecting and would not be available to play in the 2007 WNBA season. That was just days before the sale was announced publicly in December, so they were a bit shocked, but both women were also very excited for me.

My pregnancy became totally public at the news conference announcing the Sparks' sale, and some members of the media questioned why I had not told the prospective owners about my pregnancy sooner than I did. Well, if I had known ahead of time that the Sparks were up for sale, I could have informed everyone involved that there was a chance that I would not be available to play, but that was not how it played out. As soon as I knew about the sale, I told Kathy and Carla about my pregnancy.

A few weeks later, on New Year's Eve, I got an excruciating pain in my stomach and was rushed to the emergency room. It hurt so badly, and honestly, I would have taken a needle in my eyeball to relieve the extreme pain. The doctor found out that I had a fibroid tumor that was outside of my uterus. I knew that I had a fibroid before I got pregnant, but I did not know that as the baby grew, the tumor could grow as well. Sometimes the tumor lost blood flow, which caused a lot of pain for me, and some of the things that I ate made the problem worse, too, so chocolate and caffeine had to be out of my diet for the rest of the pregnancy and maybe the rest of my life.

My doctor also told me to stop working out, so I was sidelined for most of my second trimester. That was really difficult for me, but some days were better than others. But I found ways to occupy my time. Michael and I traveled a bit. And we set up the baby's nursery.

The whole pregnancy process was amazing. When Michael and I saw the ultrasound images and 3-D video of the baby during the second trimester, we were convinced that I would be having a boy. It looked like a boy for a while, but near the end of the trimester, the doctor said, "No. We are pretty sure that your baby is a girl, or a really unhappy boy." It did not matter to us. We just wanted a healthy baby.

I had to start shopping for bigger clothes because my stomach kept growing and growing. Nothing that I owned fit me anymore because I'd gained about thirty-five pounds. I popped the buttons off of two pairs of slacks, and I felt weird wearing XL shirts, but that was what I needed to cover my big belly. Some people said that I looked like I was hiding a basketball under my shirt.

Things continued to go smoothly into my third trimester. I was allowed to start working out again, so Michael and I would go to the gym, and I also got to work some with my trainer. The worst days were when the fibroid was bothering me or when the baby was kicking the tumor. The baby was seven and a half pounds by my ninth month, and that put pressure on my back. My feet started to swell, too, and I had all the symptoms of a full-fledged pregnant woman. Fortunately, I did not have them throughout my entire pregnancy, the way some women do.

All in all, I had a very blessed pregnancy. My attitude and energy were good, and I did not get too moody (in fact, my husband says that I was the best pregnant woman ever!). I had a few uncomfortable days, but overall, the experience felt like one big miracle. I think every woman who wants to get pregnant and can handle it should experience having a baby at least once.

People certainly treat you differently when you are expecting. Once my pregnancy became public information, folks would come up to me and say, "I didn't know you were pregnant, Lisa. You look so beautiful pregnant, and you have that glow about you!" I got a lot of those kinds of comments, and they made me feel really good. People were very nice to me, but I had to be protective when they wanted to rub my stomach. Most of them wound up rubbing my fibroid tumor instead of my baby. The fibroid was so large that it made me look as though I was carrying twins. Sometimes when people would rub my stomach, it would irritate the very sensitive fibroid, so I had to break out my post moves and get my elbows out to keep them away.

I got lots of cards and gifts, some from people that I did not even know. We had a beautiful baby shower, too, and my teammates, family, and friends all showed up. We had an awesome time, and the baby got so many nice gifts and outfits that before she was even born, there were enough clothes and toys to last for years. We stocked up on sports equipment. We got a basketball and a tennis ball because Michael wants to teach the baby to play tennis like Venus and Serena, and I want a basketball player like me. In anticipation of a girl, we bought lots of dresses, too. Our daughter needs to know that it is important for her to be a little lady first, but she will definitely be a die-hard athlete, too.

As my due date in June drew closer, I really did not feel nervous. I knew that I was going to be doing something that millions and millions of women had done before me. A lot about having a baby is instinct, but I had read a lot of books and had done some online research, and I had watched a few videos. I think I was as prepared as I could have been.

I was looking forward to actually experiencing the delivery and then the breast-feeding. I think motherhood is a blessing. It is a tremendous opportunity to make a baby and feel her grow inside you. It is also a blessing to have a supportive husband, and Michael was extremely helpful. He rubbed my feet and my back, tied my shoes, helped me in the kitchen, and, some days he even had to help me put on my undies, because I could not reach them. It really makes the process a whole lot easier when you have a caring and understanding man by your side. Michael was there for me 100 percent. I really appreciated all the little things that he would do, and I was so thankful to have him with me as we went through this very exciting time.

Chapter 16

Special Delivery

While we prepared for the coming baby, the Sparks were again going through a major reshuffle. The new owners rehired Michael Cooper to come back and coach the team for the 2007 season. Coop had been with the NBA's Denver Nuggets for a while after he left the Sparks, and he had spent two seasons coaching the Albuquerque Thunderbirds of the NBA Development League. Coop's T-Birds won the NBDL championship in 2006, so he added that trophy to the five NBA championships that he had won as a player with the Lakers and the two pieces of WNBA championship hardware that he had won while coaching our team.

But when he came back for the 2007 season, he had major holes to fill. I was out on maternity leave. Tameka Johnson was out with a knee injury, and Chamique Holdsclaw, the four-time All-Star, had to play out of position and handle the point guard job. She was a good enough athlete to do it, but Chamique was never comfortable at the point, and she had some troubles with turnovers. The Sparks started the season 3–2, and then Holdsclaw abruptly announced her retirement. She was only twenty-nine years old and was an excellent player, but she said she was not happy playing anymore and wanted to spend time doing other things and more time with her family.

Losing one starter would cripple most teams. Losing three starters signaled almost certain doom. But there was not much I could do about it from my position besides cheer for the team from the sidelines at games . . . which I did. A few days after Chamique's retirement, *it* happened. Michael and I were watching Game Four of the NBA finals with Tiffany, Gabrielle, and Mikaela, and I began to have contractions. They started about forty-five minutes apart, then twenty minutes, then fifteen. Ooh! I had another one. "That was only eight minutes," Tiffany said.

Everybody started checking their watches. Everybody started feeling my stomach. It felt like a ball. I was not in pain, but I could feel tightness. The next thing I knew, Michael got up and started running around in circles.

I had heard stories about erratic first-time mothers going to the hospital for false alarms, and I was determined not to be one of those women. We knew ahead of time that the baby was going to be breach, but I did not want to overreact. I wanted to go only when I was sure I was in labor. And I was not sure. There was no pain at all, just tightness every few minutes.

"Okay, this is serious," Michael said. My husband started cleaning up the office. He was cleaning the kitchen. He was cleaning up everything, like a chicken running around with its head cut off.

"Babe, what's wrong?" I said, trying to calm him down.

Tiff interrupted. "Wait a minute. This *is* getting serious."

Everybody was going nuts, while I was just sitting there. I told them, "You guys. It's okay. I'm okay. It's not time yet."

Tiffany called Mom. "Mom, it is serious. Lisa is having contractions. We are going to the hospital."

The bags were ready, and just in case it was necessary, Michael put the baby seat in our truck.

I had to chime in again. "We're not going to the hospital. Calm down. It's NOT time yet."

Things calmed down for just a bit and Michael started getting tired. I think all the cleaning up and running around had worn him out.

"When it's time to go, wake me up," he said and then went to lie down.

I wanted to wash up before things went any further, so I took a shower, and I was fine while I was standing up. I put on some sweats and still felt okay. But when I sat on the bed, I had a contraction, and then another one and another. Now I knew it was time. With my contractions down to just six minutes apart, I woke Michael up and told him it was time to go. Mom, Tiffany, Michael and I headed to the hospital, and as soon as we got there, they hooked me up to a machine that would monitor my contractions.

The unit was showing contractions, but I was not feeling them. Everyone would watch the monitor and say, "See that?" and I would say, "I didn't feel anything." There were two things that the doctors were looking for. They were watching my contractions and monitoring the baby. At the time, she was sleeping and not showing enough activity. They gave me an IV to get some sugar to the baby, and when she gradually started getting more active, the doctors decided it was time for her to come out. I was having a C-section, so they had me in a different room than the delivery room.

Michael was the only nonmedical person who could go into the room with me, so they gave him a set of blue scrubs to put on. I guess they do not get too many fathers his size at the hospital, because the scrubs looked like capris on Michael. He squeezed into them, and we were ready to go.

I did not know what to expect. I was just sitting there, with this big belly. I was not in pain; I was just ready. The room was so cold. I got on the table and started to shake. I mean, it was all-out shivering, like I was in a freezer. I was given a blanket, and Michael was waiting for me to be prepped so that he could join me. There was a female nurse ready to administer my epidural. She basically told me to hug myself and lean forward, and when I did, I felt the needle like a bee sting in my back. I have a really high tolerance for pain, so it was not too bad.

With that out of the way, they laid me down and started giving me an anesthetic through an IV. They pinched me and stuck me with little pins to see if I had any feeling. "Yes! I can still feel that," I told them. So, they gave me a little more anesthetic.

The anesthesiologist tried it again. "Okay, Lisa. You can't feel anything now, can you?"

"I can still feel that." I guess I needed more painkiller because I was so much larger than the average person. But eventually, I started to feel light-headed and drowsy. I yelled, "Wait a minute. We can't start without my husband. Where's my husband?"

Then Michael said, "I'm right here, babe." I did not know when he came in, but somehow he was right next to me.

Everybody in the room was wearing blue. They put a blue cover-up screen in front of me so that I could not see the operation, and they asked me to put my arms straight out at my sides. I was lying there and looking straight up when the procedure began. I was pretty numb, but I kept feeling movement. "I can feel that," I told them. "I can feel you guys digging. What are you doing?"

The doctors all stopped. "You can feel us?"

"Yeah."

My doctor had to clarify what I was supposed to expect. "Lisa, you are still going to have some feeling," she said. "You are going to feel us touch you, but you should not be feeling any pain."

"Okay, but it feels like you guys are digging in me," I said.

Michael looked over at me and said, "Babe. They are not touching you now."

"Well, I still feel digging," I replied.

I was given a little more anesthetic, and then I felt like I could not breathe. The painkiller was numbing me from my toes to my waist, but because they had to give me so much, it was creeping up into my lungs. I told everyone, "I can't breathe!"

The anesthesiologist said, "You may feel a little shortness of breath because your lungs are getting a bit numb."

I definitely heard what he said, but it did not help me breathe any better. Tears were running from my eyes. I felt like I was dying.

Michael asked me, "Babe, what is wrong?"

"I am dying!" I cried.

Michael tried to comfort me. "No, you are not dying. You have to think positively. We don't think negatively. You are going to be okay. God didn't bring you this far to leave you."

I heard Michael and understood what he meant, but I could not breathe! I was feeling every attempted breath, and I was truly losing control! That was the hardest part about it. I had no control. I could not really feel anything. My breaths just kept getting shorter and shorter. I was lying there, with my arms stretched out at my sides, and I started thinking about Jesus on the cross. The more the doctors worked on me, the less control I had. I could hear my own breath. That was all I could hear. I kept trying to breathe.

I looked over at Michael, and he had his camera out. My husband was taking pictures while I was trying to hang on for dear life. Then, all of a sudden, the doctors and nurses were all rushing around. They took the baby out of me, and Lauren Jolie Lockwood was born at 4:05 AM on June 15, 2007.

The ultrasound indicated with a fair degree of certainty that we were having a girl, but we wanted to have names ready for both sexes just in case. We had narrowed it down to Michael II for a boy and either Lauren or Logan for a girl. I was fond of Lauren because I had always liked the musician Lauryn Hill, and I had heard the name Logan on a soap opera and had thought it was a cool name. Michael was not sold on Logan, though.

For a girl's middle name, we both liked Jolie. There is Angelina Jolie, of course, but Michael's dad's name was Joe, and my father's name was Lee. So it was "Joe Lee." It did not hurt that Angelina Jolie is a good humanitarian, and I like that she is independent and a little bit different. I do not care for everything she is into, but she walks to her own beat, and I respect that.

So we loved the name Lauren Jolie Lockwood. It was a very good name—one that everybody would know and could spell. Lauren Jolie Lockwood also had a ring to it, and it had the same first and last initials as my name. It even sounded a little presidential. Lauren Jolie Lockwood. *President* Lauren Jolie Lockwood. That worked for us!

When some people heard the name, they asked, "Why would Lisa name her child Lauren, when Lauren Jackson is her biggest rival? Why would she want her daughter's first and middle initials to be L.J., like Lauren Jackson's?" The answer is very simple. My daughter is *my* life. I was not thinking about Lauren Jackson when I picked a name for my baby. I did not think about Lauren Jackson enough to even consider it.

Speaking of names, a lot of people wondered if I would hyphenate my last name on my jersey after I got married. I did not change my name from Leslie to Lockwood in the basketball world because I thought, *I am going to stick with Leslie because that is how people know me. It took me a long time to build that name and it sounds good, too.* I have always had traditional values and I took my husband's name at marriage. I did not want Lauren growing up and wondering why her last name was different than mine. She did not need the confusion, so I decided to take Michael's last name and become Lisa Lockwood, without any hyphens.

When you see me in my Sparks jersey, however, or in my Olympic jersey at Beijing, it will say LESLIE on the back, because that is how the worldwide basketball community has recognized me for almost twenty years. When it comes to autographs, I sign "Lisa Leslie." After all, I started practicing that signature when I was seven years old. I had no idea then why anybody might want my autograph, but they seem to want it now. Besides, "Lisa Leslie" is comfortable and easy; it makes sense to stick with the name I have had my whole career.

But, at the end of the day, it was important for Lauren Jolie Lockwood's name to look like mine. When Lauren was born—and I did not know this until later—her umbilical cord was wrapped around her throat and legs. No wonder they were digging into me like that. And when I did not hear her crying when they took her out of me, I immediately spoke up about it. "I don't hear her crying," I said. "Why isn't she crying?"

Michael told me later that everyone's hands were in motion. Every person in the operating room was moving very fast. He had a better view of the action and was not loopy from anesthesia.

Michael's Version of Lauren's Birth:

I was watching the whole thing. While they were cutting Lisa, I was trying to keep her calm and let her know that everything was okay, but as I was looking over the other side of the screen, I was thinking, It sure doesn't look all right to me! It is serious on this other side.

They reached in there and grabbed the baby, and when they pulled Lauren out, everybody just stopped. The doctors had been moving so fast, and then, for just a moment, everything stopped. When the baby came out, she was not breathing, and she was not moving. I heard the doctor say, "The cord is wrapped around her neck. It is wrapped around her leg and around her body."

I could see them removing the cord from around her. The baby was not crying or anything, so they started shaking her around and suctioning her out. There were so many hands going at the same time. I was like, "Oh my God. Something is not right." I could tell because everyone started working frantically.

When Lauren finally screamed and jabbed both hands over her head, everyone in the room went, "Yeah. All right!" You could tell that they were really stressed about the whole thing. I could not be stressed, because I was trying to keep Lisa calm. I told her that the baby looked beautiful and everything was good.

Lisa was a little spacey during the delivery and afterwards, too. I was all excited when I took the baby over to her for the first time. I tipped the baby so that Lisa could see her, and my wife looked over groggily and said, "Whose baby is that?"

I told her, "It's our baby!"

She said, "No. Whose baby is that?"

That is the honest truth.

Michael is right. That was the very first thing that I said. My husband told me, "Babe, that is our baby. She is so beautiful." He showed Lauren to me. She was very, very pale. She had a head full of hair. I do not know what was going on in my mind. I was so out of it.

"Is that our baby?" I asked Michael. "Where did you get that baby?" Then I kept telling him, "Stay with our baby. Don't leave her."

Michael assured me, "I am not going to leave the baby." He gave her a kiss and then gave me a kiss, and then Lauren was taken to the nursery while I was getting stitched up.

The first time I got to hold her was in the recovery room. She was wrapped up like a burrito. I kept looking to see that she had all her fingers and toes. She had a really nice head. Her face was not all scrunched up like those of other babies I had seen. She was really pretty to look at. I could hear the nurses talking to my mom in the hallway. They were saying, "Wow! She is a really beautiful baby." Then Mom, Tiffany, Gabrielle, and Mikaela came in. It was the first time I got to see everybody. My family was with me, and it now included a brand-new baby girl. I kept looking at Lauren, and she kept looking at me. That was the start of our new life together.

Once we got Lauren home, it was time to put to good use all the reading and online research I had done. It was on-the-job training for me, but my maternal instincts kicked in, and I caught on pretty fast. Michael thought it was important for me to breast-feed the baby, and I was fine with that. I knew when Lauren was hungry. I could hear her cries from far away, but I did not know that when a woman is nursing, her milk refills naturally when the baby cries. Isn't that amazing? Any woman who has had a baby has got to be baffled when she hears someone say that there is no God. My baby whines, and my breasts automatically fill up with milk. That is incredible! The first time it happened, I had no idea what was going on. It was like a balloon blowing up in my chest.

Our girls, Mikaela and Gabrielle, loved having a little sister. They were really excited when the baby was born, and they were very helpful. They took pictures of Lauren all the time. We wanted to spend more time with the girls, but that was difficult with Michael based in Miami, me in L.A., and Gabrielle and Mikaela with their mom in Dallas. So Michael and I decided to build a house in Dallas. We were all looking forward to going there after the Sparks' season ended because then we would be able to take the girls to school and pick them up, plus Gabrielle and Mikaela could come home to their other house and do their homework. I think they really liked that idea. I was lucky that the girls and I liked each other from the start. I know that it is not always that way with stepfamilies. I understand that the girls have existing relationships with their mom and their friends. I just want to be an addition to their family, and so far, it has worked out very well for all of us.

The girls are already asking about when Michael and I are going to have the *next* baby. Truthfully, it would be nice to have a boy, but I want to play some more basketball before I think too seriously about it. For now, I am very content with my baby girl.

After Lauren and I had been home for a few weeks, I started really looking forward to getting back on the court. I worked out a few times during my pregnancy, but for the most part, I had been sitting around for about six months. The doctors told me that I had to wait six weeks after Lauren was born before I could start working out. I was only allowed to walk, and I did a lot of that, but it got to be really boring. After five weeks, I got cleared to start swimming, but I could not wait to lace up my sneakers and get back to basketball.

I think it is good for the WNBA when our players get married and have babies. We are professional women in sports. It is a good thing for people to see that female athletes can have family lives, just like other working women. A lot of us have gone to college and have advanced degrees. Many of us are wives and mothers, and we can identify with any woman who has a busy job and tries to get home by bedtime each night to be with her family. We are great role models, and more women can identify with us than people probably realize.

There is that nagging stigma, of course, about rampant lesbianism running through women's basketball. I do not know if people avoid the WNBA because of this perception, but if that is the only thing keeping someone from coming to a game or tuning in on Saturday afternoons, then that is just silly. A lot of people were shocked when Sheryl Swoopes came out of the closet. Obviously, I have known Sheryl for many years and I know her better than the average fan, so her news was no secret to me. But who cares, anyway? Let he who is without sin, cast the first stone. I think, statistically, there are more straight women in the WNBA than gay women. But really, who cares? As long as a player comes to work and does her job, she can live her life the way that she chooses.

That said, the players are responsible for the WNBA's image, and I believe the best and strongest image is one that shows the unique beauty and strength of women. I think it is important for us to have our hair combed and to look presentable when we go out on the court. We are not playing in little gyms anymore. We are playing on a national stage. I think we need to take responsibility for the way that we present ourselves. What happens in the bedroom needs to stay in the bedroom, regardless of a player's sexual orientation. Just focus on upholding the integrity of the game and the positive image of the league. If more players took that approach, the WNBA could flourish indefinitely.

While on maternity leave, I went to several of the Sparks' games at Staples Center, and it was really different for me. It was strange being out of uniform and sitting at the end of the scorer's table, holding Lauren, instead of running in with the team. I wondered for a moment if I wanted to continue to play basketball, but the more I watched, the more I realized just how much I loved the sport and how much passion I still had for the game.

During one game, the Sparks were getting knocked down and pushed around. It was hard to watch. I was not going to say anything, but one of the forwards, Jessica Moore, saw me sitting in my seat and shaking my head. She came over, kind of teary-eyed, and asked, "Lisa, what do you see?"

"Do you really want to know what I think?" I asked.

She nodded.

I handed Lauren over to Michael, got out of my seat, went over to the team huddle, and told the team exactly what I thought.

"First of all, you are just letting them shoot jumpers," I began.

The players seemed to be paying attention, so I continued. "It's just a real shame that you are gonna let this team come in here and kick our butts on our court. You are doing a disservice to our crowd. It is one thing to lose, but at least lose with some fight, and let the other team know that they are in our house. Come on now. Show some heart."

It was really hard to sit on the sidelines and watch the Sparks struggle through the 2007 WNBA season. There were certainly reasons for their problems, but reasons cannot be excuses. In the past, when teams played in Los Angeles, they always knew that they were going to have a battle on their hands. That was something that we had established, and to me, that was what the Sparks lacked most in 2007. When I looked at our team, player by player, I did not feel that it had the kind of heart and fight that we needed to be successful. This made me even more eager to get back in the gym.

I started going to the Sparks' practices the moment I was cleared to do so, but it was a slow beginning. I started by shooting about two hundred jump shots in each practice. Michael was my rebounder. It was a relief when I realized that I could still shoot. Then I started taking hook shots and doing ball-handling drills with Chris Mihm, Brian Cook, Kwame Brown, Andrew Bynum, and some of the other Lakers players. It was good to get in some work and get my heart rate up. Thirty-five minutes was all I could handle when I first got back on the court, but it was fun.

I went to my first official practice with the Sparks when they got back in town in August 2007. The team was already on the court when I got to the arena. I was ten minutes late because I had been pumping my breasts, so I went straight to the locker room and started putting on my gear. It was exciting. I walked into the gym and went over to Coach Cooper. He looked at me and said, "Smooth. How you feeling?" He gave me a high five and was really excited to see me. I gave high fives to everybody and then hopped on the elliptical machine to warm up.

Before I knew it, I was out on the court, doing full-court press breakers with the team. The action was moving a little quicker than I had anticipated. I could not really move that fast right away, but I still had my technique. I was just trying to help the team, and it was fun to be out there with the girls. I did block a shot by Sidney Spencer, the Sparks' rookie out of the University of Tennessee, so there was a glimpse that I still had some game. I was pretty excited, until Taj McWilliams-Franklin blocked one of my shots. I was finding out exactly where I was physically after having a baby, and where I was now was nowhere near where I wanted to be.

I was glad that Taj was there, because that meant we had great veteran leadership. I looked at Mwadi Mabika. We had come into the WNBA together when the league began in 1997, and when the 2007 season was over, there were only five other "originals" remaining: Sheryl Swoopes, Tina Thompson, Tamecka Dixon, Wendy Palmer, and Vickie Johnson.

We had all been around at the beginning, but it does not seem quite right to me when people say, "Lisa, you are a pioneer in women's basketball. You have really paved the way." Not really. The true pioneers in women's sports are people like Babe Didrikson Zaharias, Billy Jean King, Althea Gibson, Ann Meyers, Evelyn Ashford, Nancy Lieberman, and Pat Summit. There was no Title IX to bar gender inequality for these women, and they battled the worst kinds of discrimination. The rest of us are riding on their coattails, and we should appreciate them every day.

If I had grown up in Compton without Title IX, I do not believe that Lisa Leslie the basketball player would exist. I could have gone to Morningside High, scored 101 points in a game, and received a lot of national recognition, but then what? Would the doors have opened for me to play professionally? Probably not. What about modeling or broadcasting? Those would have been unlikely, too. I might have been just another tall lady.

But I had great opportunities and was able to pick from all the colleges in the entire nation. I got to play all over the world. I really did not pioneer anything. I just reaped the benefits of the work that so many female athletes had done before me, and I kept my head on straight through it all.

Epilogue

I still write down the goals that I want to accomplish, and one of my big ones in 2008 is to help the Sparks get back to their championship level. I also want to contribute to renewed success for USA Basketball at the Summer Olympics in Beijing, China. That would be my fourth Olympic appearance, and to win one more gold medal would be phenomenal. Sometimes I ask myself why I continue to play so hard. But that answer is easy: my passion for the game has not diminished. I like to compete, and I have a drive to win at the highest level, and there is the extra incentive from knowing that our U.S. team settled for bronze when I was not with them at the 2006 world championships.

It is also important to me to mentor some of America's younger players. USA Basketball, on the men's and women's sides, has been getting away from what it used to be. I hope that I can help us put less emphasis on individual skills and more on the team concepts that have made USA Basketball so formidable for so many years in international competition. Beijing will be my last Olympics. I want to make it my best one. I want to stand on the podium again and hear our national anthem playing as the Stars and Stripes are raised. I want to feel that Olympic gold medal around my neck one more time, and I want to prove once again, to every little girl or boy that has goals and works hard, that they can do and achieve anything. Absolutely anything.

I am who I am, and where I am, by nothing but the grace of God.

Acknowledgments

From Lisa:

I am in such awe of my Lord and Savior, and I am thankful that He has allowed me to share my story at last. The many blessings I have received from Him are humbling, and I am grateful for all of the experiences, both good and bad, that have brought me to this point in my life.

I am very thankful to my mother, who has always been my own personal *shero*. Mom, I am the woman I am today because you made a conscious decision to love me and to reinforce that love from the inside out. Your commitment to teaching me to think positively and always to stay away from negativity allowed me to achieve success even when times got tough. You are a special person who loves all of God's children, and your warmth and sensitivity make it sometimes seem like you have never met a stranger. You have made sacrifices for all of your children, and you represent what a mom and a dad should be. You are a wonderful role model, and I am so thankful that you taught me to see the beauty in myself. You are a soldier, and I pray to be a great parent to my children, as you have been to me. Thank you for being my rock. This book salutes you, Mom, for a job well done. I love you to the core of my soul, and I thank God every day for choosing you to be my mommy.

To my big sister, Dionne, I love you and I will always have a special place for you in my heart. If we could turn back the hands of time, I would try to make all the wrongs right.

To my baby sister, Tiffany, God knew how much we needed

each other growing up—not only to survive, but to love and nurture one another. Everything I have given you in life you have given right back to me. Thank you for always being by my side and truly having a sistah's back. You will always be my "ride or die" chick!

To my entire family, it really does take a village to raise a child. And my village has been truly instrumental in molding me. Thanks to all my aunts, uncles, and cousins, who have loved me unconditionally and have supported me over the years. And thanks to Grandma Dear for producing the whole clan!

Special thanks to my wonderful daughters Gabrielle and Mikaela. It has been a God-given gift to have you both in my life. Thanks for being so sweet and for welcoming me into your lives. May God continue to bless our family as we grow together.

To baby Lauren, Mommy is so thankful for you. Your smile is heaven-sent. I pray that God keeps a hedge of protection around you. May you become all that Christ intends for you to be. You will undoubtedly be tall, but it is a unique and beautiful gift. I hope that you will embrace it, because along with being tall, you will also be tan and terrific! So take all your gifts, and turn them into your successes. Mommy loves you!

I am deeply appreciative of all my coaches that helped me become the player that I am. Thanks to Coach Scott for being so fatherly to me and for protecting me during my wonder years. Thanks to Coach Stanley and Coach Thaxton for teaching me how to give the game my all. Your incredible work ethic has been invaluable to my career. Thanks to Tara VanDerveer for pushing me beyond my limits and to the next level. You are truly an amazing coach. Thanks to Coach Cooper for your time and efforts. I am thankful for the time you took to help me turn my weaknesses into strengths. Thanks to Coach Thompson for always telling me what I needed to hear and not what I wanted to hear. The truth always brought out the best in me. You are missed.

ACKNOWLEDGMENTS

Thanks to Larry Burnett for working so closely and diligently on this book. It took several years to get it together, but we did it! Thanks for all your hard work, L.B.

I also want to extend a very special thanks to Rakia A. Clark at Kensington for her hard work and professionalism. Thanks for adding the golden touch, Rakia. You are awesome!

And last but not least, my bone of bones, my Luv Bug: Michael Lockwood. I am so thankful that my loving husband found me. Our steps have been ordered, and it is wonderful to have a man who knows how to lead. Thank you, sweetheart, for encouraging me to share my story. I could not have done this without you. Love, your Lucy!

From Larry:

Many thanks to Lisa for her time and effort, and for trusting me with her life story. Her openness and candor made this book more compelling and exciting than I had even imagined. Thanks to Lisa's husband, Michael, and her mom, Christine Leslie-Espinoza, for their contributions as well. And a big thank you to Frank Scott, Lisa's high school coach, who was a tremendous help to me.

On a personal level, I send gratitude to my mom, for teaching me about words and language and love, and for always reheating those many dinners when, as a kid, my games and practices ran late. Thanks to my dad, who taught me a love of sports, and to my brother, Ray, who put up with little brother tagging along and butting in.

I want to thank my wife, Barbara, for not hitting me over the head with a frying pan while I was constantly typing away on the computer until 2:30 AM to get this book finished. Also, thanks to my daughters, Katie and Jenna. Katie was my proofreader on this project, and both girls are a constant source of pride and happiness to me.

ACKNOWLEDGMENTS

Thanks to Mrs. Schwartz and Mrs. Dickerman, who taught me that "creative" and "writing" were not mutually exclusive terms.

You would not be reading this book right now if not for the incredible efforts of Frank Scatoni of Venture Literary. I am so pleased that Kensington "got" the significance of Lisa's story and that no matter what, our tireless editor, Rakia A. Clark, was 110 percent behind this project from start to finish.

So many thanks go out to so many people, such as Earvin Johnson, Michael Cooper, Kobe Bryant, Bill Walton, Carla Christofferson, Kathy Goodman, Craig Miller, Caroline Williams, Jenny Maag, Marianne Stanley, Tara VanDerveer, Mark Scoggins, Tammy Warren, Catherine Sebring, Karleen Thompson, Lon Rosen, Tim Tessalone, Darcy Couch, David Tuttle, Matt Bialer, Jonathan Daillak, Karen Case, Ron Howard, Margaret Kendall, Jimmy Clark, Linda Dodge Reid, and Bev Smith, for helping to make this book and this dream a reality. One more goal written and accomplished.